THE SECULAR SQUEEZE

Reclaiming
Christian Depth
in a Shallow
World

JOHN F. ALEXANDER

INTERVARSITY PRESS
DOWNERS GROVE, ILLINOIS 60515

InterVarsity Press® is the book-publishing division of InterVarsity Christian Fellowship®, a student movement
active on campus at hundreds of universities, colleges and schools of nursing in the United States of America, and
a member movement of the International Fellowship of Evangelical Students. For information about local and
regional activities, write Public Relations Dept., InterVarsity Christian Fellowship, 6400 Schroeder Rd., P.O. Box
7895, Madison, WI 53707-7895.

Scripture quotations, unless otherwise noted, are from the New Revised Standard Version of the Bible, copyright
1989 by the Division of Christian Education of the National Council of the Churches of Christ in the U.S.A. and
are used by permission.

Cover illustration: Roberta Polfus

ISBN 0-8308-1341-1

Printed in the United States of America ∞

Library of Congress Cataloging-in-Publication Data

Alexander, John F., 1941-
    The secular squeeze: reclaiming Christian depth in a shallow world
/John F. Alexander.
        p.   cm.
    Includes bibliographical references.
    ISBN 0-8308-1341-1
    1. Apologetics—20th century.   2. Civilization, Modern—20th
century.   3. Secularism—Controversial literature.   4. Christian
life—1960-   5. Alexander, John F., 1941-   I. Title.
BT1211.A44   1993
239—dc20   93-18086
                                                  CIP

---

17   16   15   14   13   12   11   10   9   8   7   6   5   4   3   2   1
07   06   05   04   03   02   01   00   99   98   97   96   95   94   93

*Don't let the world squeeze you
into its own mold,
but let God remold your minds.*
(ROMANS 12:2 PHILLIPS)

To Francis Schaeffer
and
Basil Mitchell
the teachers of my youth
who did what they could to teach me
to feel more deeply
to reason more precisely
to see more widely
and
to think more Christianly

Acknowledgments

This book has been eight years in the writing, all my life in the making, and in that time I have become indebted to far too many people to mention or even remember. My greatest debt is to my wife, Judy, who for most of the last eight years took jobs she didn't always like so I could work on this book. This is especially remarkable since she doesn't give a rat's tail about epistemology or metaethics. I sometimes think her belief in me is misplaced, but without it I would have quit long ago (and not just this book). Perhaps even more important is that in the struggle to be the church, she has often led the way.

My debt to my teachers is nearly as great. At almost every stage of my life I have had mentors of a stature that I can scarcely comprehend and certainly did not deserve. At Stony Brook School, Frank E. Gaebelein took a special interest in me, and in the process set standards for me of excellence and the love of beauty and justice that still mark who I am.

At Malvern College (which I assumed would be a secular den of iniquity), I was astounded to discover that my primary teacher, G. S. B. Sayers, was a student and friend of C. S. Lewis—and more to the point, a man of Christian depth (although a Catholic!). It was from Sayers that I learned to love Shakespeare and Wordsworth.

During my time at Oxford I spent many of my vacations with Francis Schaeffer at L'Abri. Without him, I probably would have succumbed to the secularism of A. J. Ayer and Bertrand Russell. He is the one who provided

me with the general framework of this book, though of course he was more
of a rationalist than I and didn't talk about stories. Perhaps even more
important, he is the one I first heard emphasize seeing the big picture and
the one from whom I learned to think dialectically. And through him I
came into contact with H. R. Rookmaaker and the work of Herman Dooyeweerd.

While Ayer was the philosopher at Oxford who was famous in America,
it gradually dawned on me that I was learning more from Basil Mitchell,
my tutor. I had never heard of him, but he turned out to be one of the
finest Christian philosophers of his generation. And he insisted that I see
the little picture as well as the big one. He soon persuaded me that neither
epistemology nor the relationship between ethics and God is as cut and
dried as suggested by the rationalistic evangelicalism I was raised on. His
mark is on many pages of this book.

But perhaps my most important teachers at Oxford were my fellow
students, especially Roger Andersen and Raficq Abdullah. With them I
discovered Ingmar Bergman, e. e. cummings, Kenneth Patchen, Zen Bud-
dhism and the Campaign Against Nuclear Disarmament. Much of this book
is trying to sort out what I learned from them thirty years ago.

At Trinity Evangelical Divinity School, my master's dissertation was in
a sense a first, vastly confused, draft of chapter four. My committee (John
Warwick Montgomery, James Oliver Buswell Jr. and Kenneth Kantzer) were
less than thrilled by my conclusions. I hope this version would suit them
at least a little more.

When I began teaching at Wheaton, my department chairman was Arthur Holmes, and in one lecture he accomplished what no one else had
been able to do: he freed me from my empiricism. Even Mitchell with years
of struggle had been unable to do that. (I must have been a very slow
student!)

In those same years, Lane Dennis (undoubtedly to his undying regret)
introduced me to the work of Art Gish and John Howard Yoder. Their work
transformed my life and provided content for the notion of church I had
acquired from Schaeffer. That is the heart of this book.

To my former colleagues at *The Other Side*, I owe much. Several parts of this book first appeared in its pages, and many of the arguments of this book first happened in its offices! Phil Harnden introduced me to Matthew Fox, and discussions with Mark and Joan Olson on the beach at Cape Hatteras crystallized my views of aesthetics.

It was Rich Read and the folks at the Church of the Servant King who provided me with the best example of the kind of church Yoder and Gish were talking about. Nothing in my life has affected me as profoundly as my experience with them. Without them, this book would have told a different story (supposing I had been able to finish it at all).

In those years and a little before, I discovered the work of Stanley Hauerwas. It is hard to assess his contribution to this book. Much of what he writes, I almost knew before reading him, and yet he had put it together and I hadn't. Reading him, I keep mumbling, "Oh, that's what I've been trying to say!" He provided the final pieces that made it possible to finish this book.

This book took so long in part because book after book, conversation after conversation, letter after letter, forced revisions in material I'd already written. I have to mention the work of Alasdair MacIntyre, Charles Taylor, Nicholas Wolterstorff and Allan Bloom. And then there are the people who made annoying notes in the margins of manuscripts I sent them: Arthur Holmes, Jack Bernard, John Sandri and Harold Commons (the finest editor I have ever had). And then endless conversations with Jack Bernard as we jogged through Golden Gate Park, and one final conversation with Steve Siebert after I thought the book was done.

I must also mention my profound indebtedness to the works of Ursula K. Le Guin, J. R. R. Tolkien, C. S. Lewis, Graham Greene, Kurt Vonnegut (stories, you know), H. R. Rookmaaker, Karl Jung, Ernest Becker, Stokely Carmichael, Malcolm X, Ian Ramsey, Stephen Toulmin and Ludwig Wittgenstein. If I were meticulous with annotation, they would be mentioned far more often than they are.

There are many others: My daughter Jenny, for whom I first wrote the story of Jah in chapter one. Joe Peterson of Eugene, Oregon, who provided my family and me with a cabin the first year I worked on this book. First United Methodist Church of Gardena, who provided me with an office for practically free for the next three years. Mike Mason and Noel King of Santa Cruz, who encouraged me and stimulated me more than I deserved. And all the folks in our church community in San Francisco, who provided us with a loving home and a reconciled church for the last three years as I finished the book.

1

Hollowness Within & Hollowness Without

I n the 1660s Rembrandt painted himself helping crucify Jesus. In the 1960s Andy Warhol painted Campbell's Soup cans. That change reflects the curious emptiness of modern culture. We have gone from the depths of God to the shallowness of technology. We seldom do statues of real people in their joys and miseries; instead we do statues of giant clothespins. When our great artists do paint people, they're likely to paint copies of Dick Tracy cartoons or pictures so abstract they appear scarcely human. Our culture has gone hollow.

Most of us sense that we are equally hollow inside. Down deep we know that something is wrong, but we're at a loss to know what to do about it. We throw ourselves further into our work or studies, we go to marriage renewal weekends, we jog, we have affairs, we try the church, we begin to meditate. Some things help, but nothing makes the difference. Gnawing emptiness remains, and nothing seems to fill it.

Hollowness within and hollowness without, a people and a culture with all the depth, all the mystery, all the passion gone.

You see, in modern, secular culture, human beings are nothing but pieces of meat—with nothing special or transcendent about us. We are not sinners who crucified God but consumers who eat canned soup. So why paint Jesus any more than sides of beef or Campbell's Soup cans?

Every culture has its symbols, its icons that reveal how it tries to fill its hollowness. Once our icon was the crucified God; now it's Campbell's Soup cans. Once we venerated Christ on the cross; now we venerate material success. We worship soup cans! We don't think of it that way, of course, but if we are devoted to getting a good job and having a nice house, we are worshiping soup cans.

Venerating *something* is central to the human condition. Not worshiping is inhuman. God gave us the hollowness within, and it means we just do worship something in hopes it will fill us. The tragedy of modernity is that we have nothing worthy of worship; the absurdity of modernity is that we go ahead and worship anyway. We worship what is left—material success or something of the sort. Imagine hundreds of millions of men and women bowing down before Campbell's Soup cans. What could be more absurdly tragic?

God gave us the gift of hollowness to goad us and guide us toward him. It's like a compass: when we're going the wrong direction, when we're worshiping something less than God, we feel dissatisfied. We're haunted by the sense that we are not yet serving anything worthy of worship, not yet serving anything worthy of who we're meant to be.

Hollowness within filled by hollowness from without is hollowness indeed.

And in the modern age it's not easy to find anything except hollowness. This loss of all that is worthy of veneration is nearly unique to our age.[1] It grows in part, or so I will argue, out of an overemphasis on what we call reason. We learned to emphasize reason from the Greeks, but for them that emphasis was not as devastating because they had a richer conception of it. But with the scientific revolution came a notion of reason so narrowly understood that our culture can see only in one dimension. We are left without the tools to see the other dimensions—the awe, the wonder, the horror.

So we are left with tools for debunking but without tools for building up.

As a result, we debunk politicians and television evangelists and sexual fidelity, but we don't know how to honor holiness or goodness. In fact, we don't even have the tools to identify people of holiness or things of beauty. So we can't tell the difference between charlatans and saints, between Rembrandt's painting and paintings color coordinated to match the furniture, between soap opera and reality, between margarine and butter. As a result, we apparently come to believe that a new toothpaste will improve our sex lives but that the universe has no room for God or beauty or anything venerable.

All of this is offensive to certain types of people, and so they react—with romanticism. Romantics emphasize feeling and choice at the expense of reason. Flower children, poets, shamans—they fill the hollowness with passion (a dimension that science excludes). But passion turns out to be as one-dimensional as reason and soon needs to be enhanced by drugs, ever more perverse sex or violence. As the Marquis de Sade and Adolf Hitler (both romantics) revealed by their very being, living out your feelings and choices is dark and hollow and sick. It lacks both a foundation and a means of discernment. So flower children slowly grow snakes within.

Not a great thing to fill yourself with.

Those two options are so ugly that many hold on to the established church. But the church has not proved terribly attractive itself. From the Inquisition to the Ku Klux Klan to Jim Bakker, the church has not been morally stellar. And the devotion of the ordinary person in the pew to job and house and nation makes it hard to believe that standard churches know much about filling the hollowness. Often it's as if churches help people hide the hollowness from themselves rather than help them fill it with God.

So churches rarely tell the story of Jesus straight. Instead, they tell versions of modernity. They preach Jesus in odd combinations with secularism and romanticism, materialism and nationalism. The church's symbol is not our crucifying God but a gold cross with no nails in it—surely as incoherent a piece of syncretism as any anthropologist ever found. Except for certain outward forms, churches (whether Catholic or Protestant, evangelical or ecumenical) are often hard to tell from the surrounding culture.

They have exchanged the gospel for a culturally acceptable cross of gold.

So modern people must choose between three empty stories: secularism, romanticism and the standard church. Campbell's Soup cans, flower children with snakes inside or gold crosses. Which turns out to be a choice between Campbell's Soup cans, Campbell's Soup cans and Campbell's Soup cans.

Our culture has lost all depth. We have been squeezed flat, squeezed from the many dimensions of Rembrandt to the one dimension of Andy Warhol. We have nothing with which to fill our hollowness but hollowness itself.

Except of course, ourselves. We fill ourselves with ourselves. Which is also hollow. This narcissism is the second and primary source of our shallowness. You can imagine what happens when you try to fill something hollow with itself. After much contortion and pain, it just disappears. The resulting implosion is quite colorful as it destroys itself and everything around itself. Like an average collapsing marriage. Or a neurosis. Or the Marquis de Sade and Jim Bakker. Filled with their empty selves.

That much the three stories have in common: the self. Like all human stories, they put the self at the center. At the center of all the emptiness, where God is meant to be. And so modernity disappears, clutching the emptiness of self. Helped along by reason, passion and the established church.

My Story

These questions aren't intellectual abstractions for me. I was drawn into them by my own emptiness and the emptiness I saw around me. I'm the son of a small-town fundamentalist preacher, but in the late fifties, I attended a Christian prep school in the East. There I was surrounded by kids who had impressive clothes and impressive status, kids from the top of the heap. I made good friends there and learned a lot, but I was not finally impressed by my friends. They had no answers. The story of the upper class seemed ultimately empty.

In the summer I worked at a ready-mix plant in the Midwest. I confess I was surprised by what good friends I made there. But once again I was

not terribly impressed. Their story had too many four-letter words, week-
end binges and dubious tales of sexual adventure. The story of working-
class males had no more answers than did that of the upper class.

That drove me back to my father. I respected him because his fundamentalist belief in the inerrancy of the Bible led him to try to live out the
teachings of Jesus rather literally. But most people in his denomination
thought he was crazy, and besides, he taught a long list of prohibitions that
I couldn't find in Jesus. I was impressed with the Sermon-on-the-Mount
side of my father, but I was unimpressed by the vast majority of fundamentalists around him. The fundamentalist story seemed empty to me.

In all these settings I knew individuals who were better than this makes
it sound, some of them much better. But none of them seemed like people
who had experienced what life was about. They weren't people whose lives
I wanted to imitate. They were as lost and empty as I was.

Meanwhile, I graduated first in my prep school class and had my choice
of universities. And I was not impressed. In fact, I felt completely, fright-
eningly empty. Neither my achievements nor anything I studied gave me
any sense of wholeness.

I decided to go to Oxford University, thinking I would throw myself into
my studies and learn something worthwhile. Since I loved stories, I set out
to study English literature. But at Oxford, you can't study stories. You study
language—Latin and Anglo-Saxon and Middle English, even Old Norse if
you want. But not stories. And certainly not their meaning for life. Maybe
you could trace historical references to the search for the Holy Grail, but
it would have been gauche to ask how to find it yourself. I was not impressed.

So I changed to philosophy, where I hoped to search for the meaning
of life. But not at Oxford. The closest I got to studying meaning was
studying how words mean: sense, reference, denotation, connotation, use.
Not the sort of meaning I was after. But I settled for it. Symbolic logic,
Descartes, Wittgenstein, the philosophy of mind, ethics. Ah, ethics. Surely
there we would discuss the meaning of life. But no, we discussed the
meaning of the word *good.* Not the meaning of goodness, I assure you, but
the meaning of the word *good.* I was not impressed. Academia had no

stories to live by. Sometimes it asked important questions but in an almost studiedly unimportant way. Finding anything worthwhile in them was mostly up to me.[2]

Now don't misunderstand me. Unlike high school, these studies were interesting. They didn't seem to me to be what life was about, and they certainly weren't what I was about, but they were interesting. Like doing enormously complicated crossword puzzles.

But was I to spend my life doing crossword puzzles? My studies were as empty as anything I would ever encounter (or did I bring the emptiness with me?).

So I neglected my studies in favor of education. I read and I talked to others who also read. We read novels and poetry, we attended plays and movies, we went to art museums and listened to music . . . and we talked. Pretentious, a lot of it, I'm sure. But pretentious or not, at least we were searching for the Holy Grail and for thinkers who might lead us to it: Feodor Dostoyevsky, Ingmar Bergman, Jean-Paul Sartre, J. D. Salinger, e. e. cummings, Kenneth Patchen, Joan Baez, George Bernard Shaw, Søren Kierkegaard.

They were asking important questions. They might not have the Holy Grail, but at least they weren't satisfied with emptiness. They were searching for some road that would lead to reality.

Somewhere along the line, from reading them, I concluded that I had to find myself. And I did. But I was not impressed. The story about finding yourself clearly was not the Holy Grail.

That opened an abyss. Perhaps there were no answers, no Holy Grail. The university syllabus required careful study of the technical writing of Bertrand Russell, and I also read much of his popular work. For the first time in my life, I seriously considered secularism. It would not be the last time. I hated secularism with all my heart. I hated its claim that the universe was empty, and I thought turning humanism into an exciting faith (the way Russell did) was jellybrained silliness.[3] I was convinced that secularism left the universe empty and pointless, but the arguments for it seemed powerful. With the help of Francis Schaeffer at L'Abri and Basil Mitchell, my philosophy tutor, I managed to hold off secularism most of the time.

Meanwhile, when I wasn't staring at secularism, I accepted a radical version of the leftist, humanistic social critique that was standard with my friends and the people we read. Those were the days of Malcolm X and Martin Luther King Jr., and so we found ourselves fighting for the oppressed—or at least talking about it. Fighting for justice for others seemed to me to fit the teachings of Jesus, even if many aspects were derived from romantics like Jean-Jacques Rousseau and Henry David Thoreau. Perhaps this was the Holy Grail.

At Oxford I encountered a version of evangelical Christianity more responsible than my father's group. But they were not at all impressed with my social critique or my commitment to the oppressed. That prompted a study of Scripture that convinced me that Joan Baez understood the social dimensions of the Bible better than did the evangelicals of the sixties. I made a more radical commitment to Christ, but a few years later I parted ways with most evangelicals. They seemed terribly empty to me.

L'Abri, marriage to Judy, seminary, teaching at Wheaton, civil rights marches, founding *The Other Side* magazine with my father (to call evangelicals to care about justice), children, living simply so others might simply live. A continuing commitment to the oppressed as the Holy Grail interspersed with occasional bouts with secularism and regular conflict with evangelicals . . . and others. That was to be my story for the next twenty years.

The left, myself included, was as divisive and hateful as my father's fundamentalist world. Since the pursuit of justice is meant to help others, we were not as empty as those pursuing wealth, but we were still empty. Judy and I helped start an organization to sell Third World crafts, another to oppose torture and another to raise money to fight the root causes of hunger; we helped organize conferences against racism, sexism and all other known forms of injustice. In several of those endeavors, we got caught up in devastating conflicts—and we weren't doing too well with each other either. This was not quite the Holy Grail.

Besides it often wasn't clear how much we helped. When we really succeeded, what we did was make it possible for poor people to join the emptiness residing at the heart of the middle class, a story nearly the opposite of what we took to be the Holy Grail. So what was so great about fighting for poor people to get into a middle class we had left? I was less and less impressed.

Midway in our pursuit of justice for the oppressed, Judy and I began to try to live it out in community, something like the church did at the beginning of Acts. We knew the government could never really do justice; so we thought we needed an alternative society as a sign of what the world was meant to be. A community to model the Sermon on the Mount, the one story that didn't seem empty. In this, we were guided by John Howard Yoder and Art Gish.

So twenty to thirty of us moved near each other in the Germantown section of Philadelphia. It went better than anything else I'd ever been involved in. But it didn't go well enough. We offered a fair facsimile of the Sermon on the Mount as far as we understood it: limited racism and sexism, genuinely simple living and a commitment to the oppressed. But our marriages weren't that much better than those of others, our simple living wasn't as freeing as we'd hoped, no one ever joined us who wasn't white, and our conflicts (though not terrible) went unhealed year after year. We weren't empty, but we sure weren't full.

I was no longer impressed, and neither was Judy; so I resigned from *The Other Side* and we left. We needed to sort things out, to reevaluate our lives. Writing helps me do that; so in September of 1984 I began work on this book. I wanted to weigh the stories again. Much of what we had done seemed right, but something was missing.

Eight years later as I finish the book, I'm surprised at how much I still believe of my old story. I'm also surprised at how it has been transformed. New approaches, like to the church and to selfishness, to romanticism and rights, have put my old beliefs in such a different context that I feel as if I have a different story. But perhaps I should let that story tell itself.

After I tell the story of Jah.

The Story of Jah

Once upon a time, Jah painted a universe of wonder, and he liked it so much that he wanted someone else to enjoy it with him. So Jah made Adam and Eve, wonderfully and fearfully, so that the three of them together could be a warm spot at the center of this universe. And Jah saw everything that he had made, and behold, it was very good.

Then Darkness came and told Adam and Eve that Jah didn't want them to have all he had. Adam and Eve rebelled and built a wall between themselves and Jah. The wall grew till it divided everyone from everyone and people from themselves to the point that the first child ever born murdered the second child.

And so it went. Racial walls, walls between men and women, walls between parents and children, wealth walls, wife-husband walls, walls between humankind and the rest of Jah's creation, walls between heart and head, compassion and self, walls between walls—these became the maze of Darkened history. Wonder still abounded, but it was twisted on jagged walls, and people didn't often attend to it because they chose Darkness, which they loved.

When Jah saw everything he had made, he was filled with horror and hope, sorrow and wonder. He swore awful judgment from that moment and forever on wall building and Darkness. And promised the end of walls. He chose a flock of geese, and he made them his and taught them how to love one another without walls. But they would have none of it. They systematically decided for Darkness and misery. Oh, here and there, for a few years, with the help of Jah, the geese would knock down walls. But that was only when they had a great knight—Abraham, Moses, Deborah, Isaiah—and even these heroes half-loved Darkness and his walls.

Then in greatness came the sorrow and the wonder. Jah became a goose and proclaimed a kingdom without walls. In rage and delight, the geese and Darkness and all the peoples of the earth conspired. They seized Jah and beat him to death against their jagged walls. For their darkness.

But that was the promise. With his own body, Jah battered down the walls. And arose broken and whole, servant-king of a universe without walls.

It's not over, but here and there little bands of joyful geese, joined by an occasional lion or owl, have become a people without walls. They live in reconciliation with each other, giving their bodies to be broken against walls (they have no concern for their rights). They don't need to prove that their story is true, for their love for each other proves it for them. They are the warm spot at the center of the universe.

Darkness tells other stories, less costly ones, but he is in fear, watching the love of the servants of Jah for each other, watching it draw handfuls of his slaves right across the jagged walls guarding his dominion.

Any minute, Jah will finish, and his people will live with him in his kingdom, happily ever after.

2

The Dimensions of Our Emptiness: Or, The Loss of the Great Questions

T he hollowness within is meant to be filled by Jah, for it's in his shape. (At least, that's how I've come to see life.) Jah and only Jah can fill us. By contrast, the things our culture offers fill nothing. They drop silently into the void, leaving us emptier than ever.[1]

Material success can no more fill the inner void than bubble-gum wrappers can fill outer space. Our hollowness is wide and deep and reaches to the heavens. It is sublime, of a majesty fitting for Jah. But our culture is thin and shallow and tied to the ground. We have money and sex and fame—bubble-gum wrappers in various forms. But you can't fill hollowness with meagerness, and when you try, hollowness turns to emptiness.

How many bubble-gum wrappers would you need to throw into the air to fill the heavens?

The dilemma of modernity is how a culture of one dimension is to fill an inner space of grand dimensions.

Signs of Emptiness
The emptiness is everywhere. We don't seem to care that each day forty

thousand children die because they're poor. Most people don't even know it, and almost no one does anything about it. We spend more on candy (not to mention alcohol and tobacco) than on world hunger, and spending on all of those is dwarfed by spending on the military.[2] That's wicked, but it's also oddly empty.

And you find the same emptiness wherever you look. Try marriage. I hesitate to recite the standard litany on divorce rates, because it may be misunderstood as moralism. But roughly half our marriages end in divorce,[3] and many of the rest are miserable. That's sad. As a people, we have no idea how to live. We don't even know how to get along with those we want to love most.

Let me put it differently. How many marriages do you know that are things of joy? (I suggest that lack of joy is a good definition of emptiness.) But what's even emptier is the way we accept joyless marriages. We spend more time watching television than we do trying to learn how to enjoy one another.

And television. Have you ever watched a sitcom? Or a toothpaste ad?

And as for jobs . . . Kurt Vonnegut spoke at MIT in 1986, and he reports that not a single person he talked to believed Star Wars would work; however, they all nonetheless said they would accept a job working on it. It offered financial security.[4] I don't know whether they were right or wrong about Star Wars not working, but I do know that it's an empty people who are content to spend their lives on something they believe futile. They've lost their way. You can't send them to hell; they're already there.

But why not work on Star Wars—if Campbell's Soup cans are the icons of our civilization? What is there but a good job, unless maybe it's a good lay? What else can *good* mean?

All the real stuff seems forgotten. Perhaps through a process of reverse sublimation, we have repressed it, and so we try to fill ourselves with shopping, baseball, Nintendo, fashion, housecleaning. I'm not objecting to those activities on moralistic grounds, but I'm sad that we tolerate their emptiness. Our culture is a one-dimensional wasteland.

So we settle for self-esteem workshops in place of confessionals, *Playboy* and "Dallas" in place of *The Imitation of Christ* and *Messiah,* cocaine instead of stillness retreats, and inerrancy debates instead of parables. Did you ever notice what a loss it is that we build nuclear reactors rather than cathedrals? That African-American singers now produce rap rather than the blues? That we don't have a new order of Franciscans who leave their possessions in awe of the numinous but a new order of yuppies who collect possessions in greed of comfort?

This emptiness in modern people is one of the great horrors of all time. It's as if we'd had a lobotomy.

The Good Old Days

But don't misunderstand me. I'm not calling for a return to the good old days. Let's face it, the good old days never existed. I don't much care for telephones and automobiles, TVs and nuclear bombs, but I'd sure hate to return to the days before penicillin and birth control, paperbacks and computers.

Any strengths in past ages were offset by weaknesses. The Western world may have been less promiscuous at the end of the nineteenth century than now, but then they were also more racist. People have fundamentally the same attraction to Darkness whether they live now or in Rembrandt's day or in the Stone Age. The desire to lord it over others, to get even, to wallow in resentment and self-pity—people of all times and all places fall for such illusions. Evil is not peculiar to our age.

Still, each age has characteristic ways of expressing its evil, ways that connect to the spirit of that age.[5] In our age, the form it takes is emptiness. A curious distortion of reality leaves us without the spiritual and moral resources to care about the forty thousand or to choose a job because it's worthwhile.

And while there's never been a golden age, some times and places have been less bad than others. The problem is that our culture doesn't seem to be one of those, and we have to wonder whether in its emptiness it can provide the spiritual resources and moral direction a people need to flourish—or even to survive.

How much can you expect of an age whose icon has been squeezed down to a soup can?

We are empty.

School

And our individual emptiness merely reflects the emptiness of our culture. I base that assertion not on any profound argument but on watching my daughter in public school. They never asked her to write a parable; they gave her multiple-choice exams.

Did you ever wonder why multiple-choice exams are the standard test these days? The reason is emptiness compounded by shallowness. We test kids for how much information they have stored away and for how well they can perform certain standard calculations. We don't test for wisdom or understanding of holiness or ability to create beauty. The very idea seems bizarre to us.

And public schools are a metaphor for our whole culture. (If you want to know what a culture is about, study its schools.) Our schools are a lot like Andy Warhol's paintings: no wonder, no wickedness, no human beings. So of course, our kids grow up into joyless marriages. And to indifference about the forty thousand.

Mind you, the fault no more lies with the tests than with Campbell's Soup cans; the fault lies with what we teach, which is information and methods of calculation and composition. The tests are reasonably accurate measures of what is taught, which is a reasonably accurate measure of our culture. Modern education is informational, not formational or transformational. That's because modern culture is informational. So teachers spend little time on beauty, truth or goodness. How could they? They're too busy teaching the names of state capitals. It's as if we'd all had part of our brains disconnected. That's called a lobotomy.

I once went to the Rodin Museum in Philadelphia with my daughter's junior-high class. I imagined that we would discuss beauty, but when we got there the teacher didn't get much beyond where Rodin was born, how you do bronze casting and what terra cotta is. He didn't ask the kids how the sculptures made them feel or which ones were most beautiful. You see, those things wouldn't fit on a multiple-choice exam.

And when they had a unit on poetry, guess what they studied? Not imagery, I assure you. Not seeing the commonplace with different eyes. Not hearing something expressed that you had always known but had never found the words for. Not even the beauty of language. No, they studied rhyme and rhythm. Which left them with the impression, I presume, that limericks are comparable to Shakespeare's sonnets. Rhythmic rhymes.[6]

This emptiness is not limited to our junior highs and high schools. You find the same sort of thing in medical school. There doctors are taught technology while people are somehow omitted. And the same is true for law school and business school.

Andy Warhol was a seer. He saw that we leave people out of our schools and our lives; so he left them out of his paintings.

Our culture requires kids to spend half their lives learning trivia that don't matter. Which would be fine if life were a game show, a sort of endless Trivial Pursuit. But how much information would it take to fill the hollowness within?

I'm not objecting to my daughter's schooling (I won't call it education) because it wasn't highbrow enough. That's not it at all. I'm objecting because the important things were left out. What I'm saying is nothing more than that the curriculum in schools is biology, algebra, English, gym, computer use and shop. Which is to say, the curriculum isn't awe, beauty and holiness; it doesn't even mention them.

That's what I'm saying. Not anything complicated.

But something elemental.

School leaves out everything that might fill our hollowness. And in that, it reflects our culture as accurately as Andy Warhol's paintings.

The Great Questions

In school we answer certain questions, information questions like what year Garfield was shot or how amoeba reproduce. But we don't deal with the real questions: What's it all about? Who am I and how should I live? What's important? Is there such a thing as wisdom? Those are the great questions, the enduring questions. Asking them is central to being human, central to filling the hollowness within.

People tell me that in the United States, values and religion should be taught at home and in church, not in public school, and there's something to that, especially in a diverse culture. That's why the Bill of Rights prohibits the establishment of religion. And in any case, if religion and values were taught in public school, I'd probably hate what was being taught more than I do now.

But the central issue isn't constitutionality or fairness. It's not just in public school that we don't deal with the great questions; we scarcely deal with them at all. It's odd, but my experience is that churches and parents don't do much better than that teacher at the Rodin Museum. Somehow, our whole culture has lost its ability to approach the great questions. Campbell's Soup cans have driven out Rembrandt.

Which is the source of our emptiness.

So Sunday-school classes are likely to be rehearsals of David's flight from Saul or moralistic lessons on behavior. You will hear that God exists and that lying is bad, but you will hear little about the fear of the Lord or the beauty of holiness. And were a class from a Christian school to visit a Rodin museum, the teacher would not be a bit more likely to talk about beauty than a public school teacher. We transmit facts (information) because as a culture we're at a loss with value (formation and transformation). Even Christians, who are supposed to major in the great questions, are often curiously inarticulate in the face of value questions.

But the word *values* is inadequate. It doesn't reach deep enough. Values are the sorts of things determined by Gallup polls, and that's not what I'm talking about. What I'm talking about is holiness and evil, hobbits and the Dark Lord, story and myth, symbols and reality, awe and the Holocaust. Even Christians have lost their sense of them.

Seminary and the Idea of the Holy

Consider our seminaries. There the Supreme Court has not encroached on religious freedom; there Christians teach whatever they believe is important. So what do we teach? The idea of the holy? How to talk to God about our messes and joys? Spiritual disciplines? The pursuit of wisdom? The construction of stories to deepen the spiritual insight of parishioners? How to become like Jesus?

Not on your life. Protestant seminaries, at least, have bought the secular model of education: information transfer, just like my daughter's junior high. Only it's different information: Greek, New Testament introduction, systematic theology.[7] If you told seminary professors that they were indistinguishable from professors in secular graduate schools, most would be delighted. They suppose that God is a topic to be studied much as you would study geological formations on the moon. And from about the same distance.

The holiness of the professors (as in contrast to a certain minimal decency) is of little concern. And it doesn't occur to anyone that the center of the curriculum should be teaching students to be holy. No, we settle for transferring information into their heads. And usually it isn't even information about holiness. Seminaries rarely even offer courses with information on Mother Teresa, let alone courses on how to *become* Mother Teresa.

As Thomas à Kempis said, "What good do you get by disputing learnedly about the Trinity, if you are lacking in humility and are therefore displeasing to the Trinity?" And a few sentences later, "I would rather feel compunction than know how to define it."[8]

Compare the idea of the holy with debates over who wrote the book of John, and you will see why I say our culture is empty. We have lost all depth. Somehow, even in religious institutions, the lobotomy continues. Soup cans have replaced the cross.

State Capitals and the Nothing Game

I first noticed that something was wrong somewhere around fifth grade. I didn't call it emptiness or shallowness, of course. I called it boring. I'm dyslexic; so I'd only just learned to read. But once I learned, I read and read. The only time I quit reading was at school. Where I was bored.

Partly it was just that I preferred play to work, and school was work (especially for a dyslexic like me). But there was more to it than that. The books I read at home were full of wonder and excitement and importance, while school was irrelevant and gray.

My books were about real things: they were about people, people who were quiet like me or people who talked, people who felt hurt, people who succeeded or failed. But school—school was about nothing. It was about the spelling of *ceiling* not being *cieling* and about the year Garfield was shot—and I didn't care. I thought *Tom Sawyer* was more important. Or walking with my dog in the woods. Now that was exciting. But in school I was bored blind.

In seventh-grade geography we were asked to memorize the state capitals, and I refused. (I suppose it was my first principled act of rebellion, obnoxious child that I must have been.) I mean, who cares what the capital of Nevada is except politicians and lobbyists and people who live in Nevada?

About that time, I started talking to my father about school. I'm not sure either one of us knew what I was talking about, but he used to let me stay home from school to read more often than my teachers liked. And one conversation ended with his paraphrasing Mark Twain: "Never let school get in the way of your education." Which I've practiced ever since.

In high school, I started playing the Nothing Game. When class got intolerable, I'd make two lists: one of things that mattered to my grade but that I believed were nothings; the other of things parallel to the nothings but that seemed to matter.

Nothings	Somethings
Who were the generals at Ft. Ticonderoga?	Was the American Revolution right?
Name the first five presidents of the U.S.	What makes a president great?
How many species of trees can you identify?	Write a poem about an oak tree.
What is the capital of Nevada?	Is a state's capital as important as its flower?
How did Rodin cast the *Gates of Hell?*	What makes the *Gates of Hell* horrible?
When was Mona Lisa painted?	What is Mona Lisa hiding by her smile?
Footnote literary references in *Waiting for Godot.*	What is the point of *Godot*'s absurdity?
Is the spelling *independence* or *independance?*	What is good and what is bad about independence?
How long do blue whales get?	How great is God?
What is the highest mountain on earth?	What on the earth is most awesome?
Quote John 3:16 word for word.	What is the love of God like?
Does the Bible have any mistakes?	What keeps you from living the Bible?
How many blind men did Jesus heal at Jericho?	Do you obey Jesus?

I still play the Nothing Game, though it's not nearly as clear to me nowadays what should be on the nothing side. Competing over who can identify the most trees is still firmly on the list, though I've found that learning trees' names helps me see them better. And by now I wish I'd memorized more Bible verses; it helps get them in your bones. Apparently, when I invented the Nothing Game, I didn't have a great handle on what makes something trivial.[9]

But I was onto something. School teaches Nothings. In soup cans.

Quality and purpose are excluded. Depth and wonder. Which is why school is boring.

And it's not just school; it's our whole civilization. Our civilization is about as deep as a pizza pan. It has little place for holiness or wisdom, for goodness, truth or beauty. Our superheroes are powerful, not wise or holy. Supermen, not Gandhis.

And if you don't believe it of yourself, ask yourself how you feel about holiness or righteousness. Are they in fact major goals for you? Have you ever even thought about them? Isn't the whole idea of holiness a little embarrassing? (I was once reading Donald Nicholl's *Holiness* on a beach in Santa Cruz when I came to his discussion of holiness being embarrassing to modern people . . . and realized I was carefully covering the title.[10])

I don't mean there's some kind of conspiracy to keep us from pursuing holiness or wisdom. It's just that our culture has given us lenses through which we can't see such things. One-dimensional people see only in their dimension; so spirituality, the great questions, goodness—all become invisible. Automatically.

Chaplains

In our culture even people who intend to be oriented toward the great questions somehow transmute them into trivia. Christians, for example, often seem able to take profound moral and spiritual matters and transmogrify them into one-dimensional Nothings that fit better in our one-dimensional culture.

Take chaplains, for example. Chaplains pray over things, and then the real participants proceed to do what they were going to do anyway: have a yacht race, vote against aid to poor children, shoot their enemies. Chaplains aren't hired to raise the great questions confronted by their employer's main activity; their job is to bless whatever their employer has already decided to do. They're not in the chain of command; they're add-ons to the real activity.

So naval chaplains advise on sexual morality in port (while distributing condoms), but in wartime they never say that any particular war is unjust; they don't speak on the moral issues raised by their employer's business. Catholic chaplains are allowed to have Mass, of course, and evangelical chaplains are allowed to try to lead soldiers to Christ, of course. As long as they don't impinge on the business—of killing the enemy.

That's what I mean by saying that today even those whose business is the great questions tend to make them one-dimensional; we tend to remove them from the richness and power of our multidimensional universe. So Christians reduce salvation to accepting certain information with little bearing on how you treat your enemy,[11] a Nothing that has lost its depth and passion. As a result, modern Christianity fits comfortably into our culture.

Let me put it another way. Chaplains are required to treat religion as a way to help people adjust to the world as it is, as a sort of societal mental-health aid. Thus military chaplains on both sides of a war encourage their soldiers to go kill each other bravely and well, and when their own people are killed, they try to soften the blow for the family.

But what should a chaplain of the Roman legion have done at Golgotha? Told the soldiers to drive the nails straight? Tried to make them feel better about what they were doing? No, a spirituality that isn't shallow would have the power to help our spiritual leaders resist and suffer in hope.

A Rabbit's Foot in the Front of Every Classroom

Perhaps the point can be made most clearly in the struggle over school prayer. Here we have people fighting for spirituality and depth. Or do we? It's not obvious to me who's shallower, Madalyn Murray O'Hair and the ACLU or their opponents. Don't misunderstand me: things are badly wrong when God isn't at the center of education. But you can't cure that by tacking on prayer at the start of school. You might as well install a rabbit's foot in the front of every classroom.

To put God at the center would require changing the curriculum and hiring teachers with wisdom and holiness. What we need is not the restoration of a formality but a spiritual renewal that will put God back at the center of our lives. Then God will be back at the center of the curriculum, and prayer will find its place in school. And that's not as a formality but as something with enough depth to fill our hollowness.

Prayer is far too precious for public school. With some teachers not even religious, why on earth would anyone (let alone a fundamentalist, by the way) want them to pray in front of kids? It's at least as sad as having Shakespeare taught by someone bored by him. The kids would be likely to conclude that prayer is the same sort of thing as saying the alphabet. Something done without passion, conviction or even much inflection. Not like having a conversation with a friend or your mom. Or the Lord God.

Don't misunderstand me. I'd love to have kids in schools where they pray. But that's just it. What's being proposed isn't prayer.

It's an empty formality.

It would only incline kids to think of prayer as an add-on to the main event. Not as a core subject like reading, writing and arithmetic, but as something irrelevant you do before getting down to business. Like at baseball games, graduation ceremonies, building dedications, even sermons: first you pray, then you do what you really came for—and everyone knows that's not prayer. I call it the chaplain's fallacy.

What's happening is not prayer; it's a Nothing. Prayer isn't dead and boring and gray. Or something to be hurried through so you can get to the main course. Prayer is where you find your center (God), where you express your deepest longings and greatest fears. Where you finally find the hollowness filled.

Secularism in Drag

The controversy over school prayer unmasks a primal problem in our civilization: the loss of spiritual depth among religious people. The controversy is sometimes seen as being between secular people and religious people. Which is to say, in our culture when religious people fight for what they believe, they fight for an empty formality. Spirituality is lost.

We seem to have our choice between secularism and religious formalism—which I think of as secularism in drag. And the odd result is that spirituality is often excluded even from religious life.

Madalyn Murray O'Hair was wrong. If she wanted to further the cause of atheism, she should have tried to *keep* prayer in public schools. The most effective way to trivialize spirituality might well be to fight over whether to have prayer as a formality. Then whichever side wins, spirituality is lost. To put it differently, we've lost the war, but the enemy is encouraging us to fight a battle—maybe it will keep us from noticing that it's all over.

Of course, not all religious people support prayer in public school. But that usually has more to do with concern over religious liberty than with a recognition of the horror of reducing prayer to shallowness. So fundamentalists aren't the only religious people who have lost sight of the spiritual: the others tend to be more sensitive to constitutionality than to spirituality.

What we need in school is not prayer at the beginning but an agenda deeper than information and methods. Kids need nurture in a spiritually sensitive environment where I-thou relationships[12] are more important than state capitals. Where the adults lead lives of grace and truth and where justice is as important as grades. Where the study of poetry does not focus on meter but on finding ways to express depths almost forgotten in our culture.

Dangerous Business

Prayer is dangerous business. You'd better not pray unless you're willing to let it challenge your narcissism. If you ask God to bless what you're going to do anyway, you may get uncomfortable results. So don't pray unless you're open to not killing the enemy, to not following the standard curriculum.

Prayer, you see, is a living, powerful thing. It's not information transfer between computers. It's communion between persons, nurture for an I-thou relationship with God, the thing that fills the hollowness within. It shakes the foundations and brings new life with added dimensions.

When Moses encountered God at the burning bush, he wasn't mumbling pleasant formalities as a prelude to what he was going to do anyway. Nor was he reciting incantations to keep the gods from messing up his plans. No, things were so awe-full that he took off his shoes and abandoned his plans. Against his will, he led his people to freedom, rocking the most powerful nation of the age. Later, when he prayed in the wilderness, it was so real it made his face glow.

I support that kind of prayer. And I'd like to see the Supreme Court try to stop it.

But let me tell you how we lost all that, how we got the one-dimensional culture we have.

3

The Implacable Tide: Scientific Wealth & Spiritual Deprivation

t started in Athens around 465 B.C. That's when a philosopher named Anaxagoras concluded that the Greek myths were superstitions. He realized that the sun and moon were not a god and a goddess but a red-hot stone and a ball of dirt.[1] That's how it all began. Very promising. But it culminated in the 1960s with Andy Warhol's soup cans and a fight over prayer in public school. Rembrandt's world was gone, taking all depth with it.

How it happened is a complex piece of history: the history of epistemology (how we know things) and, secondarily, the history of metaphysics (what exists and what it's like). And if you look at this history honestly, the reasons for accepting its conclusions are quite compelling. Once you grant a few harmless-looking assumptions, ones which most of us think are obvious, you are caught in an implacable tide. And without noticing how or even when it happened, you are reduced to one-dimensional emptiness. And it all seems natural. I call it the secular squeeze.

Like the proverbial fish that can't see the water it swims in, so we don't see the shallowness of the water in which we live and move and have our being. We scarcely notice the narrowness of the stream that we have come to tolerate, scarcely recall the depths from which we have been taken.

Old Stories: Of Dragons, Fairies and Gods

Those we call "primitive" explain things by stories. If they were trying to understand the sunrise, they might say that it's the result of a battle between darkness and light that was won by the sun god.

This kind of story making has more to do with poetry than with the objective approach of science. It's connected to the emotional experience of those who fear darkness and need sunlight for their crops; for them sunrise ends a struggle between chaos and order, good and evil. For them, reality is personal; so the sunrise is an encounter with the person of the sun.

The only possible result is stories. Not critical judgments or analytical statements or mathematical formulas, but stories—generally epic stories in the form of dramatic poetry. The stories are told and enacted not just as entertainment or to convey abstract information, but as ritual intended to influence the behavior of gods and human beings.

Intellectual Distance: The Loss of Dragons, Fairies and Gods

Those stories are not designed to answer questions like, How do you know the sun is a god? What's your objective evidence? They scarcely even allow people to ask such questions. But the time comes when people ask them anyway. And when that happens, we no longer call those people primitive. The first and biggest step toward science, toward becoming modern, has been taken.

Ancient Greek philosophers started the process. At least in the West they were the first to break away from mythic explanations and begin to make critical judgments about reality. They introduced intellectual distance and tried to be emotionally detached from the questions they asked. They didn't go far enough to suit modern scientists: often their basic ideas were intuitions for which they offered little evidence, and many of them held observation in low regard. Plato even used stories. Still, their ideas were the sorts of things that people could, and did, argue about.

This was a titanic shift in our worldview, one of the biggest of all. It was what philosophers call a paradigm shift. We see exactly the same world as before the shift, but we see it in a different way.

This particular shift certainly seems like a good thing. Modern people can't possibly argue against it. To us it seems obvious that scientific explanations are better than mythological ones. At least it does to me.

But this was an early step toward secularism.

I suggest that we must find a way which does justice to both science and stories, or we'll be trapped forever in a universe empty of everything but soup cans.

And we'll never escape the secular squeeze.

What's the Universe Made Of? Or, Disenchanting the Universe

Now as the epistemology changed, so did the metaphysics. That is, as views changed on how you know things, so did views on the nature of reality, on the furniture of the universe. As views on how you know things narrowed, fewer things were thought to exist. The universe got flatter and flatter.

Primitive people used a broad range of human abilities to make their stories (imagination, observation, dreams, prayer, mystical states, intuition, action, emotion, choice), but the new epistemology used mostly observation and reason.[2] If the old epistemology used human beings mostly from the mouth down, the new one used human beings mostly from the eyes up. The old epistemology used dramatic poems, the new one mathematical formulas. The new one, at least in its modern form, is limited to a mechanical brain—not a whole person confronting a thou, but a machine scanning unconscious matter. And that is bound to make the universe a less luxurious place. The advantage is that the superstitions that haunt primitive people are gone. The dragons are gone, but so are the fairies—and, before long, so too is the Lord of the universe.

These metaphysical changes started immediately in Athens. Almost as soon as people started asking "How do you know?" Anaxagoras asked, "How do you know that the moon is Artemis? It looks like a bunch of dirt to me." Modern people are so used to his conclusion that it's hard for us to imagine how primordial the change was.

Before Anaxagoras (and for a good long time afterward), people thought of the universe as spiritual. They saw God and spirits behind every rock, or rather they saw every rock as a spirit. The sea god doesn't live in the sea; he *is* the sea. They saw the moon not as a bunch of dirt or even as a bunch of dirt inhabited by a spirit, but as itself an embodiment of an angel or of the goddess Artemis.

The moon wasn't an it but a she—or rather a thou. Not an object to measure telemetrically, but a being to address, or even to commune with. As a personal being, the moon didn't move blindly, regularly, merely in accord with the abstract law of gravity. She moved by her own choice and with a purpose.[3] Her movement was not certain, predictable and impersonal, but the act of a god who could be supported, or perhaps even bribed, by human rituals and gifts.

So before Anaxagoras's way of thinking was accepted, the universe was sacred and personal, and each thing in it was spiritual and had a purpose. But when the process Anaxagoras began was completed in modern science, the universe was simply a piece of machinery, impersonal and meaningless, like a windup watch. There were neither dragons nor fairies.

But there were lots of machines to make soup cans. We were squeezed flat.

Anaxagoras began a process of disenchanting the universe. Before him, people experienced the universe as an enchanted place (in both good and bad senses of the word). In that worldview there might well be a warm spot at the center of the universe, but when the consequences of Anaxagoras's ideas were worked out, we experienced the universe differently. It had no center, let alone a warm and friendly one.

Anaxagoras began the process of explaining the universe with less reference to gods or spirits or persons. That is secularism, and taken to its limit, it necessarily means losing some dimensions: at least the spiritual dimension and the personal dimension. Taken to its limit, it means losing the warm spot at the center of the universe, losing all sense of purpose, losing a cross with nails as your icon, losing everything that might fill the hollowness.

"Lose all hope, you who enter here."

But let's be clear; Anaxagoras was right. The moon is not Artemis. We may not like the consequences (Anaxagoras had to leave town hastily), but that doesn't change the truth of the matter.

Where Do You Stop?

The process had begun. Can it legitimately be stopped at any point?

Perhaps *the* crucial intellectual question for modern civilization is, Once you introduce intellectual distance, can you have a personal universe, one with values? Can you ever get back? Can you ever be a whole person again? Can you ever have a personal relationship again, or are both the I and the thou eaten up? Can good and evil and the personal be explained scientifically without reducing them to something that destroys them? Can modern people accept some mythopoeic process without loss of intellectual integrity?

The Late Middle Ages and the Loss of School Prayer

But I have jumped over two thousand years. Few people in the ancient world accepted secularism. Neither Plato nor Aristotle had any time for it, and even Anaxagoras assigned an important place to spirit.

And in the early Middle Ages, after the West was "Christianized," theology was the queen of sciences, the foundation of knowledge. Augustine made light the key epistemological metaphor (it was found in both Plato and the New Testament). Truth was something you got through divine illumination. Reason was important, but everything was seen in the light of faith; so reason apart from God was limited, and the senses, though reliable enough for everyday practicalities, yielded no truth—or rather, no Truth.

This dismissal of observation as a source of knowledge is as incredible to modern people as our dismissal of most everything else would be to medievals and ancients. It wasn't that they didn't trust their eyes to get them across the street but that they didn't consider that kind of information knowledge; they didn't consider it worth knowing. Plato, for example, acknowledged observation, but he said its results were opinion rather than knowledge. It didn't lead to eternal truth about the sublimity of spirit but only to changing information about the temperature outside. He was emphasizing its irrelevance as well as its uncertainty.[4]

So till the late Middle Ages, insight, revelation and mystical experience were accepted throughout Europe. People studied theology and didn't bother to study ants or smallpox; God and the good were what mattered, and knowledge of them came by divine illumination. (Multiple-choice exams would have made no sense.)

Then something happened. Who is responsible is hotly debated. I believe Thomas Aquinas laid the foundations for it, but Thomists deny this furiously.[5] In any case, people came to believe that God created reason and our senses; therefore, both can function reliably and independently of divine illumination. Though theological and spiritual things require special illumination (revelation), philosophy and science don't. Theology and knowing God aren't necessary for "secular" knowledge; so pagans can do science as well as saints, and what they learn is as true as what Christians learn in theology.

As with any paradigm shift, it's hard for those of us who live on this side of it to imagine what it was like before. That is partly because we accept the change totally. But we should remember that medieval people took the Bible at face value where it says, "The fear of the LORD is the beginning of knowledge" (Prov 1:7) and in Christ "are hidden all the treasures of wisdom and knowledge" (Col 2:3). Now, however, even devout Christians overlook such biblical teaching.

Imagine education prior to that. At its best, it consisted of learning to read the Bible and the official prayers, learning theology and morality under a teacher who was a model for life as much as a conveyer of information. Any biology and physics were mixed haphazardly with theology, which was the integrating point for your studies and your life. Who cared about biology and physics? They were Nothings, mere opinion.

But in the new view you could study physics apart from studying God. Seminary was separable from the university, or rather the university was separable from seminary. Theology was one part of the curriculum rather than the organizing and controlling principle that undergirded everything else. It was a separate topic, on a level with philosophy, science, rhetoric.

And people studied it differently. As I said in the last chapter, they supposed that God is a topic to be studied much as you would geological formations on the moon. And from about the same distance. First the moon was changed from a person to a stone; then God was changed from a person to a stone. The personal relationship, the thou, was being lost. Nothings were all that existed.

Eventually, in this dis-integrated setting, you could have school without any mention of God, without any prayer, certainly without any personal relationship to God. It's not that education was the same as before only without morning prayer; it's that education became a collection of bits and pieces of Nothing with no center, like in my daughter's class. It became the sort of thing where prayer and the personal were not of the essence.

If the topic is how to get to know God personally, then school without prayer is not one of the options. But if the topic is the sum of two plus two or the date of Plato's birth, then school is meaningless and prayer is optional. And if you have prayer, it will be an impersonal formality rather than a way to develop a relationship.

But that took a long time to develop. To start with, this epistemology was broader than earlier medieval epistemology. It allowed both observation and the older forms of knowledge; so for a time Western metaphysics and thinking got quite broad. For a while it looked as if we might have both science and theology. But the new knowledge eventually took over. It began to insist that its Nothings were the only proper form of knowledge. If you couldn't see something, it didn't exist. Leaving us with a narrow epistemology and therefore a narrow metaphysics. Leaving us, to be more precise, with a one-dimensional universe with nothing but Nothings. The secular squeeze was on.

But let's be clear. All that its advocates were saying to start with was that reason and observation, apart from God, were possible ways of knowing. And that's hard for modern people to question, though I'll come close to doing it before we're done.

Calibrated Instruments and the Flattening of the Universe
Part of what made modernity was the acceptance of observation as a source

of knowledge, but it was observation with a special twist. Scientists like Galileo and Newton narrowed observation to one sort of observation. Their problem was that Plato was right about our senses: they *are* unreliable and imprecise. When some people feel cold, others feel comfortable, and others hot. So how do you study temperature?

Scientists solved the problem by using machines, by observing with calibrated instruments; that way we have to rely on our senses for little more than reading dials and scales. So observation very nearly came to mean observation by calibrated instruments like thermometers, balances, clocks, sextants.

That has the advantage of objectivity in the sense that science no longer has to rely on my evaluation of my consciousness of temperature or whatever: distortions by an individual's senses are almost overcome. This made repeatability possible: if someone reports a result in Rome, it's testable in London using similar instruments. Even more important, calibration had the enormous consequence of making it possible to do science in the precise and powerful language of mathematics.

Going hand in hand with this basic epistemological change was, of course, an equally basic metaphysical change. What is it you can observe with a calibrated instrument? What is it you take the temperature of or weigh on a balance? What is it you can express in mathematical language? Not spirit, not God, not goodness, not persons. All you can measure is mass, extension and time.[6] In clearer but oversimplified language, all you can measure is particles in motion or, in more modern terms, wave-particles in motion.

Secularism was about to devour us in all its shallowness.

But this change in metaphysics was central to the advance of science: it changed reality from infinite chaos to a uni-verse. It reduced the number of sorts of things from infinity to three. Instead of seeing rocks as their own sort of thing and stars as their own sort of thing and light as its own sort of thing (and so on almost forever), it reduced the universe to mass, extension and time. Three possibilities is rather simpler to deal with than millions. That simplified the universe enough that the human mind could deal with it better. So science took off. This may well have been the most staggering intellectual leap in human history.

The Greeks had made a comparable move, reducing reality to fire, air, earth and water, and that view was common in the Middle Ages. However, reducing things to these four hadn't led to the discovery of patterns. It didn't work. But reducing reality to mass, extension and time worked. Boy, did it work. Suddenly patterns in the universe began to come clear. Scientists explained sound, for example, as particles hitting your ears in a certain way. Sound was not its own sort of thing alongside particles; rather it was made of particles in motion. *Everything,* at least in the physical world, was made of particles in motion.[7]

Scientists explained gravity as nothing more than mass and distance, and temperature as the speed at which particles were moving. Later they explained electricity as particles moving at the speed of light. And on and on. Although in the end this didn't deal with light or the behavior of subatomic particles, it was quite a start. A start that no one can fault.

Of course, it was a big step toward materialism and secularism—toward an impersonal universe. The new metaphysic was reducing all sorts of things to the physical, to particles, not to thoughts or feelings . . . let alone to spirits or persons.

Its advocates didn't mean to apply it to the soul or to the spiritual world. In fact, many of them were devout Christians; they still accepted other ways of knowing. Nonetheless, here was an approach that explained an awful lot of reality in secular terms—without any reference to spirits or God or persons. And that inevitably raised the suspicion that perhaps spirit and persons were not needed to explain any part of reality. Perhaps all the talk of spirits and God was superstition. At least, honest people had to wonder.

Soup cans were upon us; it just took a couple of centuries to notice.

Scientific Wealth, Spiritual Poverty

Now it's obvious that God and spirit are in trouble in this framework, but it goes deeper than that. All kinds of other things are in trouble too, things that even the bravest atheists cherish. What can be mechanically measured is quantity, not quality. So for the purposes of science, you have small particles or heavy particles, but you don't (and can't) have bad particles or wonderful particles. Scientists don't measure things by their quality. And they're right in some sense. Can you imagine a painting being measured as having twenty-seven units of beauty per square inch?

Since quantitative measurement was what mattered, quality decreased in importance. When you looked at a great painting under a microscope, the details of the patches of color increased in clarity; the beauty didn't. So since a microscope or telescope didn't show beauty as a separate item, beauty got decreasing emphasis.

As did good and evil, wonder and horror, wisdom and folly, spiritual depth and moral deprivation. You couldn't measure them with any kind of meter or scope; so what were they? Do beauty and goodness exist at all? Are they a projection of our imagination like goblins? Maybe you can measure IQ, but what about wisdom? If you can't discuss virtue in terms of calibrated instruments, if it's not analyzable into wave-particles, you have to wonder about it. And no one ever managed to invent any sort of ax-iometer (instrument for measuring value).

But you can measure certain aspects of poetry (rhythm and rhyme). You measure the meter of a poem in feet—meter and feet, the two modern European measures of length. In fact, *meter* means *measure*. So, of course, when modern schools teach poetry, they tend to reduce it to what they can measure. We are inarticulate about everything else, for we have a vocabulary for measurement but not a vocabulary for the heart.

Earlier, in the Middle Ages and the Renaissance, beauty and truth and goodness had been about all that was worth studying; they were the essence of learning. But by the end of the secular tidal wave, they had little place in the curriculum. How could they when no one could figure out how to measure them with a calibrated instrument? How could they when their metaphysical foundation was unclear?

The secular squeeze has succeeded. We are flat.

This prompted e. e. cummings's lines,

> While you and I have lips and voices which
> are for kissing and to sing with
> who cares if some oneeyed son of a bitch
> invents an instrument to measure Spring with?[8]

But more on that later.

The Abandonment of Purpose

Another aspect of this central change in modern metaphysics was the abandonment of purpose. In earlier, less successful attempts at science, the purpose of things had been central. But purpose requires consciousness, some sort of personal universe; so if scientists limit themselves to particles in motion, they are not able to ask what the point of things is. They can only specify cause and effect, and those only in terms of correlations, only in terms of mathematical equations—nothing more.

The theory of gravity, for example, merely states that bodies attract one another in proportion to their mass and in inverse proportion to their distance; it doesn't explain what force does the pulling—whether gravity is bodies sending out tentacles toward each other or what. To speak of the "force" of gravity is merely to state that bodies move toward each other according to a mathematical formula. In science, that's all explanation is.

I remember hearing Newton's law of gravity explained when I was a kid. I didn't consider it an explanation at all. I was annoyed. I already knew that apples fell toward the earth; now I wanted to know *why*. What force produced this attraction? Years later, I realized the value of the sort of explanation I had found so unsatisfactory. First, it tells you not just that apples fall but the precise mathematical rate at which they fall. Second, it states a regularity (a correlation) found in all bodies—not just that apples are pulled toward the earth but also that the moon is pulled toward the sun and the earth toward an apple. That kind of explanation may not tell why, but it has tremendous power. It simplifies our understanding of the universe by fitting movement among all bodies into one mathematical formula.

Which formula says nothing about purpose. That whole dimension is lost. It's not observable under a microscope or weighable on a balance scale. The meaning of *why* is forgotten.[9] We just are—no reason.

What science does is notice regularities and put them in mathematical formulas. And those formulas allow accurate predictions about the physical world, which makes possible everything from penicillin shots to sending rockets to the moon. In that sense, science is rich. It greatly increases intellectual grasp of patterns, which greatly increases control of the universe. That is, science increases knowledge and power. Which is an awful lot.

An awe-ful lot. The lot of the West is aweful Knowledge and aweful Power. And nothing else. Nothing else.

Can you imagine what happens to a soul with knowledge and power and nothing else? Faust, I think his name is. What we get in return for our souls is soup cans. With atomic bombs inside.

Science has given knowledge and power . . . without divulging how to use them. Nothing evil here—just a profusion of knowledge and power pushing everything else out, leaving only the crevasses for wisdom and purpose and spirituality . . . And they eventually die from lack of attention. Leaving evil to take over.

That is the secular squeeze. The intellectual crisis of modernity. And why we are so shallow.

But It Feels So Normal

But by now this shallowness seems normal—the way it is, the way it was, the way it has to be. The change has come so gradually that we scarcely notice. It is so pervasive we can't imagine anything else.

We're the famous frog sitting in a pot of water on a fire. It never notices any change and . . . never jumps out. We're not being boiled alive, of course. We're just having a dimension or four removed. And by now we're unable to imagine what any of the removed dimensions were like. Or even to remember that they ever existed.

A Little Lower Than the Angels: Or, What Are Little Girls Made Of?

However, I'm ahead of myself. Up to this point, scientists hadn't reduced human beings to particles in motion. The physical world may be mechanical and impersonal, but few scientists maintained that people were.[10] A little girl was still a person and therefore enchanted. A thou.

So let's go back. The stage was set to change all this by Copernicus (before calibrated instruments were central). The change he introduced was not exactly a metaphysical one, nor was it as basic as reducing the world to particles in motion. But what he figured out had a similar effect:

he figured out that the universe didn't revolve around human beings.

Of course, he didn't put it that way. From his point of view, all he figured out was that the sun and stars don't revolve around our planet. Now that's no big deal. It's an interesting fact from astronomy, but it has little intrinsic metaphysical import. It's like it would be to find that in an atom, protons circle electrons rather than electrons circling protons. Big deal.

That's if you look at it as a fact about the physical world. But if it's experienced as a fact about human beings, then it's another story. It means not just that the earth isn't the center of the universe, but that our home isn't the center of the universe—that *we* aren't the center of the universe. And before too long people realized that *nothing* is the center of the universe—nothing.

As always, it's hard to feel the importance of a change that came before our time. However, if you believe that your planet is the center of the universe, it's easier to believe that God cares about you and your planet. After all, you're in the middle of everything, and that's a sign of God's special care. But if the universe is a vast place that doesn't even have a center, no warm spot is suggested by its shape. The idea of Jah coming to love us and die for us is harder to believe if we live on one of millions of rocks hurtling through the universe.

Our home address used to be Number 1 Main Street. Now it's not even Number 7231 Third Street. We have no address. No home.

Perhaps the fundamental human desire is to find a home, a warm spot at the center of the universe where we feel we belong. But we are lost in space.

Hearts and Pumps

About a hundred years later came William Harvey. People believed that the heart was the seat of our emotions, the center for compassion, anger, romantic love. Then Harvey discovered that the heart was a pump—no different in principle from any old water pump. Nothing romantic about it, nothing mysterious, nothing spiritual. Just a pump. You open human beings up and right at the center you find . . . nothing. In the form of a pump. Are our bodies simply machines?

If people felt lost in space after Copernicus, now they felt lost in their own bodies.

Purpose and Design

But the idea that our bodies are machines was not terminal. After all, no one had a mechanical explanation for where human beings came from. We might be machines, but we were extremely well made ones—clearly the work of a creator. So people who rejected Christianity tended to be deists, not atheists. To explain our wonderful design mechanically was unthinkable; in fact, to explain *any* design apart from a designer was logically impossible.

Then Darwin did it.

He pointed out that natural selection and survival of the fittest would give the appearance of design. Some may not find his explanation convincing,[11] but survival of the fittest did the unthinkable: it offered a *conceivable* mechanical explanation for design. Darwin's explanation was logically possible.

At that moment, secularism won the day. The paradigm shift was complete. The secular tidal wave overwhelmed an entire civilization. People were no longer a little lower than the angels; we were a little higher than the monkeys. Rembrandt and Warhol were monkeys who not too long ago stopped swinging in trees.

And your daughter is just a bunch of protoplasm.

If the moon is what's at issue, it may be no big deal that it's merely a thing. But if it's your daughter . . . ? In the secular paradigm, if a tree falls and crushes your daughter, it doesn't mean a thing. It's not by design of the gods or of anything else. All your daughter's death means is that the tree was diseased and the wind was blowing and your daughter happened to be there. An unfortunate correlation of events. Nothing more. A meaningless accident in a cold, centerless universe—an impersonal event that squashed a piece of protoplasm called a daughter.

If secularism is true, we are alone in the universe. Alone with red-hot stones and balls of dirt. No spirits to protect us. No gods to rail at. No God to weep with us. The universe is a coldly impersonal machine. We cannot say with Isaiah:

Thus says the Lord,

he who created you [and] formed you, . . .

"Fear not, for I have redeemed you;

I have called you by name, you are mine.

When you pass through the waters I will be with you;

and through the rivers, they shall not overwhelm you. . . .

For I am the Lord your God. . . .

You are precious in my eyes, and honored,

and I love you." (Is 43:1-4 RSV)

That is how Isaiah felt, but he was wrong, at least according to secular people. The world is not in the hands of a caring being. It's all a one-dimensional accident:

A man said to the universe:

"Sir, I exist!"

"However," replied the universe,

"The fact has not created in me

A sense of obligation."[12]

God is not at home—and neither are we. The secular metaphysic has eaten human beings up.

The Psychology of Moral Irresponsibility

The major area still not explained mechanically was human behavior and feelings. But Pavlov and Freud plus the study of brain physiology and cybernetics soon began to change that.

Pavlov took a giant step toward mechanistic psychology: he discovered that some of what appears to be intelligent choice is conditioned reflex. Ring a bell just before you feed a dog, and soon the dog salivates whenever it hears the bell. This was the beginning of behaviorism, and since then people like John Watson and B. F. Skinner have tried to explain all behavior as the result of reward and punishment—without reference to consciousness or choice. If human beings are rewarded for obeying the Bible or seeming to like art that hangs in museums or voting their father's politics, soon they'll salivate at the mere mention of them.

And Freud's very different analysis put to rest any remaining illusions that human beings are but a little lower than the angels. Morality is merely a censorious superego, and love, art and religion (humanity's highest creations) are sublimated sex. Romantic love, which is supposed to set human sexuality apart from animal copulation, turns out to be an excuse for lust— our breeding drives are different from animals' mainly in that we're not honest about them. Being in love is a euphemism for being in heat, and what's worse, we don't know why we do things because it's all controlled by the unconscious. We're so loaded with ego-defense mechanisms that we can only sort out why we do things by going to a psychoanalyst and having our dreams and free associations analyzed. And it turns out that we're not responsible for our behavior—Mom and Dad are.

Not too much later, physiologists located specific areas of the brain that controlled not only bodily movement but also things we thought of as mental. By stimulating a particular spot on the brain electrically, physiologists could move a person's finger, revive a visual memory or produce anger. And chemicals acting on the nervous system turned out to have every bit as much influence on emotions as choice or training. Even our deepest feelings are not an outgrowth of the soul but the result of chemical interactions.

Meanwhile, transistors in computers began to outperform the human mind in some respects. Since Aristotle, human beings have been said to differ from everything else in that they are rational. But are you sure computers aren't rational? They can certainly do math more quickly than people can, and they can beat almost everyone at chess. Psychology (the study of the soul, you know) was reduced to the study of semiconductors. Semiconductors were all that was left of Adam, Plato and Jesus. And of Rembrandt.

And of you and me.

The Death of Humanity

The final chapter on modern psychology is not yet written. What parts are true and what parts nonsense will take decades to sort out. We can say that behaviorism and psychoanalysis (the two dominant schools early in the century) are not compatible with each other and are both on the wane in academia. Meanwhile, cybernetics and the study of brain physiology are in their infancy, and no one can know how much behavior they will succeed in explaining.

But we do know that all four of these schools have brought profound insights that we use all the time, so dismissing them would be folly. The unconscious, rationalization, superego, conditioning, the effect of chemicals on our moods—all are ideas we couldn't do without. We also know that in certain respects they all point in the same direction. They suggest that the reasons for our behavior and feelings are not what we think they are, and they agree that we are less responsible for our actions and feelings than we used to imagine. And there is truth to all that.

What is happening here is that the stance of science and secularism is being applied to one more area, the human psyche. This stance has succeeded everywhere else; so it isn't silly to suppose that human behavior too will be explained in such terms.

But notice the consequences. If you take any of these schools to their logical conclusion (and their originators tend to), humanity is dead. Here is an evaluation of Freud that could be a summary of all the developments since Anaxagoras:

> [Freud] depicts society as a mass of isolated individuals whose most natural emotion is hostility, pushing and jostling each other in the name of the survival of the fittest, but willing under certain circumstances to band together for self-protection. Their ivory towers conceal their stinking cave by the entrance of which they ruthlessly trade physical needs or personal relationships for private gain, returning to their innermost recesses to enjoy them without interference—and this after all is not surprising since they ceased to develop emotionally at the age of five and any trait presented in later life is merely camouflage to conceal what goes on within. Outside their tower are displayed their paintings, their collections of *objets d'art*, their musical skill and wit, or their scientific curiosity, when the psychoanalyst knows perfectly well that inside they are smearing the walls with ordure or enjoying "retention pleasure," satisfying their autoeroticism, or preparing to bite and rend any source of frustration. . . . Freud believed in the person as a social atom requiring

community only as a means to the satisfaction of his needs; in a primary hostility so strong that only sheer necessity or common hatred directed elsewhere could join people in love.[13]

This is the conclusion of the process that began with Anaxagoras. In which view, we human beings are a little lower than dogs. So Brahms's violin concerto, Shakespeare's love sonnets, Jesus' parables and Leonardo's Mona Lisa—all are products of neurosis. According to Freud, healthy people wouldn't do such things. Leonardo's desire to paint Mona Lisa in oil was merely a childish desire to play with feces. And the same for Rembrandt's painting himself crucifying Jesus.

And even if you reject Freud's explanation of behavior, most alternative psychological explanations are only more mundane, not different in kind.[14] The love of violin concertos and of the parable of the good Samaritan are reduced to conditioning or to some sort of electrochemical reaction. Don't ask, What's it all about? The answer is clear: nothing.

The Implacable Tide

Partly because of the horror of these conclusions, Christians and other critics of modernity often fail to acknowledge the power of the historical march of science or of its logical development in secularism. We claim for ourselves the parts of science that we like, and we dismiss as scientism the parts we don't like—without really grappling with the legitimacy of doing so.

And we point out that the really great scientists haven't been secular. Copernicus and Newton were serious Christians, and Einstein and Heisenberg were mystics. Secularism is for petty scientists, for technicians not capable of seeing the grand sweep of the universe in their telescopes. Now that response is important and exciting. It suggests that in missing the grandeur of the universe, secularists have missed even what science is about.

But we must say more than that. We must explain where it is that secularism has gone astray. We must explain the force of the historical tide. Secularism has swept religion before it like so many dust balls. In one area after another, religious assumptions have been shown to be irrelevant at best. God hasn't been a useful hypothesis in astronomy, dynamics, optics, chemistry, electronics or physiology. Secular assumptions have worked for science; religious and personalistic assumptions haven't. In the mathematical formulas of science, God doesn't appear: there is no x that stands for God. Ever.

That is just a fact.

The same is true for virtue, wonder, beauty, wisdom. They aren't useful in scientific formulas. They just don't appear there.

Einstein may have been a mystic, and quantum mechanics may give comfort to spiritual types, but the fact remains that God is not one of the factors represented in $E = mc^2$, nor does quantum mechanics use purpose to explain anything.

As long as people supposed that the sun was pulled by the chariot of a god, as long as they imagined that wheels fell off because a spirit was offended, as long as they tried to explain the physical world in personal (not to mention theological) terms, they got nowhere. Science muddled along for centuries precisely because it used those ideas.

There is something inexorable about secular science: first God was excluded from astronomy, then from the physics of motion, then from physiology, then from all biology. Where does it stop? Is God only for those areas that science hasn't yet got around to? A God of the gaps?

There is no logical place to stop. The scientific model has been so successful in the obviously physical sciences that it's natural for people to try to apply it to everything else. To try to treat psychology and literary criticism the way Galileo did motion is a little odd, but it's not stupid. It's being driven before an implacable tide. Perhaps it's refusing to bury your head in the sand.

And those quick to say that secularism is wrong merely show that they don't understand. Secularism makes it hard to believe the story of Jah.

Perhaps soup cans are the only possible icon.

The Implacable Consequences
But let's be honest about what that means. About the spiritual deprivation that follows the implacable tide.

Science is fine when we ask scientific questions. (We are geniuses at technology.) But what about when we ask the great questions: What's it all about? Who am I and how should I live? Answering them is not something that science does. It makes atomic bombs brilliantly, but when it comes to guidance on using them, science isn't in the business. It can tell us the effects of dropping a bomb, but it has no comment on whether those effects are good or bad, wonderful or vile.

Now perhaps that's fine—if someone else can comment. But the logic isn't just that science has no answers but that no one has answers, that the questions don't make sense. Values themselves have been ruled out, and questions like "What's it all about?" assume purpose, which has also been ruled out. It's about nothing. Nothing at all. Absolutely nothing.

Which leaves a thinness of mind and soul. A great thinness.

Implacably delivered.

Our emptiness is complete. We are squeezed flat. And the arguments for it are as implacable as empty soup cans.

4

Secularism Triumphant: Or, On Not Living Happily Ever After

By the 1700s and the dawn of the Enlightenment,[1] the triumph of secularism must have seemed certain to its supporters. Science was a source of brilliant light, and it was dispelling the confused muddle of prejudice and ignorance, superstitious fear, idle conjecture and theological dogma that had held humanity captive since the beginning of time.

Applying math to the measurable properties of what you could observe was the route to truth, and recognizing that fact was bringing not only knowledge but also freedom and happiness. The emotional dictatorship of the church and the iron heel of kings were going the way of alchemy and astrology. People were beginning to be able to say what they believed while doing what they wanted, and they weren't having to look over their shoulder to see if God, a black cat or a government spy was at hand.

True, much remained to be done. But more progress had been made in physics by Galileo and Newton than by all prior scientists; so why not comparable advances now in history, biology, psychology, politics? A Frenchman named Julien La Mettrie wrote a book entitled *Man the Machine,* and his colleague Pierre Cabanis said that the brain secretes thought as the liver secretes bile. All that had to be done was to work out the details, and in France a group called the *philosophes* set out to prepare an encyclopedia that would attempt just that. Alexander Pope expressed the mood of the age: "Nature and Nature's Laws lay hid in Night: / God said, let Newton be! and all was light!"[2]

The social and political impact was profound. Medieval metaphysics had lent itself to hierarchical structuring: God, king, lord of the manor, knight, serf; God, husband, wife, child, slave. But when people approached questions by "applying math to the measurable properties of what they could observe," they found no evidence of a hierarchical structure for reality. So democracy was established in the United States, Britain and France, and peasants began to rise throughout Europe.

And that was only the beginning. The rejection of hierarchy was a major factor in the profound cultural transformation still remolding civilization.[3] Abolition, women's suffrage, child labor laws, communism, labor unions, colonial revolts, the civil rights movement, women's liberation—all owe their existence in part to hierarchies' being hard to defend by applying math to measurable properties.

Human beings aren't born into niches where they find their lifelong role and contentment. Hence freedom, individualism, rights and equality. Without this foundation, Thomas Jefferson could never have written, "We hold these Truths to be self-evident, that all Men are created equal, that they are endowed by their Creator with certain unalienable Rights, that among these are Life, Liberty, and the Pursuit of Happiness."

Another sort of hierarchy central to the Middle Ages was the hierarchy of the spiritual over the physical. Spiritual and rational activities were at the top, while the physical and especially the sexual were at the bottom. But applying math to measurable properties also weakened that hierarchy, thereby producing further fundamental cultural changes—everything from affirmation of manual labor to the sexual revolution to aerobic dance.

Also challenged was traditional morality. What was the observable basis for all these rules? Old moral regulations began going out the window along with constricting priests and smothering hierarchies. We can do as we please! We may have lost the ability to answer the great questions, but who cares? Condoms are practically free, and there is no god to complain if we use them with whoever strikes our fancy.

The loss of the great questions is not a loss but a freedom, a great freedom—right there alongside freedom from smallpox and freedom from kings. No gods, no black cats, no bubonic plague . . . and no constricting moral regulations. The Puritans are dead. We're finally free to do what we really want, the things that conventional parents and constipated priests never allow. It's like summer after sixth grade with a strict teacher. This is the Holy Grail.

By the end of the 1700s the king of France had been executed and, in an elaborate ceremony, reason (in the person of a prostitute) had been crowned—not at the Sorbonne but at Notre Dame Cathedral itself, the religious center of France. God and king were dead. Something approaching religious fervor was generated for Enlightenment reason. And understandably so. When had there ever been anything so obviously and rapidly beneficial?

Denis Diderot, leader of the *philosophes,* had hoped for the day when the last king would be strangled with the entrails of the last priest, and now the time was at hand.

The Secular Story: And They Lived Happily Ever After

Once upon a time, people were ignorant and superstitious. A priest ruled their souls by telling them stories that fanned their superstition into hatred and their fear into subservience. And, with the help of the priest's stories, an emperor ruled their bodies by cruel power. A few knights fought the priest and emperor during those dark ages, but they were all killed. Then came Science, the greatest knight ever known. He slaughtered the priest and strangled the emperor. He put his Rationality in the place of their subjective stories and seated Democracy on the emperor's throne.

Then progress began—and was without end.

Rationality and Democracy brought total freedom. They strangled inquisitions and ignorant village elders, replacing them with freedom, equality and the computer. They attacked the oppression of peasants, blacks and women and supported any minority fighting for its rights. Meanwhile, Science worked great wonders—banishing smallpox, polio, false teeth, gangrene and near universal poverty. And in their place he graciously gave a cornucopia without limit: cars, jet planes, stereos, flush toilets, television, inexpensive books. To make pain unnecessary, he created Valium and self-esteem psychologists (whom he allowed to wear white coats). He also provided a Six-Shooter of Power to obliterate remaining problems. Admittedly, Scientific Rationality has not solved the problems of pollution and war, but in time he will offer a technological solution to them too—as he has to all problems.

Scientific Rationality banished Story to never-never land by demanding its scientific credentials, which of course it did not claim to have. And without Story, God and Taboo and Spirit slowly smothered. Scientific Rationality sensibly replaced them with a utilitarian understanding of feelings and rights.

So people were free at last—free to pursue their right to life, liberty and of course feelings. The focus on rights and feelings justified resentment and free love while Utilitarianism shone on success, power and money. Combined, those things were what life is about. So that people could live in the fullness of Rationality, they were given many models of true life—like on the cover of *People* magazine.

And they lived happily ever after.

The Most Successful Story Never Told

What you have just read is a story, the story of secularism. The one that killed God and made soup cans our culture's icon. It's the most successful story ever told. Wherever it has gone, it has smashed other stories and made them seem ineffectual and silly. Except for "primitive" people, readers of the *National Enquirer* and a few intellectuals, it rules the world.

Of course its purveyors don't admit that it exists, since they say they don't believe in story, only in rationality. So I had to dig it out myself from philosophy books and *Reader's Digest* and from silences I heard in school. I've never heard it as a story, and I hate it; so I may not have told it fairly.

But it is a story. False, hideous—and monstrously powerful. Never before in history has a story crashed through every culture and almost every person it met. But this one has. It is the secular squeeze—whose icon is a soup can, whose idea of spirituality is a brief prayer said at the start of school. It grips some of us all the time, and all of us most of the time.

On Not Living Happily Ever After

But things didn't go as planned. The secular story undermined not only prejudice and superstition but everything. As promised, it ate witches and astrology for breakfast, and kings and priests for lunch, but it then proceeded to eat human beings for dinner and itself for a midnight snack. No one noticed exactly when it happened, but (somewhere around dinner it must have been) the universe went one-dimensional and soup cans appeared faintly on the horizon.

Not many secularists noticed, of course. Self-deception keeps us human beings from noticing anything too upsetting to our agendas, and the fall of monarchies and colonialism and the flourishing of technology kept most of us satisfyingly opiated. Voting and heart transplants may not be all they're cracked up to be, but enough to eat and birth control are, and television and jogging at least distract us from the emptiness.

Secularism has changed us from people like Rembrandt—who could picture himself as an evil man crucifying God—to morally irrelevant chunks of protoplasm of no more significance than sides of beef. Were we to crucify someone, that act would not be evil but sick, and we would be sent not to confession but to psychotherapy.

Hierarchies have been got rid of—not by raising us all to the highest level but by pushing us all to the lowest level. We're all equally valuable— because we're all totally valueless. We are Nothings.

We are rid of the Inquisition—and also of Rembrandt.

Plato's Forms and a World of Depth

Our predicament will be clearer if we go back to Plato. Plato believed in what he called Forms. For each thing in the universe there was a Form, a sort of spiritual DNA. This Form determined the shape and nature of the thing and also the ideal it should strive for. Things are made of matter, which imitates the Form, but unfortunately matter tends not to hold the Form well. Hence error and evil: things imitate their Form, their ideal, to a greater or a lesser degree, which is what *good* and *bad* mean.

All we can see with our eyes is the matter of which things are made. However, by using reason, we can come to know the Forms themselves. The Pythagorean theorem is a good illustration: the square of the hypotenuse of a right triangle equals the square of the other two sides. You can't see that by looking at a triangle, but you can come to "see" it intellectually by using reason. In fact, just by asking questions, Socrates got an uneducated slave boy to figure out some complex geometry for himself.[4]

By using a dialectical approach ("the Socratic method"), the teacher becomes a midwife who draws out knowledge of eternal truth. This is possible because people are born already knowing the Forms. Matter and our senses obscure them, but by using reason to clarify the confusion, we remember the Forms themselves: we come to know the Truth.

We are like people in a cave, chained with our backs to a fire. As things move between our backs and the fire, they cast a shadow on the wall in front of us, and we mistake these shadows for reality. That's what we're doing when we use our senses instead of our reason: all we then see is a shadowy imitation of the real. Unlike in geometry, we see a physical shape without grasping the essence.[5] As a result, we can't live up to our ideal, to our Form, because we don't know what it is. So we need to use reason and have a teacher draw out of us what we already know, or we are limited to Nothings.

Scientific Epistemology and a World of Shallowness

Views related to Plato's ruled till the late Middle Ages.[6] Then William of Occam mounted an attack on Forms, and later the triumph of the application of math to measurable properties made the idea of Forms seem so odd that few even bothered to refute it. Both the strengths and the weaknesses of Platonism are obvious and enormous, but at the moment that's not the point.[7] The point is rather to illustrate why things are different for modern people. Comparing Plato to modern thought illustrates the interconnections between epistemology, metaphysics and ethics in a way that reveals a major source of our shallowness.[8]

You see, the lack of anything as handy as Plato's Forms leaves modern people inarticulate about morality (at least unless we have some religious account of ethics). The scientific revolution makes us articulate about quarks and electricity, but it offers no vocabulary or method for morals (or for the other great questions). The great questions are what Plato and Aristotle, Augustine and Thomas Aquinas would have taught in school, but after the Enlightenment we have no obvious way to talk about them.

Let me put it another way.

Scientists can build nuclear bombs, but they have nothing to say about whether to use them. They can set up experiments to determine roughly how many human beings would die and how severely property would be damaged if a bomb of a certain size were dropped on Hiroshima. They can put buildings on a test site at increasing distances from ground zero, and they can tie goats in various locations. Then they can drop a bomb and correlate the damage with the probable destruction at Hiroshima.

But what experiment could scientists perform to show whether that destruction was evil? What if someone claimed that Japanese lives were valueless, and so it didn't matter how many were killed? What experiment could scientists perform to determine the value of a Japanese person's life? Tying Japanese people up at a blast site would tell how many would die, but it could never tell you whether their lives were more or less valuable than the lives of white people . . . or of white mice.

Science has no way to discover the "Forms" of whites and Japanese, no way to approach moral questions, and therefore modern people have no way to approach them. The only questions we can approach are questions about Nothing. We have no Forms.

We know how to answer questions like, How far is the earth from the sun? What is the molecular structure of the rocks brought back from the moon? But science offers no way to answer questions like, What's worth doing with your life? What is the good? What is the value of a life? What is the Holy Grail? With Platonism, you could cross-examine your ideas until you came to a knowledge of the human Form, but nothing like that is possible for modern people. Nothing. We are stuck in a cave.

That is the intellectual crisis of modernity. Plato's metaphysic and epistemology produced a different world—a different ethic, a different education, a different aesthetic. A Rembrandt wouldn't have been possible under Plato,[9] but the art produced was closer to him than to Warhol.

We have lost our compass.

Enlightenment Subjectivism and a World of Shallowness

But the problem is not just the loss of our compass. That's the epistemological problem, but deeper than that is the metaphysical problem. The Enlightenment leaves us not only with no epistemological approach to ethics but also with no metaphysical basis for ethics—no metaphysical explanation for moral obligation, no metaphysical depth. We've lost not only the compass to find the North Pole but the North Pole itself.

In the Enlightenment world, what comes closest to Plato's Forms? What is there that could possibly be relevant to moral questions? Few ever suggested wave-particles; the only possible candidate was feelings. So the Enlightenment replaced Plato's Forms with feelings. Our moral North Pole was how we felt.

Which is to say, for all its emphasis on objectivity, the Enlightenment was oddly and radically subjective. I've said that for the Enlightenment, wave-particles were all that existed. But that's not quite right. There was also the subjective experience of wave-particles: sight, memory, hearing, emotion, kinesthesia, pain.

When Descartes wrote, "I think; therefore I am," he wasn't making a claim about rationality (as is sometimes suggested). Rather he was claiming that you can be certain about your subjective experience and about nothing else. So if you believe you're looking at a red rose on your desk, you know for sure that you're seeing redly, rosely and deskly, but you don't know for sure that a red rose and a desk are three feet from your eyes—or even that you have eyes. And if you're mistaken and are dreaming or hallucinating, you still know you're experiencing certain colored shapes.

So you can be certain only about subjective experience. You're shut off from the world and from others by being shut into yourself: the objective Enlightenment had a radically subjective underside.

Now in a world composed of particles and perceptions and feelings, feelings are the obvious candidate to guide behavior. If children touch a hot stove, it hurts, and so they're less likely to touch it again. If they hug their father and it feels good, they're more likely to hug him again.

That didn't mean that people were supposed to do what they felt like, at least not at first; it meant rather that ethics tended to be understood in terms of feelings rather than Forms. So you know that murder is wrong because when you encounter it you feel horror and moral repugnance.

Soon, utilitarians took the obvious next step. They identified goodness with pleasure and badness with pain. Murder is bad because it ordinarily increases the amount of pain in the world. Unlike intuitionism, this is a scientific ethic. You don't need to intuit some mysterious something called goodness or badness. All you have to do is measure pleasure and pain, happiness and unhappiness.[10] And in principle, some instrument like an electroencephalogram should be able to do that. Jeremy Bentham even suggested a unit of measure: the hedon. An act is good if it increases the total number of hedons in the world.

Changing the Question

We have here a primal paradigm shift: feelings replacing Forms in epistemology, metaphysics and ethics.[11] And that has been overflowing into ethics and life ever since, into culture and sex, politics and art, education and the search for meaning. Since then, even people who try to act morally have devoted themselves not to living up to their Form or to obeying God's law but to maximizing people's happiness and minimizing their pain.

And that hasn't been all bad. From that perspective, many previously accepted social practices are seen as obviously evil. Slavery, war, poverty, racism, killing for the sake of honor, sexism—all are unmasked as terrible evils, as are most forms of discrimination and oppression.

And some things once thought to be evil turn out to be OK. Consider sex outside marriage. In a utilitarian framework, the key question is, Does anyone get hurt? It's not immediately obvious that the answer is always yes. As long as all concerned are consenting adults, as long as disease is prevented and no child is born, what's the harm? That can perhaps be answered (though it won't be easy), but the point is that the question is different now. Not, "Is X wrong?" but "Does X maximize pleasure/minimize pain?"

And since the question changed, so do at least some of the answers. Our ethic has tended to change on the whole range of sexual issues: from birth control to homosexuality to striptease to sadomasochism. And the same is true on questions about women's roles, slavery, euthanasia, abortion,[12] war, animal rights and on and on.

If the Form of people is to be rational or holy, then we behave in certain ways, but if we are to maximize pleasure, the story changes. And since most of the changes brought by utilitarianism are enthusiastically supported by the majority, we're liable to think we're well rid of Forms and depth and God's law.

And it's not a silly claim. But neither is it living happily ever after.

Mana and Taboo

One way of explaining this is to examine little words like *ought* and *good*. What does it mean to say we *ought* to maximize happiness? *Happiness* and *maximize* are harder to explain than you might imagine, but explaining *ought* in a scientific, utilitarian framework isn't hard—it's impossible. In a world of wave-particles plus feelings, why ought we to maximize the feeling of happiness? Indeed, why ought we to do anything? In such a world, what is moral obligation? Where does it come from?

Some form of the problem has been recognized by almost all modern philosophers.[13] If *good* means maximizing happiness, then what does it mean to say, "It's good to maximize happiness"? The sentence then reduces to: "It maximizes happiness to maximize happiness." And surely it means more than that. Something is missing.[14]

What's missing is that *good* has a normative force not in the description *maximizing happiness*. And that normative force can't easily be accounted for in purely secular, scientific terms. Scientists can provide descriptions, but how do they explain anything normative? They can perform experiments to determine what maximizes pleasure, but what experiments could they perform to determine whether you *ought* to maximize pleasure?

Where do they get something with morally binding force? How do you move from *is* to *ought*?

Why *ought* we to oppose slavery—when science and secularism have no moral North Star? Science may provide no defense for the hierarchy used to justify slavery, but neither does it provide a reason to oppose it. From a scientific point of view, slavery (and all other forms of "injustice") are morally neutral, merely topics to be studied. Female slaves may have been sold away from their husbands and children, but that's nothing to get upset about. Nothing at all.

Let me put the problem this way: we aren't human without a clear sense of taboo and of mana, and feelings alone can't provide an account of them.

By *taboo*, I mean that some things are just wrong no matter how we feel; no matter how we feel, we are morally obligated not to participate in them and morally obligated to oppose those who do. To participate in them is an accursed abomination, an ominous defilement, a loathsome emptiness. It's to build jagged walls against others and ourselves, against the personal.

Such things aren't understandable in the glare of calibrated instruments and scientific notation, but they're readily understood in the nighttime of murder and trench warfare where we are in intimate touch with children's intestines, menacing guilt and tarantulas from hell. Freud and Jung knew the terrain well—as did Tolkien, Oedipus and the victims of the Nazis, not to mention punk rockers and viewers of *The Exorcist*. Taboo is the power both for and against the horror of all we're meant not to be. Breaking taboo makes jagged walls, boredom, hollowness and stupidity. It is death.

By *mana*, I mean the light and power surrounding all we're meant to be.

Some things are just good, and there is around them something that empowers those who love them and confounds those who reject them. To participate in them is the joy of revering what calls us to fulfillment in the warm spot at the center of the universe. It's an endless delight, a sublime wonder, an exalted jubilation. Mana is wildflowers and that which imprinted the hollowness within that keeps us yearning for the fullness of the stature of Christ. It's springs of living water, the awe-ful wonder of a crucified God, the distance of the stars, an ideal of life that draws us beyond our selves.

Such things aren't understandable in the midst of the pursuit of money and success, but they're readily understood in the light of love and self-lessness, where we are in intimate touch with beauty, justice and mystery—where the wolf will lie down with the lamb, and children will hunger no more. They will not hurt or destroy in all God's holy mountain, for the earth shall be full of the knowledge of the Lord, as the waters cover the sea. Jung and Tolkien knew this terrain well, as did Wordsworth and the residents of Eden, not to mention children on Christmas Eve, Buddha and *Pretty Woman*. Its marks are walls broken down, joy, hope and love. It is life.

"Trailing clouds of glory do we come, from God who is our home."[15]

Explaining Clouds of Glory and Befouled Orcs

But secularists can give no account of these clouds of glory or of befouled orcs: they have only wave-particles and feelings. For this many of them are thankful. They want nothing to do with guilt feelings—which lead to nightmares about tarantulas from hell. Orcs are only a projection of our own hatred and anxiety over Father hurting Mother in bed. We're well rid of all that.

Or so they say. And it's certainly true that Plato and historical Christianity brought baggage we'd be better off without, but we need to be careful that in getting rid of that baggage we don't accidentally get rid of ourselves.

For there are befouled orcs slaving for the Dark Lord of Mordor. That's why concentration camps exist. And we deny it at the price of being human. They're not an illusion, and neither is their horror. How are secularists to explain their horror? Perhaps they can describe the physiological happenings, but in what scientific language do they describe the horror? Once having accurately described the mechanics of a gas chamber, where do secularists get a taboo on using it?

Imagine that instead of ordering the death of all Jews, Hitler had ordered the destruction of all Mercedes-Benzes. Suppose he had had them all shipped to Auschwitz and put in a giant smelter to be made into Volkswagens. We'd think it very impractical, to say the least, but we wouldn't react with the horror and revulsion we do to smelting Jews. (Businessmen, of course, would have run him out of office immediately; all the tragedy of war would have been unnecessary.)

Smelting cars just isn't in the same category as gassing Jews. But if Jews are merely particles in motion with no clouds of glory, then we have no more reason to get upset over their being killed than over sending a car to the smelter.

I'm told that fathers often molest their daughters, but after all, if human males are just animals usually in heat, then fathers' having sex with their little girls is no problem. Dogs do it all the time, and we don't call it rape. The forty thousand may die each day, but if kids are merely something with height, weight and motion, then forty thousand of them starving is no big deal.

The things we care about most, the things most central to being human, are illusions. It's meaningless to say that genocide is evil. Our horror over it is odd. Why should scientific, secular people get upset over the destruction of some protoplasm?

For secularism lacks the category of the personal, and so it has no legitimate grounds for distinguishing between persons and things. Remember, secularism explains reality without reference to the personal or the spiritual; so it explains the sunrise without reference to gods. And without such categories, perhaps you can explain things on a scientific level, but you can't explain them on a moral level. On a human level.

However, if the universe is more than wave-particles and feelings, then the door is open to enchanted realms: realms of personhood and spirituality that can be the foundation for treating others well and for rejecting not treating them well. So, for example, the neglect of other *persons* takes on horror and taboo, and care for other *persons* takes on mana and wonder—hence the awfulness of concentration camps and the glory of a father taking care with his daughter.

Wherever the personal encounters the personal, I suggest that we have the metaphysical category of the personal and the moral category of the invaluable. The personal (spirit) is as real metaphysically as wave-particles in motion (both are presumably an aspect of the same reality),[16] and this metaphysical reality is what morality grows out of. Wherever we have the potential for an I-thou relationship, there we have the personal, and therefore the potential for good and evil, wonder and horror, mana and taboo. For the personal is real. That's why concentration camps leave us with such a sense of violation. Treating persons that way is taboo beyond imagining and brings us face to face with the horror and power of the realm of the dark. We are not dealing here just with protoplasm and soup cans but with people and principalities and powers.

A Delightful Concentration Camp: Or, Can a Feeling Be Wrong?

Secularists don't see a need for any of this, of course. They believe they can explain morality as feeling. The feeling of horror you have on learning about concentration camps is all you need for morality; that's the source of the taboo.

But there's another question: Is that feeling of taboo correct? Suppose a sadistic guard guided you around a concentration camp commenting on the delightfulness of it all. Would his feelings of delight be correct, or would your feelings of horror? It's not at all clear what it could mean for a secularist to say your feelings are more correct, and therefore it's not at all clear that your feelings are normative for the guard's behavior (or yours). If torturing people turns him on, why shouldn't he do it? How can other people's feelings put a taboo on his actions?

Physiologically, nothing is right or appropriate about feeling taboo over the Holocaust. If my outrage is detected by an EEG, that's interesting, but it doesn't justify the taboo. I may feel a taboo on male gynecologists, but that doesn't make them taboo—it only makes me confused. Taboo is not the same as the feeling of taboo.

For feelings are not Forms. Only if our feelings are a way of discovering a metaphysical something like the personal or like Plato's Forms do they have moral force—only if our feelings reflect something in reality that makes them right or wrong.

But for a secularist that cannot be. Like the experience of the color black, feelings are not out there; they're in me. In fact, they're out there less than the color black. When I read a newspaper, an image of the black words is in my eye, but the words are in the newspaper. But horror (like beauty) is in the eye of the beholder—and nowhere else. To make some sense of concentration camps (and roses), we need some notion of reality that overreaches wave-particles and feelings. We need something spiritual, something enchanted. We need the personal.

Is horror *just* my subjective reaction, or is my subjective reaction an *accurate* gauge of what's out there, an appropriate response to persons? Is the torture of Jews itself a horror, or is horror just my overwrought response? (Is a rose itself a wonder, or is wonder just the quaint response of an effete aesthete?)

In the secular story, to say that a painting by Rembrandt is great is only to say that I have certain feelings when I look at it and that lots of other people have comparable feelings. Beauty isn't in the world to be noticed by the sensitive; it's added by them. You can't be right or wrong about such things, only different from others. And the same is true for the horror of concentration camps.

There are no clouds of glory and there are no orcs. Except in overexcited imaginations.

Insensitivity Training

But if nothing is physiologically right about feeling horror over the Holocaust, then perhaps those of us who feel horror should go to psychiatrists to get our feelings straightened out. Feelings of moral outrage have no different standing physiologically from feelings of depression when everything is going well. How about electroshock therapy to get our emotions more rational?

In an impersonal world, sensitivity to the suffering of others is silly. If the world is not the kind of place that includes the personal as well as particles, then the thing for sensitive people to do is to stop being sensitive. We need to learn to look at Jews as we look at cars.

Horror. Nausea. Dread.

But maybe I'm naive and sentimental. Maybe what I need is to go to business school. Then I could write a self-help book, *Insensitivity Training in Thirty Easy Lessons.* I could get rich starting a Bleeding Hearts Anonymous. Then those who care about others could join my twelve-step program to cure people of their addiction to being human. They'd have to pay

for the service, of course—all the market would bear.
I'd rather strangle myself with the entrails of the last priest.
What'll it be, God or insensitivity training?

The Moral Clarity of Consistent Secularism

Christians commonly argue that secularism causes moral confusion: because of secularism, the world doesn't know whether to devote itself to helping starving babies or to getting rich on the stock market. The world wonders if people can properly have sex with anyone, providing they care about them, and it's not sure whether it's OK to lie or get divorced, to cheat on taxes or to steal "little" things from employers. All because of secularism.

And there's something to accusing secularism of causing confusion. But only because secularists don't face the consequence of their beliefs. Let's be absolutely clear: consistent secularists aren't confused on moral questions. They have answers. Boy, do they have answers.

Their answers are horrible, but they aren't the least bit confusing. Starving babies, getting rich, Japanese people, the stock market—all have exactly the same value. The same value as Volkswagens, redwood trees, garden rakes, dog turds and soup cans. No value at all. None. Nothing. Absolutely nothing. In none of them do you find value when you try to apply math to the measurable properties of what you observe.[17] The whole idea of value is a superstition on the level of belief in goblins and fairies.

We can have sex with whomever (no matter how we feel about them), we can rob whomever, we can kill whomever. We can torture people recreationally if we feel like it. We've gotten rid of hierarchies and morality—by making everything junk.

Without some replacement for Forms, some sort of numinous spirit, we live in hell.

Doing As We Please . . . to the Weak

If we're merely wave-particles that feel, we're free to do what we really want. And that freedom feels great.

Especially to the powerful. And the shallow.

The powerful love it because it means they can do as they please. It's not so nice for the weak . . . having the powerful do whatever they please . . . to the weak. The heck with strangling kings. How about strangling the weak with their own entrails?

We can do not only what moralistic, harsh priests prohibit; we can do what the sensitive and wise prohibit; we can do *anything*. If we're merely animals, we're free to behave like animals. We're free not only to eat, drink and be merry . . . but also to kill, torture, rape and smash. And others are free to do the same—to us.

So endeth common human decency. Right around dinnertime.

Having fun yet?

In a universe that's not enchanted, we're subject to the biggest bullies. And can object only on the ground that they're too big for us to bully. Of course, the people in charge may try to persuade others that certain rules are morally binding, but unless values are real, that's just a trick to get people to do what the folks in charge want.[18]

The movie *Alphaville* is a parable about a consistently secular world. In it, the hero tells a sort of joke about a man going to a restaurant one morning for a cup of coffee. When the owner asks him to pay, the man says, "I'm not afraid of you; why should I pay?" And he walks out. He does this every morning till finally the owner hires a thug. The next morning the man comes in and orders his coffee as usual, and the thug comes over and demands payment. The man replies, "Neither of us is afraid of the owner. Here, have a cup of coffee on me."[19]

Before, I told you what I called the story of secularism. But that story was propaganda. *Alphaville* is the real story of secularism.

If we're alone in a mechanical universe and heaven is only the sky, then we are in horror. Anything and everything is allowed—no matter how horrible. And Nothing is all there is.

The sounds of secularism strangling on its own entrails.

Not quite what the folks of the Enlightenment had in mind.

Popes and Sides of Beef

Of course, secularists rarely see it that way. They don't have the courage to face what they're saying. Except for a few. Like Jean-Paul Sartre and Ingmar Bergman. Like the painter Francis Bacon and the playwright Samuel Beckett. They portray the terror of humanity in a cold and empty universe . . . they look it in the eye and shriek abandonment.

Contrary to the general rule, Bacon is a modern painter who paints people. In his paintings, people are "paralytic, neurotic, leprous schizoids [who] move in cages"; they "become animals and yet remain human," and having "lost their heads, [they] cry out for help, for reality, and yet are real even if lost in the void."[20]

Bacon has a series of paintings reinterpreting a portrait of a pope painted by Velázquez. Velázquez's painting is beautiful; the pope is impressively dressed and appears to be a great man. In Bacon's paintings, the pope is still dressed in full regalia, but he is sitting in a cage, his face melting down like in a nightmare, and his mouth open in a scream. In the 1960s I saw these paintings at the Tate Gallery in London, and alongside them were hung a series of paintings by Bacon of sides of beef.

Why not? For what is the difference between a great man and a side of beef?

Bacon can explain himself:

Man now realizes that he is an accident, that he is a completely futile being, that he has to play out the game without reason. I think that even when Velázquez was painting, even when Rembrandt was painting, they were still, whatever their attitude toward life, slightly conditioned by certain types of religious possibilities, which man now you could say, has had cancelled out for him. Man now can only attempt to beguile himself for a time.[21]

Christians complain about the bleakness of such work, and we should. It's terrible. But we should complain quietly. Mainly we should rejoice. Secularists are the ones who should complain loudly, for it unmasks them for what they are: dressed in fancy regalia while secretly screaming horror at being no more than sides of beef. Christians, by contrast, should hail it as a courageous and accurate portrait of a universe without God. For in facing reality lies truth. There lies release from secularism.

And return home to the God who wants to fill us all.

The Case Against Secularism: Or, Better Dead Than Empty

Deep within each human being is a yearning to be filled. We feel incomplete and are always reaching for something more. Something is missing. Sometimes we reach for it in a fast car or a cheap TV evangelist, but we're always reaching for it. Secularists are no exception. They tell us it's to be found in reason and technology, rights and equality.

Well, they're wrong. At the end of that rainbow are caged people hung next to sides of beef. The fervor with which most secularists deny that end is an indication of how deep the human longing for meaning is.[22] They see the horror of that conclusion. And they're right. As secularists, they should proclaim the meaninglessness and hopelessness of life, but as human beings they know better. Down deep, they know they aren't meaningless.

And so do I. God made us to know that much. So I refuse to accept a story that says that the beauty of the sunset is not in the sunset but in the beholder's eye. I refuse to accept a story that says the murder of my daughter would not be a horror but merely a reorganizing of protoplasm.

I pointed out in the last chapter that God does not appear in a single, scientific formula and that that is the main argument for secularism. Now I'd like to point out that wonder doesn't appear in a single, scientific formula either. Or horror. Horror doesn't appear in a single, scientific formula.

And that's the main argument against secularism. Any set of formulas that omits beauty and horror, wonder and holiness, wisdom and veneration is silly.

So I conclude that secularism is an unnecessary hypothesis.

This is no criticism of science; it's a criticism of those who think science is everything and then carry on as if beauty and horror were real. Science isn't about beauty and horror but about applying mathematical hypotheses to the measurable properties of what you observe. We need to see measurable properties as one rather small aspect of reality. And like any one aspect, if taken alone they produce flatlanders who live in one-dimensional, dessicated desolation. If we think that science is all, we'll eventually become narrow and dry, squeezed nightmare empty, shrieking headlessly, whether we understand the reason or not.

We must decide whether Macbeth is right that "life . . . is a tale told by an idiot, full of sound and fury, signifying nothing." If that is what we decide, then we should live that way. What we can't do is decide that Macbeth is right, that secularism is true, and then carry on with life as if it made sense.

But we aren't capable of believing that life makes no sense. At the very least, life is "a beauty chased by tragic laughter."[23] A beauty and a tragedy that make no sense in secularism—for that which merely is cannot be tragic. So we must find a better story. One that makes sense of both science and tragedy, measurement and love.

I understand why some people think that the hope for such a story is wish-fulfillment, but it seems to me that our deepest longings are one key to the nature of reality, a key quite as important as reason. Surely our yearnings tell us something about what the universe is like; surely, the fact that a cold and empty universe flies in the face of my very being is an indicator of its falseness. The aching within tells something about the structure of reality. On what grounds is that realm just excluded from epistemology? Feelings have an epistemological role too; reason isn't all.

Would we really be given a telephone and a longing to use it if it weren't connected at the other end?

5

A Feeling of Passionate Mercy: Or, A Hitchhiker's Guide to Romanticism

At one time people were appalled by the superstition of the Middle Ages and enthralled by the rediscovery of classical learning and by the huge advances in science. But before long that began to wear off, and a reversal set in. Some people began to think of science and classical learning as the start of their problems. They began to think of the Middle Ages as the good old days and of the time before Greek philosophy as even better.

These people (I'll call them romantics) were so revolted by the horrors of science and secularism that they rejected them flat. They often didn't bother with a critique intelligible to rationalists; they just vented their rage that people should ever have had to deal with anything so silly and destructive. They spurned the Enlightenment and its children for putting life into neat little see-through boxes and carefully labeling each one in precise handwriting—like sorting rocks for a museum display. They found secularism stupid, insensitive and superficial, and that's all they felt the need to say.

The Romantic Story

Once upon a time, there was a great serpent who lived in a soup can. He was a nice serpent as long as he stayed in his can, but one day some Greeks let him out. Right away, the serpent, whose name was Reason, started killing reality in order to squeeze it into cans, which of course was where *he* felt most comfortable. He was always a terrible tyrant, but he got worse during the Enlightenment when he merged with science. Science gave him power.

The power to destroy. Empowered by science, Reason formed huge nation-states and immense corporations that funded enormous armies. They forced people to live in square, numbered houses in cities that had straight, numbered streets. There people worked on straight assembly lines that squeezed everything into cans with straight sides. The kids went to schools with straight hallways and numbered classrooms where they sat in straight lines to learn straight thoughts served from cans by straight teachers. After school, they marched in straight ROTC lines.

Violence was OK. How else could you make things fit into the cans now made by the *Fortune* 500? Natural curves had to be chopped off children, redwoods shortened, and whales killed for parts that could be sold in cans. Anyone and anything that wouldn't or couldn't be made to fit the cans was burned, and the smoke was vomited into the skies till the smell of earth-murder overwhelmed joy, and darkness covered the face of the deep.

Naturally, the people in cans soon lost contact with reality and had to use a lot of corporate deodorant to cover the smell of the rot from their amputated souls. Most everyone died, though out of habit most kept moving inside their cans.

A few heroic misfits survived, and after peeling away layers of reason and convention, they found their feelings and their true selves. Replacing their cans with self-determination and self-expression, they slowly learned how to go their own way and feel deeply and freely. Fed up with the hollowness of the daily grind, they moved to the woods, danced barefoot in the grass, and earned only enough for basic needs. "Tune in, turn on, drop out." They were joined by all those fed up with the rat race and all those following their hearts, and together they formed a counterculture, nonviolent and kind and free, where everyone loved everyone.

Kids didn't have to go to schools with straight rows but stayed home where they learned only what interested them naturally. Instead of learning how to make machines that killed, they learned how to let things grow, how to release their feelings in poetry and painting and stories. They spontaneously questioned authority, fought for their rights, and didn't hurt others, for people are good when not corrupted by civilization.

Naturally, straight civilization tried to repress these people because it was terrified by their spontaneity, especially about sex and drugs, but the beauty of their lives compared to the smell of souls rotting in cans revealed the grandeur and intricacy of a universe yearning to be free.

They had little interest in politics, but their revolution spread from the bottom to the top till the serpent and his culture of cans collapsed under the weight of its own hollowness. And free of reason and rules, government and clothes, everyone lived happily ever after.

The Vengeance of Poetic Souls
Or so the story goes.

Historically this hatred for rationalism came mostly from poetic souls who despised the shallowness of Enlightenment culture. Surprisingly perhaps, this reaction began before the Enlightenment proper was born. Almost a hundred and fifty years before reason was crowned at Notre Dame, Blaise Pascal (a younger contemporary of Descartes) began the attack.[1] If the way of thinking that led to rationalism is symbolized by Descartes, then the revolt against it is symbolized by Pascal with his famous line, "The heart has its reasons that reason does not know."[2]

Pascal had made lasting contributions to mathematics and physics, but while he was still a young man, he concluded that math and science were unimportant. He became absorbed in the great questions about life's meaning, which he understood not as matters for reason as Plato had but as questions of the heart. He was more concerned about the meaning of the vast emptiness of space than about measuring it accurately: "The whole of natural philosophy [the physical sciences] is not, to my mind, worth an hour's labor."[3] It was a Nothing.

Pascal didn't dismiss reason but limited it to a narrow realm—the realm of science and mathematics. He distinguished between the geometrical mind and the intuitive mind.[4] Some things you know by reason, but the important things you know by the heart, by intuition. Exactly what he meant is unclear (somehow he failed to explain the intuitive spirit with geometric precision!), but he rejected the imperialism of reason. He insisted that we know the important things another way.

In arguing this, Pascal was articulating a broad stream older than himself. On the one hand is math, science and logic, along with systematic, analytic approaches that test things by reason. It emphasizes the mind—objectivity, hardheadedness, clarity, precision, head knowledge. On the other hand is poetry, story, dance and art, along with imagination and creativity, which test things by living them. It emphasizes the heart—sensitivity, choice, commitment, paradox, dialectic, personal experience, subjectivity.

Pascal's stream, the stream that emphasizes the heart, I'm going to call romanticism; the stream we talked about before, the one that emphasizes the head, I'll call rationalism.[5] In Pascal's stream are romantic poets, most modern artists, existentialists, neo-orthodox theologians, mystics East and West and in certain respects many recent analytic philosophers. In Descartes's stream are social scientists, biologists, engineers, empiricists, early analytic philosophers, liberal and evangelical theologians and many (but by no means all) physical scientists.[6]

The distinction between what I'm calling rationalism and what I'm calling romanticism has been popularized in the distinction between left-brained and right-brained. According to this theory, the two hemispheres of the brain process the same things in different ways. The left hemisphere functions sequentially and abstractly,[7] breaking things down into parts and labeling them verbally. The right hemisphere functions spatially and creatively, seeing the same things but experiencing them as unnamed wholes evoking unnamed feelings.[8] We do science and sort through facts with the left brain, but we encounter God and beauty and friends with the right. Whether the right brain/left brain distinction is valid physiologically or not, the two tendencies are clear.

Table 1. The Left and Right Brain

Left Hemisphere	Right Hemisphere
Head	Heart
Reason	Passion, Choice
Arithmetic	Art
Words, Labels	Pictures, Nameless Feelings
Calculation	Imagination
Accuracy	Creativity, Beauty
Fact, Information	Meaning
Dispassionate	Committed
Objectivity	Subjectivity
Analytic, Dichotomous	Synthetic, Holistic, Integral
Parts, Segments	Wholes, Gestalts
Digital, Binary	Analogical
Abstract, General	Concrete, Specific
Sequential	Total
Linear	Dialectic, Circuitous
Formula	Metaphor
Coherence	Paradox, Ambiguity
System	Poetry
Organization	Chaos, Anarchy
Discipline	Freedom
Program	Spontaneity
Intellect	Body
Achievement-Oriented	Being-Oriented

The two tendencies[9] lead people rather naturally to talk about two kinds of truth: the facts (obtained by scientific and rational means) and a deeper spiritual truth that transcends science and reason. (How this deeper truth is thought to be known varies from thinker to thinker; it may be through feelings or choice, through a blind leap or a mystical surrender.) This in turn leads rather naturally to two metaphysical realms: the finite world of matter and necessity and science, and the infinite world of spirituality and freedom and art.

So science is not the only approach to life. We can also use our hearts. (Science left us only with matter and feelings, and limited by the choices of their age, the romantics chose feelings.) We can *feel*; we can *choose*. We can take a blind leap of belief that the furniture of the universe transcends particles in motion. This sort of stance is an obvious response to the problems of rationalism and secularism (*the* obvious response if you accept the Enlightenment paradigm that feelings and matter are all that exist). A way to give depth to life. And get beyond soup cans.

Following Your Bliss

The problem of knowledge, says the romantic, is not what Descartes supposed. It's not that we're irrational, passionate or ignorant. It's the opposite: we're too logical, not passionate enough, brainwashed with massive amounts of meaningless information from a technobarbarian culture. To discover truth, we need to follow our hearts.

Since spirit is free, we must shape our own lives—freely and without concern for social conventions, family expectations or religious rules. (Here we are already on more radical terrain than was Pascal.) Nothing is prohibited that brings authenticity. The trouble is that civilization has imposed on us literally thousands of social roles and institutional structures. These conceal us from ourselves, and we must escape them in order to find our true selves—for spontaneous self-expression is what it means to be human.

The spirit of romanticism is well expressed by e. e. cummings's poetry (not to mention the way he wrote his name):

since feeling is first
who pays any attention
to the syntax of things
will never wholly kiss you[10]

All we need do is to live our hearts, and life will be rich and full. Then we will escape the secular squeeze.

In Defense of Romantics

For what is perhaps still a majority of modern people, the left hemisphere is so in charge that romanticism seems strange. We have been so overpowered by science that we can scarcely picture alternatives to it even if that means looking frozen desolation in the face forever. Many of us are too ready to reject romanticism. So we must struggle to grasp its spirit before criticizing it.

Romanticism offers an escape for those who have grasped the devastation of secular rationalism. It opens a way to persons and to God—a way out of the shallowness of explanations limited to the mathematical and the impersonal. That's why some form of it has been embraced by so many good people—William Wordsworth, Ralph Waldo Emerson, Henry David Thoreau, Victor Hugo, Johannes Brahms, George Bernard Shaw, Teilhard de Chardin, Ursula K. Le Guin.

The early romantics were people well versed in the spirit of rationalism. They had tried it and despaired of its ever leading them to depth of life. It seemed to get stuck on the surface of things. The rest of the world was glorying in the growth of science and seemed to think progress was assured: justice and reason were right around the corner. But Pascal and Co. were frightened. For they had looked into rationalism and seen the abyss.

In the midst of an immense mechanical universe where death can snatch you at any moment, what is the point of living? If things are so wonderful, why do people spend so much time distracting themselves from reality with sports and entertainment? Science and math don't even approach the fundamental problems that human beings have always faced: fallenness, death, aloneness, evil. Pascal had done brilliant physical experiments proving the existence and weight of the atmosphere, but those experiments wouldn't help him if he were thrown out of his carriage into the Seine. We need to get beyond that sort of reasoning to the reasons of the heart.

So Pascal wrote, "Metaphysical proofs of God are so remote . . . and so involved that they fail to grip."[11] Logical proofs just aren't enough; they still have to take root in your heart: "What a distance between the knowledge of God and the love of him!"[12]

You may think that Pascal's talk about the heart is hopelessly vague, but while others were partying for progress he was penetrating the human predicament. And he did it, not by geometric or scientific method, but by some sort of emotional insight into who we are. People of romantic temperament keep helping us to see what it means to be truly human, and that should make even rationalists question themselves. With few exceptions, the Descarteses of this world have little to tell us about life; they don't even try; all they have to say is *Cogito, ergo sum.*

Rousseau and the Noble Savage

The most influential of the romantics was Jean-Jacques Rousseau, who lived nearly a hundred years after Pascal (1712-88). He was at the heart of the French Enlightenment with its mechanistic optimism and atheistic scientism, and he rebelled. He rejected the sterility of the Enlightenment's arid intellectualism, nice manners, conventional behavior codes and prostration before power and pragmatics.

On intimate terms with its leaders, he saw the Enlightenment for what it was—one of the shallower movements in human history. From his point of view, their endless intellectual salons, supposedly searching for truth, masked preening in stylish clothes and clever lines. Too sophisticated to boast about themselves, they accomplished the same thing by belittling others. (It was the romantic, not the rationalist, who penetrated the moral façade of the day.[13])

A Genevan artisan transplanted into Parisian literary and social circles, Rousseau was not impressed. He concluded that the human predicament was culture and science. In a state of nature, human beings are naturally good and free, but civilization brings property and therefore inequality and slavery. "The first man who, having enclosed a piece of ground, bethought himself of saying, 'This is mine,' and found people simple enough to believe him, was the real founder of civil society"[14]—and therefore of human woe. From then on, people wanted more and more, and those who got it were able to enslave others either by violence or by promising possessions that made people love their miserable state.

Rousseau himself advocated attempting to reform society, disgusting as it was, rather than returning to nature. Nonetheless, he fathered the back-to-nature movement, the idea of the noble savage and all those who believe in one form or another that "great things are done when Men and Mountains meet. This is not done by Jostling in the Street."[15]

Rousseau was contemptuous of rationalism and materialism. To those who thought that living was thinking and that feelings were glandular secretions, he said, "To exist is to feel."[16] We may find this extraordinary, but it's no worse than the alternative notion that to exist is to think.

To those who were too sophisticated to know right from wrong, Rousseau said, "What I feel to be right is right; what I feel to be wrong is wrong. . . . It is only when we haggle with conscience that we have recourse to the subtleties of argument."[17] This may help license the atrocities of zealots, but for most people seeking moral advice, don't you often suspect that the answer is "You know what you should do; stop arguing and do it"?

To people who mocked belief in God, Rousseau said, "The world is governed by a wise and powerful will; I see it or rather I feel it, and it is a great thing. . . . I see God everywhere in his works; I feel him within myself."[18] Rationalists may find that unintelligible, but some people, myself included, in fact experience things that way.

Many years ago I was struggling with whether God existed; I had heard and weighed all the rational arguments, and I was getting nowhere. Then one night walking alone in Switzerland, I saw the moon reflecting off the snow on the mountaintops, and I saw (or rather I felt) God in those works and in myself. It was an intuitive grasp of the invisible background of what I could see with my eyes. I might never have submitted to God if evidence were limited to rational proofs.

A Return to Primitivism

However, romanticism does not necessarily lead to the God of the Bible. Historically the attempt to get around the shallowness of rationalism has led to an attempt to get back before rationalism. If rationalism has disenchanted the universe, then what do you do? You go back to primitivism, to before Plato. You revive the original, pagan stories.

As usual, Wordsworth puts it better than anyone else:
The world is too much with us, late and soon,
Getting and spending, we lay waste our powers:
Little we see in nature that is ours;
We have given our hearts away, a sordid boon!
This sea that bares her bosom to the moon;
The winds that will be howling at all hours,
And are gathered now like sleeping flowers;

For this, for everything, we are out of tune;
It moves us not.—Great God! I'd rather be
A Pagan suckled in a creed outworn;
So might I, standing on this pleasant lea,
Have glimpses that would make me less forlorn;
Have sight of Proteus rising from the sea;
Or hear old Triton blow his wreathèd horn.[19]

We waste ourselves in the pursuit of Nothings and soon can't hear our hearts or be moved by wonder. We are out of tune with reality and would do better with primitive gods.

That way, we get beyond wave-particles to a universe that is once again magical and enchanted, like before Anaxagoras. The earth isn't dead matter but rather the essence of spirituality; it's to be loved as your mother and cared for as your source.

Kierkegaard and Existentialism

Working in Denmark in the 1840s and 1850s, Søren Kierkegaard had much in common with Pascal and Rousseau and also much not in common with them. He wasn't a romantic in the technical sense (by most accounts, he was the founder of existentialism), but he was a man of passion who rejected rationalism.

It was in Kierkegaard that I personally first found someone who understood me.[20] My senior year in high school, I took a course in philosophy. There I met Plato, Descartes and Kierkegaard. I suppose it sounds silly, but at seventeen I was disillusioned with life. Although I was successful academically, it all seemed empty, useful for little more than making money or seeming clever. I could see nothing significant in the things I was expected to know for College Boards, for example; they were only a slightly more sophisticated form of my seventh-grade geography test on state capitals. What was the point? What did all this have to do with life?

Nothing.

It was all Nothing. Plato's story about the cave interested me. Here was someone trying to see toward things that were real. But he seemed to think you found the real through mathematics, and at that very moment I was studying sines and cosines and was not impressed. So Kierkegaard came "like the cry of a wild bird in the silence of the night."[21]

He attacked learned people who know "a thousand historico-literary facts." Talking to them "is almost like reading a cookbook when one is hungry." "While Don Juan seduces girls and enjoys himself—Leporello notes down the time, the place, and a description of the girl."[22] His *Journals* were full of such comments: "Like the man caught in the quicksands who began by calculating how far down he had already sunk, forgetting that he was all the while sinking still deeper."[23] Here was someone who saw the pointlessness of studies the way I did, who could tell the difference between the real and Nothing.[24]

Meanwhile, my father was a fundamentalist pastor whose congregation paid no attention to his talk of the Sermon on the Mount. Kierkegaard saw that the way I did, too:

Try to imagine for a moment that geese could talk—that they had so arranged things that they too had their divine worship and their church-going.

Every Sunday they would meet together and a gander would preach.

The sermon was essentially the same each time—it told of the glorious destiny of geese, of the noble end for which their maker had created them—and every time his name was mentioned all the geese curtsied and all the ganders bowed their heads. They were to use their wings to fly away to distant pastures to which they really belonged; for they were only pilgrims on this earth.

The same thing happened each Sunday. Thereupon the meeting broke up and they all waddled home, only to meet again next Sunday for divine worship and waddle off home again—but that was as far as they ever got. They throve and grew fat, plump and delicious—and at Michaelmas they were eaten—and that was as far as they ever got. It never came to anything. . . .

Among the geese were several who looked ill and wan, and all the other geese said—there, you see what comes of taking flying seriously. It is all because they go about meditating on flying that they get thin and wan and are not blessed by the grace of God the way we are; for that is why we grow fat, plump, and delicious.

And so next Sunday off they went to divine service, and the old gander preached of the glorious end for which their maker (and at that point all the geese curtsied and the ganders bowed their heads) had created them, and of why they were given wings.[25]

Kierkegaard was a man who saw life the way I did, and so I believed him when he said:

The thing is to understand myself, to see what God really wishes *me* to do; the thing is to find a truth which is true *for me*, to find *the idea for which I can live and die*. What would be the use of discovering so-called objective truth, of working through all the systems of philosophy and of being able, if required, to review them all and to show up the inconsistencies within each system . . . if it had *no* deeper significance *for me and my life* . . . ?[26]

Our job is to be passionate individuals; we must stand apart from the crowd. The task of science is to be as objective and universal as possible, but we are subjects, and so our task is to become as passionate and as individual as possible. But we don't become subjects by anything as simple as following our bliss or returning to a state of nature; we do it by struggling to get rid of illusions. We're always trying to act objectively and unfeelingly or like members of the crowd, but all that is illusion. We must strip away those illusions and be ourselves—passionate individuals.

However, this is a terrible burden. Since we're subjects and not objects, we can never be objectively sure of anything. We're free, but that means we must act without conclusive evidence. In fact, at times we must act against the evidence—we must take blind leaps. We're on our own, never arriving, always journeying. Like Abraham deciding whether to sacrifice his son, we must forever choose without the luxury of objective criteria. One thing is needful: a decision. This is done in fear and trembling, dread and anxiety. And we have no promise of living happily ever after.

I was never convinced of the blind leap, but the rest felt right. It explained the nothingness that seemed to surround me, and it fit my sense of anxiety about life. (It also fit my adolescent autism and the standard confusion of my generation over who we were supposed to be. Besides,

I didn't mind feeling superior to the geese surrounding me.)

Kierkegaard also fit the age I was born into. His pessimistic outlook could make little headway in the midst of the "progress" of the nineteenth century, but after World War I the tone changed. All of a sudden, the fruit of science seemed to be mechanized death for millions followed by economic collapse for those who were left, and then before long, concentration camps, radioactive holocaust and the Cold War. The optimism of both rationalism and the other romanticisms seemed pretty silly. For a generation or two, Kierkegaard and his descendants (Heidegger and Sartre, Barth and Bultmann) became the gurus of half the intellectuals of the West.

Sartre

Jean-Paul Sartre was the most accessible of the existentialists, and I read almost everything he wrote. I remember where I was sitting when I found his discussion on a waiter not *being* a waiter.[27] People aren't the roles they play in society. A waiter may precariously balance his tray above his head, but that's not who he is; it's merely who he's pretending to be; it's merely a role he has adopted for the moment.

I immediately found myself peeling away my various roles to discover who I really was. Who was I if I wasn't the roles I played as intellectual, boyfriend, political dissident? While several generations of narcissistic postadolescents got lost asking these question, it was a great deal better than allowing ourselves to be absorbed into roles as chemists inventing napalm or teachers peddling symbolic logic.

But then Sartre did me one better. No sooner did I acquire the wonderful idea of peeling away roles to discover my true self than he said that when you do so, you discover . . . nothing. It's like peeling the layers of an onion till you get to the middle where there's nothing, no self—true or otherwise. This is scary; so we give ourselves a solid, comfortable identity in some artificial role. But that is self-deception, bad faith. We must have the courage to see that we have no purpose, no self, no identity, no meaning. Knowing that, we must choose to act, inventing our insubstantial self as we go, blind leap after blind leap. Only by now, it's blind staggering after blind stumbling and in no particular direction because no direction is right or wrong.

Sartre's conclusion was as horrifying as his start was exciting, but he wasn't just blowing hot air. Whatever else may be said, it was better than the self-deception I believed those around me were practicing. The Christians I knew my age never questioned themselves—they were Christians because their parents were Christians (they'd have been secularists if their parents had been secularists). And the rich kids who were my friends were mostly in career tracks, hoping to make themselves as comfortable as possible, with no sense that joy didn't lie in that direction. Everyone was playing status games with everything from clothes to grades to friends to sex to religion.

All those people seemed solid and real, in contrast to me, who I felt could float away at any moment. But I was convinced that they were solidly empty. Some day they would discover they'd been quietly pursuing illusion, Nothing. The people who seemed real to me were like me, reading Sartre and Kierkegaard, cummings and Dostoyevsky, and going to movies by Bergman and Fellini. We were confused, but we were trying to be real.

The Great Divide

Near the heart of all this was the distinction I'd been looking for, the distinction between something and Nothing. It was clear in existential writing that Western education was nearly always a Nothing.[28] Facts and information were on one side of a great divide, and on the other side were self-knowledge, passionate commitment, the struggle against illusion, freedom, the decision to act.

This became not just a commonsense point but a metaphysical claim. There are two sorts of being, two sorts of stuff. One is factual, space-time things, wave-particles in motion, stuff that is solid and accessible to logic and scientific observation. And on the other side of the great divide is what rises above the facts: spirit, God, consciousness, the individual—passionate and free.

The whole Enlightenment tradition was committed to truth, truth of the sort you looked up in the answer section at the back of a textbook, truth that was coolly and calmly ascertained by checking a handbook. (It's no accident that the primary work of the French Enlightenment was an encyclopedia!) By contrast, existentialists were committed to Truth, Truth of the sort you sought passionately on a long journey and caught only faint glimpses of as you struggled to live out what at that moment was True for you, the individual.

Theologically, this was revolutionary. (Existentialists probably had more influence on twentieth-century theology than did Jesus!) Previous theologians had been concerned about facts; so when secular science questioned the facts as the Bible recorded them, many abandoned those facts and became "liberals." That is, they denied the resurrection, creation, the divinity of Jesus and anything else miraculous. Having accepted secularism, they baptized it and trivialized Christianity by making it whatever part of secular culture looked good at that moment. And what looked good tended to be whatever their own culture was up to at the moment. So for German liberals the good turned out to be Kaiser Wilhelm's war, and for American liberals it turned out to be Woodrow Wilson's response to that war. And on and on.

How trivial can you get?

From an existential point of view, fundamentalists weren't very different. They too were especially concerned about the facts, and although they championed different facts, they were still hung up on . . . facts. Another version of Trivial Pursuit. Fundamentalists were so busy fighting evolution and liberalism that they forgot about justice for the poor; they were so busy fighting for the factual inerrancy of the Bible that they didn't give their inerrant Bible spiritual authority in their lives.

The existential solution was simple. Forget about the facts; go for the *meaning for you.* It doesn't matter about evolution or about how many blind men were healed outside Jericho. All that matters is what the creation story means for you, what Jesus' healing stories mean for you. This can't be determined just by exegesis; that's relevant, but in the end the text must be brought to life *for you* by the Holy Spirit. So the Bible isn't God's word in and of itself; it becomes God's word for you as the Spirit works in your life.

This, of course, meant that insofar as the resurrection was a factual question, a question of resuscitation, it was of no importance. That bothered me. But it had been the logic of my own position since that junior-high geography test. Facts are Nothings.

Besides, existential Christians were the ones fighting for justice for the oppressed, one of the major points of the text of the Bible and one which had been conveniently overlooked in the evangelical and fundamentalist traditions. It was Karl Barth,[29] the greatest of the existential theologians, who had gone around Germany in the thirties preaching that Jesus was a Jew. His sense of God beyond the facts had been big enough to lift him above the Führer while the God of liberals and fundamentalists hadn't done so well.

Hippies and Beyond

For me the whole thing reached crisis point in the late sixties. Oddly enough, I was teaching symbolic logic at an evangelical college in the Chicago area. Although I was more of a romantic existentialist than I realized (I had bought the social analysis entirely), I held on to the resurrection and to an objective interpretation of the Bible. As for teaching symbolic logic . . . well, you have to earn a living somehow, and I enjoyed logic and teaching.

Before I ever taught my first class, I marched in a housing demonstration sponsored by the NAACP, and I heard about it. Even when the school began to admit significant numbers of blacks, the administration was unable to accept that the middle American dream seemed like a nightmare to many ghetto kids. Meanwhile Chicago burned with some regularity. And after teaching all day, I was supposed to be writing a doctoral dissertation on G. E. Moore.

Meanwhile, the war in Vietnam was escalating. During the 1964 election, Johnson had lied about what he intended in Vietnam. Before it was over, *The Pentagon Papers* documented a whole complex of lies from officialdom, and tiger cages and Operation Phoenix showed that the communists weren't the only murderers. The color of those Americans who died showed the depth of privilege and of institutional racism. Official morality was a hypocritical façade that required no Pascal to smell out. Yet the war had the unwavering support of the college administration and the evangelical establishment.

I hated communism; so at first I reluctantly supported the war. But the photographs of napalmed children devastated me. The standard line was that war is hell—implying that it was also necessary. I might have bought that if the people who said it had shown signs of feeling the irremediable horror of it all. Babies maimed, sons and husbands killed, girl-children turned into prostitutes. Meanwhile supporters of the war seemed to feel nothing. They talked about it like a stock report. Body counts, the number of tons of bombs.

Facts, information. All measurable.

I went around saying that I didn't care too much whether people supported the war or opposed it as long as they felt its horror. But few supporters of the war showed any sign of feeling the horror. All those who let themselves feel the horror seemed to oppose the war. So I came to understand the difference between those who opposed the war and those who didn't as the difference between the sensitive and the insensitive, between those who felt and those who reasoned.

And evangelicals were among those who reasoned. All reason and no feeling, it looked like to me. Evangelicals were clearly not secular in the full sense of the word (they believed in God and in miracles), but increasingly it seemed to me that they had secular minds that had happened to come to a different conclusion about God. The difference between secular rationalists and evangelicals was not in how they thought but in the conclusions they reached. This was a disagreement between varieties of rationalism. Was it this rationalism that kept the college administration from feeling the pain of others?

Romanticism, with its stress on feelings, was looking better and better.

I gave a lecture to ROTC defending just war, and in the process I said that a war could be just only if the soldiers killed weeping.[30] The officer in charge informed me with considerable passion that war was possible only if you trained the soldiers to hate the enemy. Here was some feeling at last, but not quite the kind I meant.

It seemed to me that a vast majority of evangelicals were insensitive and uncaring. I was officially informed that the Republican understanding of the war and of civil rights was the logical outworking of Christian faith. Perhaps the administration had a better sense than I did of my romanticism and its dangers, but that didn't excuse their defense of wickedness. I gradually became so angry I was disabled.

Meanwhile, I knew the irrelevance of teaching symbolic logic, especially with Chicago burning and thousands dying in Vietnam. School might not have to be irrelevant, but the Enlightenment curriculums we had inherited even in Christian schools were as hollow as government self-righteousness and opposition to drugs from adult alcoholics. So if college was the home of reason and it had no bearing on reality, well then, reason could take a flying leap into "feeling is first who pays any attention to the syntax of things."[31] It took no Pascal . . .

I left teaching and graduate school to became the editor of *The Other Side* magazine. I hoped to keep the rationalistic theology of evangelicalism while being able to feel the horrors of racism and war. I had huge doubts about it, but I was going to give it one more try. The response of evangelicals to *The Other Side* was somewhat less than euphoric, but that didn't bother me too much. It didn't bother me much either that few evangelicals would work for us. (It wasn't exactly a great career move, and we paid hardly anything.) So we hired who we could, mostly people who felt deeply and didn't give a rat's tail about rationalistic theology.

The Precipice
Somewhere along there, I fell off a precipice. At least I nearly did. It took me years to find a way home—which I'll describe in the next three chapters. But before going on to that, I hope you appreciate the strength and attraction of romanticism, perhaps especially in its existential forms. I have no intention of defending it further, but it is a powerful and understandable response to the shallowness and unfeelingness of the dominant culture and of rationalistic theologies.

At the moment, the cycle is happening again in our culture, and so we're hearing earth-goddess talk from parts of the feminist and ecological movements. On the one hand, we're devastating the environment for the sake of ticky-tacky possessions, and it looks oddly like the logical outcome of Enlightenment science. And on the other hand, we have a church that has done little to stop the exploitation of creation, even when that creation is human, let alone when it's redwood. So what can we expect . . . but a revival of paganism, an attempt to return to a time when nature was not being destroyed and when people could at least tell themselves that human beings weren't being oppressed?

Gaia (the earth-mother goddess) is upon us.

6

The Romantic
Dead End:
Is Feeling
Enough?

The first thing to hit the fan for me was abortion. Non-Christian
radicals supported abortion almost universally, but many radical
Christian pacifists considered it murder. I wasn't sure what to
think myself, but the pacifist position at least seemed compassionate and
reasonable. However, such pacifists were often greeted by the rest of the
left with a hatred that achieved almost physical force; some secular peace
groups went so far as to refuse them membership.

I'll never forget breakfast one morning at a conference of radical Christians. I was at a table with one of America's most prominent feminist
theologians and a soft-spoken radical priest who opposed abortion. I was
struggling with the topic, and not being too clever, I thought that by getting
them talking about it I might acquire some wisdom. And I suppose I did.
But the talk was brief. It ended with the theologian throwing her tray and
screaming she'd never again attend any event the priest attended.

Perhaps feelings are not an infallible guide to life.

If evangelicals had thought police, the left had feeling police. You were
required to feel compassion for napalmed Vietnamese babies, but you

weren't allowed to feel compassion for babies who hadn't been born.

Whose feelings were you supposed to trust?

The next problem was sex. Within an ideology of rights and feelings, people can express themselves sexually any way they like as long as no one else's rights are violated. Well, it was pretty clear that Jesus didn't agree.

At first I thought that this was a question that Christian romantics would automatically take a different stand on from other romantics. But then it turned out that some of my Christian friends were "broadminded" about sex. I had been fond of saying that for evangelicals fornication was a felony but racism only a misdemeanor. Now it turned out that for much of the Christian left, racism was a felony but fornication only a misdemeanor—if that.

I was not impressed. Then it gradually dawned on me that they were right . . . In an ideology of rights and feelings, especially the feelings of men, you have a right to express yourself sexually however you please as long as no one else's rights are violated.

Now I was really confused. My attempt to synthesize romanticism and biblical authority was in question. Either I had to abandon all semblance of biblical authority and rely on feelings alone, or I had to find another approach altogether.

Feelings no longer seemed so attractive. I began to ask a question of romanticism that I had asked of secularism: "Suppose a sadistic guard guided you around a concentration camp commenting on the delightfulness of it all. Would his feelings of delight be correct, or would your feelings of horror? It's not at all clear what it could mean for a [romantic] to say your feelings are more correct. If torturing people turns him on, why shouldn't he do it?"

Well, after a couple years of vacillation, I took a sabbatical to write a book. The claim of the book was that Christians didn't take Jesus seriously about things like money and power. In the process of writing, I became convinced of two things: that Jesus was far more powerful than Rousseau or Wordsworth, and that if I was going to call people to take Jesus seriously on money and power, it would be pretty silly to ignore him on sex.[1]

I was on the way home.

A Feeling of Passionate Mercy

However, I had always loved the passage where Jesus tells the Pharisees, "If you had known what this means, 'I desire mercy, and not sacrifice,' you would not have condemned the guiltless."[2] Jesus seemed to me to be rejecting rule-based ethics; he was telling us that what mattered was feeling with hurting people. That, it had seemed to me, was exactly what wasn't done by the administration both in Washington and in the evangelical college where I'd taught. Rather than hurting when others hurt, they cut themselves off from them by hiding behind rules.

What Jesus was saying seemed central, but how was it to be used in a way that didn't justify anything anyone happened to feel? Here was a passage he quoted twice (one of the few), and something close to it was found ten times in the Old Testament.[3] I had put Kenneth Patchen's version of it over my desk: "A feeling of passionate mercy; the rest doesn't matter a damn."[4] It was the verse of the decade for me.

And wasn't the Golden Rule nearly the same thing? "Do to others as you would have them do to you; for this is the law and the prophets" (Mt 7:12). You can do that only if you feel with others; you can do what you'd like done to you only by entering into the situation emotionally from the other person's point of view.

Are Feelings Enough?

Now I was faced with people who had the "right" feelings about racism and war but who disagreed with each other's feelings on abortion, and at the same time I was faced with other people whose feelings on sex didn't fit Jesus' teaching. What was I to do?[5]

Well, it still seems to me that you get a long way by feeling with others. In fact, if you're to treat people decently, let alone with goodness, feeling with them is a necessity. But is it enough? Is it the whole story? Who do we feel with: the unborn baby or the pregnant woman who doesn't want the baby? Do we need an exceptionless set of rules? Or is something else needed?

I'm still skeptical about the possibility of devising an exceptionless set of rules to cover every detail of life, but that's not the only alternative. Now

I'd say we need a good story to help shape our feelings. Feelings aren't autonomous; they aren't infallible guides to reality any more than rationalism is. No, our feelings are shaped by the story we've lived.

How we feel about things is integrally connected with the actions we've chosen, with our parents' feelings, with our personal experience of reality, with what movies and books we've allowed to shape us. So the feelings of Victorians about extramarital sex just *are* going to be different from those of modern people who in hundreds of movies see extramarital sex portrayed as the standard. So it's hardly even interesting that people have conflicting feelings about how we should behave; it depends too much on their story.

Besides, Jesus gave us a story with quite a bit of detail. He didn't *just* tell us to feel with others; he also told us to turn the other cheek, to sell our possessions, to take up the cross as he did. And not many of us would have figured those things out just by feeling with others; at least I wouldn't have. Our story informs how we feel with others.

So I gradually concluded that romantics like myself had overreacted. We had assumed that left-brained functions were inferior and that only right-brained feelings and intuitions (that agreed with ours!) could bring depth. So I began reaching more firmly toward the obvious conclusion that we need *both* reason and feelings.

Intensity of Feelings, Emptiness of Feelings

I think I've always known that the romantic emphasis on feelings easily gets off balance. Poetic glorying in unrequited love was something I'd never been able to get into. It seemed silly to me. Rousseau's "To exist is to feel" soon leaves nothing but feelings. And when your feelings leave you hollow, as I found they soon did, what's left? Well, more intense feelings, that's what. So romantics have a constant need to escalate intensity of feeling.

In romantic poets, you again and again find this need to feel more deeply. Think, for example, about the Wordsworth sonnet in the last chapter. It's a favorite of mine, but there's something unreal about it. He complains, rightly, that "the world is too much with us" and says that "we have given our hearts away." But what is it that we no longer have? Compassion for the poor? Love for God? Hardly. It's that we no longer feel the crashing sea with intensity.

Now it's tricky to say this right. On the one hand, our culture is shallowed out by its preference for Disneyland over the crashing sea. No doubt about that. But on the other hand, if we remember an intense experience of the beauty of the sea and then go back to the sea to relive the experience, we're going to be disappointed. We can then go home and write tragic poetry about the shallowness of modernity, but the problem is merely that human beings aren't given the gift of reliving past wonders, aren't allowed to devote ourselves to wonderful feelings. It's like people who keep getting divorced because they're no longer "in love." Intense experiences are gifts that cannot be long held, surprises that come when not sought.

Consider Gauguin with his lush paintings of tropical women and his call to return to nature. He's typical: he wanted to overcome the rationalistic approach to reality with its loss of all feeling "for the mystery and the enigma of the great world in which we live."[6] In the process, he abandoned his family for his artistic freedom—so he could express himself. "Before an easel a painter is no slave, neither of the past, nor of the present, neither of nature, nor of his neighbor. He is himself, himself again, always himself."[7]

Big deal. That's what Hitler was doing too—being himself.

That's just an alternative lobotomy. An alternative result of the secular squeeze.

If we forget that, we'll be like Rousseau who sent all his children to a state orphanage where he knew almost all children died.[8] Or like Rimbaud who left France and poetry for the intensity of gunrunning in Abyssinia. And remember the personal lives of Shelley and Byron and their cruelty to their "women," the ones they wrote beautiful poetry to as long as the feelings lasted. They were on a frantic, deadly search for intense feelings. If a child gets in the way, kill "it." If a woman gets in the way, dump her.

Where do you get intense feelings? The obvious first answer is falling in love. The next answer is sex. And when sex fails, try drugs. And when drugs fail, try guns. And when guns fail, try death. More and more excitement, always more. That's what romanticism is, even in its New Age variants. Dissatisfied with life as it is (it's not intense enough), people escalate the search for feeling to psychedelics and beyond. Which I assume accounts for the importance of drugs in the lives of romantics from Coleridge and Poe to Faulkner and Ginsberg and for the obsession with sex from Byron and Verlaine to Oscar Wilde and Henry Miller. And don't forget the Marquis de Sade. Combining sex with violence seems to offer an especially intense high.

But on that route lies insanity, and we know it. We may identify with Gauguin vicariously, but we don't follow him to the South Seas, at least not for long. On some level, most men may think they'd like to be surrounded by beautiful naked women, but even among males, few believe that the South Seas were ever really like that or that life's problems would be solved if they were.

Or try Woody Allen's solution. He took as his lover a twenty-one-year-old girl he'd adopted when she was a child. Here's his explanation: "The heart wants what it wants. There's no logic to these things."[9] Hey, can he help who he falls in love with? "The heart has its reasons that reason doesn't know."

Feelings by themselves are one-dimensional. They don't fill the void; they just make the emptiness more obvious. Human beings need more than passion. Otherwise the personal is lost as surely as it is in rationalism. No matter how intense, feelings are superficial and impersonal outside lasting relationships in which you lay down your life. (At least, that's the story I've found worth living.) Pursuing feelings yields snakes devouring your insides.

Romanticism fell into a ghastly trap left by rationalism. Matter and feelings, reason and passion: that's all there is. And if matter and reason don't work, well, that leaves passion, doesn't it? So into the hole dug by rationalism go the romantics. And it's a deep hole. A very deep hole. An abyss.

Harmonic Convergence: Or, A Heritage of Gothic Garbage
On August 16, 1987, the universe's vibrations changed, resulting in a harmonic convergence that altered the spirit of the age and would bring disaster unless counteracted by thousands of people sending out good vibes at the right moment. At least, that's what José Arguelles told us.[10] He

based this on the ancient Aztec and Mayan calendar and a good deal of intuition. Others who know about those calendars said his calculation of the time was off and his interpretation of what Aztecs and Mayans believed was surprising. But tens of thousands of people believed him and gathered to experience it together—in Mia Pia, Bolivia (where the vibrations were strongest); Central Park, Manhattan; London, England; Pella, Iowa; and of course, Boulder, Colorado (where Mr. Arguelles himself blew a conch shell 144 times), and Santa Cruz, California.[11]

Well, baloney. For Arguelles to come to that conclusion was humorous, but for anyone to buy it other than Shirley MacLaine and Arguelles's father freezes the heart and paralyzes the mind. As for tens of thousands . . . let's hope they went along for the lark.

If rationalism left us with a heritage of dessicated desolation, romanticism leaves us with a heritage of Gothic garbage. If rationalism omits living, romanticism offers in its place cheap feeling. Just consider: the drug culture, the age of Aquarius, sensitivity training, charismatic TV evangelists, Esalen, the joys of sex, multiple maharishis, the back-to-nature movement, mantras for purchase, witches' covens, punk rock, the primal scream, Rolfing, astrology. Some of these have a place in the larger context, but none by itself gets us anywhere near home. They're just jellybrained Siamese twins of rationalism.

And for all romanticism's ability to see through the shallowness of rationalism, it has rarely done well seeing through its overenriched self. It can be as softheaded as rationalism is irrelevant. Its apparently rich garden of wild and wonderful vines doesn't yield fruit that nourishes. It too lacks depth. For how deep can gibberish be?

José Arguelles is, of course, the lunatic fringe of romanticism (though the library of the Graduate Theological Union in Berkeley has his many books!). And it isn't fair to dismiss romanticism because it attracts loonies. Every worthwhile movement does. The question is whether romanticism attracts more than its share of loonies, whether perhaps it has something at its core which feeds overripe folly.

I fear it does. Romanticism has deep internal flaws. At heart I'm a romantic (at least, some of my best evenings are reading Wordsworth and cummings), but romanticism is rotten at the core.

Means of Discernment

After all, the Nazis were romantics. And that's not a cheap shot. Of course, if romanticism hadn't been available, Nazis would doubtless have found some other ideology, but the fact remains that romanticism served Nazism well. And here's the point: romanticism had nothing in itself with which to question nationalism and anti-Semitism.

Nazism is as appropriate an outcome for romanticism as is hippie war resistance—the swastika as appropriate as the peace symbol. And in fact, as the Nazis gained power, the flower children of the day flocked to the swastika—and rationalistic logical positivists had to flee. Hitler, after all, felt passionately. He loved good music and beautiful scenery; so the mere fact that his feelings were wicked and his thought processes irrational scarcely counted against him. Romanticism had nothing of its own by which to discern that Nazism was feelings run amok.

Romanticism lacks an anatomy of feelings. So it's unable to distinguish between good feelings and bad, between hatred and compassion. Surely the point isn't just that we be passionate; it's that we be passionate in good ways. Otherwise, you can't distinguish between Nazis and the Confessing Church—after all, both felt passionately. We can scarcely overdo compassion, but we surely can overdo fear, jealousy, hatred . . .

The solution is not to denounce feeling like Plato and Descartes tended to do, nor is it to enthrone feelings like Rousseau and cummings did. At least in part it's to sort out what feelings are good and what feelings are bad. It's to find a story like the story of Jah that guides us toward good feelings and away from destructive ones.

For without that, romanticism frees us from Campbell's Soup cans by subjecting us to feelings. And that's a squeeze as tight as secularism.

The hollowness left by the pursuit of feelings is at least as great as the hollowness left by the pursuit of reason.

On Not Falling into the Abyss on Either Side

I argued before that when science and its methods become all, we get something one-dimensional and death-dealing. Now I'm suggesting that the same thing happens with romanticism. When feelings and the heart become all, we get something equally one-dimensional and death-dealing. If it's lethal to build up reason at the expense of feeling, it's also lethal to attack reason to save feeling. Those with reason and no feelings soon lose their reason, and those with feelings and no reason soon lose their feelings.

We walk with a precipice on each side, and if we fall off either way, the bottom turns into a curiously similar horror. If reason helped the bomb along, feelings helped Hitler along. Which do you prefer, concentration camps or nuclear war? Which is sillier as the ultimate source of truth, mathematics or a European's view of Tahiti?

When secularism deifies science, we fall into the abyss, and when romanticism deifies feelings, we fall into the abyss. Only God is God; and *whenever you treat something (anything) as God that isn't, you limit yourself to its one dimension.* That's what one-dimensionality is: making something God that isn't.

From Plato to today, we have had a series of pendulum swings between reason and feeling. People seem either to hail reason as savior and spurn feelings or else to hail feelings as the center of life and spurn reason. But we need both. We need both halves of ourselves: left brain and right, rigorous logic and passionate intuition, analysis and imagination, penicillin and the crashing sea. We need a synthesis between heart and intellect, between science and art. We must affirm their essential unity.

I'm not talking about finding a balance here, a balance between feelings and reason, with just a little of each. No, I'm talking about both full-blown. Deeply rational, deeply passionate.

Not necessarily in the same person. That's the ideal, but some people are going to be thoroughly right-brained and others thoroughly left-brained. Those people need to try to develop the other part of themselves, but we'll all be different. What matters is that we see our need for each other.

Freud and the romantic poets have taught us to reject people who reason more than they feel (repressed and constipated males), but feelers need reasoners. And those who emphasize reason tend to be contemptuous of feelers (silly women), but reasoners need feelers too. We have to feel and feel deeply, but if we don't also think and think hard, we're going to talk gibberish and live nonsense. And if we don't have compassion when we start thinking, we're quite likely never to rise above trivia.

When Wordsworth says, "We murder to dissect," he's wrong. We must reflect carefully on our feelings, and the thoughtful analysis of flowers is valuable. Without hardheaded analysis, poetry becomes babble, and the resulting unexamined life isn't worth living. On the other hand, botany should be taught only to those who are struck with awe at Wordsworth's daffodils; the laws of motion taught only to those who stand in wonder as the petal of a flower falls to the ground; and physiology taught only to those who go stiff with horror at Mengele's physiological experiments.

Wonder and analysis, horror and dissection are equally real, equally important. We are forever shallow if we allow only what can be measured by scientific instruments—forever trapped in a Gothic garden of gibberish inhabited by snakes if we allow only what we feel passionate about. We need both the aspect of stars which fits Newton's laws and the aspect which poets write about.

So we must recognize it as folly when cummings says, "the blond absence of any program except last and always and first to live makes unimportant what i and you believe."[12] Filling the hollow within is central, but what people believe determines whether they fill it with psychedelics, work or Jah. And cummings is telling only half the story when he says, "its brains without hearts have set saint against sinner; put gain over gladness and joy under care."[13] We must also tell the other half: hearts without brains have set saint against sinner; put sex over troth and joy under drugs.

The history of modern culture underlines the importance of both head and heart. Philosophers like Descartes and Hume who value only reason never get anywhere. Those like Rousseau and Schleiermacher who value only feeling wind up in weird and silly places. Home is approached by people like Socrates, Isaiah, Augustine and Einstein who have a healthy regard for both. You find the real power among people (like the Hebrews) who never had a mind-heart dichotomy to become the gulf it did for the Greeks or the chasm it did after Descartes.[14]

The same sort of thing is true for literature. I love many romantic poets, and their rejection of the formal standards of Pope and Dryden was a step toward depth. But Sophocles, Chaucer, Spenser and Shakespeare are greater than the romantics, and I suspect that that is partly because they never got caught in the pendulum swing between reason and feelings. Mark Twain is better than Nathaniel Hawthorne, Balzac than Hugo, Goethe than Hölderlin or Kleist—partly because they have a greater respect for more parts of who we are.

I resonate with the romantic rejection of technique and of accuracy in painting. Rationalist painters like David[15] and Poussin are minor figures; romantics like Delacroix and Turner are better. But once again Da Vinci, Michelangelo and Rembrandt, who knew little of a conflict between reason and feeling, are in another league altogether. And the failure of modern art to find its way through the conflict has left it as shallow as the rationalism it despises.[16] Isn't Brahms's superiority to Liszt and Wagner partly that he overcame the conflict between romanticism and classicism?

If the head is not enough, neither is the heart.

Telephone Numbers and the Texture of Reality

But of course most people who say we need both head and heart seem then to fall back into rationalism. So let me point out the blindness of rationalism once more. Rationalists want to narrow reality down to what can fit into Newton's laws. But to suppose you know all about a thing when you've got its measurements is like supposing you know all about a man when you've got his telephone number. To know a man's telephone number is something—but to suppose that that is the total person is psychotic. You have left out quite a lot.

To narrow reality down to Newton's part of it (particles in motion and maybe proofs for God) is sheer prejudice. Wonder and awe are just as real. How could anything else ever have been imagined? The universe is not the sort of place science imagines: there are more things in heaven and earth than science ever dreamt of.

Galileo and Newton left some significant numbers about the stars, and poets left us some important words about the wonder of the stars. Who

is to say that the aspect of stars which fits the laws of science is all there
is to say about the stars? Who is to say that the numbers are more real
than the aspect of the stars which poets write about? (Or vice versa.)

You see, the rationalist mind assumes that reality can be described the
way you describe a telephone number: 213-555-7358. That's it. Nothing
more to be said. It's fully described, and either incorrect or else fully correct.
You prove God's existence and your job is done.

But the actual world is not as simple as that. Nor as impoverished. Reality
is not one-dimensional—science is (and so is romanticism). You can give
many descriptions of the same person, multiple interpretations of the same
event. They may have little in common, and yet all may be correct.

How many descriptions of a rose would it take to give an exhaustive and
true description of it? One from a botanist, one from a microbiologist, one
from a nuclear physicist, one from a rose fancier, one from a little kid who
had fallen into a rose patch, one from a theologian, and, well, how many
from poets? Even then, you'd be oh, so far from a complete description.
If the reports were verbal, people who'd never seen a rose still might not
know a rose when they saw one.

Our words never describe reality exhaustively. The world doesn't con-
form to reason the way a series of digits does to a telephone number. And
if some scientists think otherwise, they're wrong. You achieve that kind of
precision only by narrowing reality. That is the great accomplishment of
science. It gives an exhaustive and accurate description of . . . very little.

If you want to give descriptions that have the texture of reality, more is
required. Wordsworth and Bach are more than quaint footnotes to Galileo
and Newton (and vice versa). The simplest piece of the world—a speck
of dust, a snowflake, a hydrogen atom—has a richness that none can begin
to exhaust.

The conflict between those who use mathematical descriptions and
those who use poetic descriptions is deep. C. P. Snow seemed to think
the problem is that people are ignorant of each other's fields. But it goes
much deeper than that. It goes to the heart of who we are and choose to
be, of what our culture is and has become. A couple of seminars where we
share information about our academic disciplines will not touch the gulf

between us. We hardly see the same world or speak the same language—even when we're trying to discuss the same topic. The concerns of rationalists seem to romantics like "the trivial labelling of punctual brains,"[17] and the concerns of romantics seem to rationalists like the histrionic sentimentality of overwrought adolescents.

An Odd Choice

In our culture we're given two options, rationalism and romanticism. Rationalism has clearly failed, yet with the likes of José Arguelles, Adolf Hitler and Paul Gauguin, few of us can maintain much enthusiasm for romanticism. So rationalism is still usually king, uneasy with it as we may be.

The weaknesses of rationalism are so well known that you'd think it would have been dethroned long ago, but no new king has arisen who is compelling, and until we have a new king, we tend to play by the rules of the old rationalist kingdom. It's like Newtonian physics in the nineteenth century. Repeatedly discredited, it continued to rule until Einstein offered a compelling alternative.

The world of ideas is no different from other parts of the world. It's like gasoline engines. We know they're destroying the environment, but we keep using them because we don't have a satisfactory replacement. And we keep using the rationalist myth because romanticism isn't a satisfactory replacement. (Except of course for those who use romanticism because rationalism isn't a satisfactory replacement.) Or we use odd, untenable combinations of the two.

A standard line, the one I've been giving here, is that we need both, and I think that's right. But it doesn't take sufficiently seriously the chasm between the two. The real question is, How do you use both? How do you close the chasm?

In a real sense the Enlightenment set up a framework that hasn't been challenged since. According to the secular rationalism of the Enlightenment, we have matter and feelings, reason and passion. And the rationalists took that to mean that reason was the way to approach epistemology. Then when the romantics launched their attack, they rejected reason while keeping the overall framework. That is, they did what reactionary movements tend to do: they bought the most basic assumptions of their opponent. They kept the duality of reason and feelings. What we need is a new framework (or perhaps an old one), a framework that gets us beyond those basic assumptions. Unless we do that, there's no way out. We're trapped forever.

How to do that is one of the enduring human questions, plaguing and giving depth to our pilgrimage. I will argue in the next chapter that you do that by reintroducing the category of story, especially the story of Jah.

7

Authenticating Story by the Lives of Storytellers

Once upon a time, people were controlled by stories told in the glow of the campfire. It was long ago when people were primitive. They didn't even have flush toilets back then or watches that beep. And they hadn't read Descartes and learned what it means to be rational and objective. Or Rousseau and discovered that feelings are all. What they had was stories. Stories the priests made up and the village elders told in the glow of the fire at night. These stories explained why the people had to obey the overclass or experience the awesome displeasure of the gods.

Today stories are at the edge of life. The outer edge. We're not primitive anymore. We're modern. We have scientific method plus our feelings. We know that the old stories were not rational. We have nuclear power and television. Stories are fine as entertainment. But like all art, they're mere ornaments and don't mean a thing. So we reject the old stories and dismiss new ones as frivolous.

The legitimate use of stories is recreation—the circus—which helps people work harder the next day. A few people write serious stories, but their stories are psychological essays with decoration. If you want the real thing, go to the essays themselves.

We modern people don't need stories to tell us what to do. When we get tired at night, we sit in the glow of the TV. We watch programs about cops and robbers. Programs about pretty young women going to bed with detectives. Programs about rich and beautiful people. Sitcoms about yuppie families. Quiz programs about money. The stars are not village elders but young and beautiful city dwellers like us.

These programs don't teach us anything, and we don't need stories. We're rational people. We have programs. We've been programmed.

Cataclysm

What you have just read is a tragedy. It degrades our lives and emaciates our culture. In losing the awareness that stories are a source of truth, we are left without access to the truth that matters most. We are left in a morass between rationalism and romanticism. That doesn't mean we're no longer shaped by stories; it just means we no longer know we are. We're forever at the mercy of CBS's entertainment division.

To a large extent, we grow out of our stories—stories about Moses and Jesus, Agamemnon and Huck Finn, about the Boston Tea Party and Jack Kennedy, about Galileo's persecution by the church and Einstein's forgetting to put on socks. And don't forget John Wayne singlehandedly overcoming crooked sheriffs and dirty Indians, and Michael J. Fox getting the girl despite his height.

The purpose of stories isn't just entertainment. They encourage, reinforce and challenge a people's lifestyle. Stories are why modern people believe so devoutly in individualism and whiteness and the scientific method—or whatever it is we believe in.

Remember all the programs about the detective going to bed with the beautiful girl? The reason it's so popular is that it reaches down to our primal selves. It allows us to identify unconsciously with light in the cosmic struggle against darkness and promises that light will win in the end. It reaches down to our yearning to heroically defeat what we fear most and to be rewarded with the promised land. It empowers us to continue the struggle against all odds, and it grants the *Good Housekeeping* seal of approval to promiscuity and to solving problems with a six-shooter of power.

But if we don't know the shaping power of stories, we have no control over which ones shape us. So we feed ourselves on nonsense from Hollywood—and don't realize that our souls are being formed. And we wind up believing devoutly in whatever nonsense we're fed.

Since we see stories as slightly doubtful distractions from the serious business (of earning money?), it doesn't occur to us to examine them seriously. The word *story* scarcely appears in school curriculums, and when used in normal conversation it usually means "lie." Mathematics and science are the important things. A school might have a course in fly-tying, but in a standard school (and what other kind is there in the West?), who ever heard of a course on stories and storytelling?

Modern people scarcely even have a way to talk about stories, let alone to test them for truth. So it's scarcely possible to decide consciously what we're going to do with our lives; rather we're grabbed on an unconscious level by some story or other—which then controls our destiny. Like the primitive people we feel superior to, we live out whatever stories our cultural scriptwriters hand us. We may be able to think critically about particular scientific claims but not about how to live our lives, not about the enduring questions.

And if our stories come from CBS's entertainment division, what kind of people do we become? What kind of culture is produced? Not one that deals with real questions, and certainly not one centered on the crucified God.

So we marry or get divorced. We vote or buy expensive cars. We spend long hours fighting crabgrass or getting good grades. We yearn to be rich or beautiful or whatever. And all because without our noticing it, certain stories infiltrated our souls and took us over. Stories it never crossed our minds to check out.

It's cataclysmic.

Socrates said, "Know thyself." I would add, "Know thy stories." (It's almost the same thing.) We need to study our stories as seriously as we study reading, writing and nuclear physics. And we need to test them at least as carefully as we test seat belts.

The unexamined story is not worth having—in fact, it's perilous. It might steal everything from us. Leaving us trash about detectives and pretty girls and dirty Indians. Leaving us Campbell's Soup cans in various colors.

To put a claim I've made all along in different words, the central intellectual task of our age is to get our stories in the light and find a way to authenticate the good ones. That will free us from the Siamese twins of secularism and romanticism, and it will allow us to put our heads and our hearts—and the rest of ourselves—to work choosing the sort of lives we will lead.

Then we can recover greatness of spirit. And the great story.

By the Lives of Storytellers

According to the story of Jah, when God came to be among us he didn't come as a mathematician or a scientist. He came as a storyteller. Not as Newton and Einstein rolled into one but as Sophocles-Dante. And he told stories people could live. At bottom, the Judeo-Christian tradition isn't a list of rules or a set of scientific theories; it's a big, long story. The hundreds of pages of story and poetry in the Bible are not an accident but the very medium through which God speaks.

But Jesus didn't stop with stories; he also gave us a way to authenticate them, a way that Newton and Einstein could have appreciated. (So perhaps he came as Sophocles-Einstein.) He told us (the whole book has been waiting for this sentence) that *you tell whether a story is true by the lives of the people who tell it.* You judge a story by its teller.

You will know them by their fruit, he said. A good tree bears good fruit, a bad one bad fruit (Mt 7:15-20). If the people telling a story love each other and live together with depth and grace, then their story is true. If they don't, then their story is silliness—or worse.

A good story enables people to lay down their lives for each other and become one. To put it in Jesus' own words, "I give you a new commandment, that you love one another. Just as I have loved you, you also should love one another. [He died for them, remember.] By this everyone will know that you are my disciples, if you have love for one another" (Jn 13:34-

35). A few chapters later he prays that his followers "may all be one . . . so that the world may believe that you have sent me" (Jn 17:21). A story is authenticated when the people who believe it go to the cross for each other.

What we have here is an epistemology with the strengths of rationalism, the strengths of romanticism and the strengths of primitive storytelling—without their weaknesses. It combines the power of mythmaking and of critical thinking, of reasoning and feeling. Here the power of imagination and the unconscious are connected to a rational way to decide truth. Which is staggering. Here is the new framework we need, or rather the old one.

Notice that Jesus doesn't require belief in his story simply on the basis of authority (as priestly classes generally do). Evidence mattered to him: here's how people will know that you are my disciples, here's how they'll know that I'm from God—that you love each other.

To put it a little inaccurately but in a way more acceptable to modern people, Jesus presented a theory and asked people to check its prediction that those who follow him love one another. That's not all that different from Eintein's theory of relativity, which correctly predicted that starlight passing the sun would be deflected by gravity.

Of course, what Jesus said isn't actually science: he failed to mention how to measure love with a calibrated instrument, and he didn't propose a mathematical reduction of his story to extension, mass and time. But his proposal is precise enough—precise enough that we know when we and others aren't living up to it.

And there you have it: an epistemology that combines mythopoeic power with critical thinking. Jesus' storytelling plus his way of authenticating is Sophocles and Einstein and Pascal combined. Here the power of imagination connected to the unconscious is backed by a rational way to decide truth. Which is staggering.

The epistemological struggles of the last two and a half millenniums are at an end. As are soup cans.

On Presupposing Most Everything
But Jesus' solution sounds odd to modern people. What kind of epistemol-

ogy centers on love? Or even on how people live? When speaking of truth, the Western tradition (at least the rationalist part of it) focuses on things like logical demonstrations and observation with calibrated instruments. So even if a story turned out to produce loving people, rationalists wouldn't necessarily think it true, and if it turned out to produce odious people, they wouldn't necessarily think it false. A story that produced love might be true, of course, but then again, it might be an agreeable falsehood.

What's happening here is that Jesus and rationalists have different paradigms. Jesus starts by assuming most everything, by telling an overarching story and then proposing a method to test the overall story. Rationalists use a fundamentally different paradigm. They start with methods (reason and observation)[1] and try to build a system one unit at a time, proving each part before going on to the next. This paradigm (sometimes called atomistic foundationalism) is totally foreign to Jesus, the very opposite of his approach.

But let's let Descartes explain atomistic foundationalism in his own words:

I was in Germany at the time; the fortune of war . . . had called me there. While I was returning to the army from the emperor's coronation, the onset of winter held me up in quarters in which I found no conversation to interest me; and since, fortunately, I was not troubled by any cares and passions, I spent the whole day shut up alone in a stove-heated room, and was at full liberty to discourse with myself about my own thoughts. . . .

Many men have their [houses] pulled down in order to rebuild them, and they are even sometimes obliged to, when the houses are in danger of falling in any case, and the foundations are insecure. By this parallel I became convinced . . . that as to the opinions I had so far admitted to belief, I could not do better than to set about rejecting them bodily, so that later on I might admit to belief either other, better opinions or even the same ones, when once I made them square with the norm of reason. I firmly believed that in this way I should much better succeed in the conduct of my life than if I built only upon old foundations.[2]

At the heart of modern thought lies the almost unnoticed assumption that you shouldn't have assumptions. (More's the pity; that's our problem). Oh, we assume a few basic methodological principles, like deduction and induction, but we argue that they're scarcely assumptions and need little justification. We then try to step right out of our lives (by setting aside our beliefs, preferences and passions) and systematically build an intellectual structure from the bottom up. That is, we start with method and then toward the end use it to justify wisdom and beauty and God or the laws of motion, as the case may be.

But there are other approaches. From the first page of this book I have rejected modernity because I dislike its consequences. That is, I started with content like wisdom and beauty and God. I didn't primarily argue that modern methods are internally inconsistent (though I think they are); instead I argued that they must be wrong because they produce one-dimensional people. People who treat Campbell's Soup cans as their icon *must* have bad methodology. That's the heart of my argument.

Which must seem strange to modern people educated into avoiding presuppositions. From that point of view, instead of starting with things of depth, I should have started by explaining a method with no content and no depth and then used it gradually to introduce things of depth.[3] (But if you start with no depth you will end with no depth, as any logician or computer programmer can tell you. To put it technically, "Garbage in; garbage out.")

So rather than presupposing only a method and going around giving rationalistic arguments for each of his points, Jesus assumed his story and then suggested a way of authenticating it as a whole. He went from village to village telling stories, posing conundrums, healing the sick, holding children on his lap, confronting religious leaders with his stories and actions, calling everyone to transformed lives.

And you find the same spirit in Moses, David, Solomon, Amos, Isaiah, John and even Paul—not one biblical writer based his message on a presuppositionless method. (Paul's argument in Romans comes closest, but read chapter 1 and notice the number of unargued insights.) What they did was come loaded with a point of view and from within that point of view spin out narratives, sing songs, compose impassioned letters, invent proverbs, write poetry, recount history.

And in the Pentateuch you find a test similar to Jesus'. The children of Israel should believe the story Moses is telling not because of a rationalistic argument for an unmoved mover or something of the sort. No, they should believe it because it transformed their lives and got them out of Egypt.

Half the Old Testament is an apologetic claiming that when the children of Israel obeyed God, they had lives of depth and joy, and when they disobeyed, they experienced death and disintegration. So when they entered Canaan, half were to stand on Mount Gerizim and half on Mount Ebal, and they were to chant blessings and curses to each other antiphonally (Deut 27:11-26). The antiphony contrasted life lived as God intended with life lived as people intend. "See, I have set before you this day life and good, death and evil. . . . Therefore choose life" (Deut 30:15, 19 RSV).

And much of the rest of the Old Testament consists in showing how that worked out in practice. The historical books record how the Israelites had real life when they obeyed and death when they disobeyed. The prophets predict disaster for disobedience and offer beautiful visions of life in obedience. The psalmists recite the wonders of obeying God (except when they are struggling with it not working out as promised!).

Which is the method of this book: set out life choices and claim that Jesus' choice produces the most life. To put it differently, I am presenting the story of Jah and asking people to see if it doesn't produce a people who love one another.

Presuppose the whole thing, and then sort out whether you've got a soup can . . . or a life.

Presuppositions as Theory Formation

The trouble is that this is presuppositional, and it's almost definitional of modernity that we think we reject presuppositions. We're likely to imagine that in biblical times people thought presuppositionally only because they hadn't yet learned to think critically and scientifically. We don't hold that against them any more than we hold it against them that they didn't know nuclear physics, but at the same time we no more set out to think as they did than we set out to adopt their physics.

That sounds sensible. But it's terribly wrong. Something primal is at issue—the very nature of thinking and deciding. I suggest that modern people in fact think presuppositionally . . . because there's no other way to think. By its very nature, knowledge is presuppositional—as everyone from Kant to Dooyeweerd to Wolterstorff to Popper to Kuhn to MacIntyre to the deconstructionists has been trying to tell us.[4]

The trouble is that we can't get past Descartes's foundationalist model, perhaps especially as explained by Francis Bacon. Bacon's understanding of scientific method, while it has had little influence on scientists, has profoundly affected the rest of us. According to him science proceeds by setting aside presuppositions, collecting observations and then, on the basis of those collections, making generalizations. The results are scientific laws. The process is called induction and could almost be done by a computer connected to a television camera.

According to Bacon, scientists add nothing from their own story or beliefs but merely calculate the mathematical averages of trial-and-error observations. Though they may sometimes cheat or make mistakes and though their data is often incomplete, the process is in principle objective and factual. It's a matter of the left brain, not of the right, and involves little by way of imagination or presupposition. And except for romantics, we Western people accept some form of this approach as our epistemological paradigm[5] (which is not to say we practice it).

The only trouble is that it's sheer nonsense. At early stages of science, when little is known on a subject, some version of induction functions, but as scientists make advances, they make imaginative leaps to theories that go far beyond anything they observe.

According to Karl Popper, science is nonetheless objective because it allows only theories that lead to precise, falsifiable predictions. So although astrology is based on mountains of observations and has plenty of theories, it isn't scientific because its predictions aren't precise enough to be falsifiable: "You have romantic possibilities with a good-looking stranger you'll meet today." Well, big deal; almost anything that could happen would fit. They don't say anything precise like "You'll choke on a piece of Styrofoam while talking to someone you want to impress."

Compare the vagueness of astrology to Einstein's theory that light and matter are attracted to each other. It leads to the prediction that when light passes close to the sun, it's deflected. And since that prediction was known to be correct, Einstein's theory was confirmed. Unlike in astrology, a "crucial experiment" was possible.[6]

The importance of theories that go well beyond the evidence is made clear by the history of chemistry. In the 1600s chemistry was proceeding slowly, scientists collecting data the way Bacon told them to and therefore not making much progress. They needed a Newton to give them an overarching theory that would point them in some direction.

Then a person named Johann Becher proposed the existence of something he called phlogiston. He suggested that all matter included phlogiston and that fire was phlogiston being released. He was wrong, but his mistaken theory, which went well beyond observed data, proved much more useful than no theory. It got chemistry functioning in the theoretical way that soon made Antoine Lavoisier's "discovery" of oxygen possible. Chemistry was on the road because chemists began taking imaginative leaps to explain data.

Some Presuppositions of Science

But this paradigm insisted on precise, mathematical predictions. And with that approach, the same things tend to disappear from the universe as in Bacon—goodness, beauty, spirit, God, wisdom . . . and science.

I suggest that science itself functions in a framework of theories that can't begin to be falsified the way Popper requires.[7] That is, science functions within a presuppositional framework. For example, reducing matter to extension, mass and time is obviously a metaphysical presupposition of no small size (no Form, no purpose, no secondary qualities like sound or color). It had scarcely occurred to anyone till the end of the Middle Ages, and it can't possibly be tested by a Popperian prediction. It's accepted for the good reason that when you do, science becomes possible. (It frees science from Egypt.) Without it, science would return to the stagnation it experienced during the reigns of Plato and Aristotle.

And that is the way to choose all stories: accept ones that make it possible to get on with life, and reject the others. (I suspect that this is a precise enough prediction to let us make the decisions we need to make, though of course it's not precise in the sense of leading to a mathematical formula that will produce predictions measurable by calibrated instruments.)

And in any case, it's what we do all the time. It's the only way we have of proceeding. Otherwise we would have no defense against solipsism. That is, maybe only I exist and everything else in the world is the product of my imagination. As bizarre as that may seem, it explains all the scientific evidence quite as well as the idea that other people and things exist. No crucial experiment is possible here. The reason we reject solipsism isn't that we have scientific or logical evidence against it or that it's meaningless; it's that otherwise we couldn't get on with a life of any quality.[8]

The same sort of thing is true for many things in science. We have no evidence for the uniformity of nature (that tomorrow will be like today, for example, or that the earth wasn't created by God in 4004 B.C. with geological strata and fossils already in place). Nonetheless, we presuppose the uniformity of nature because otherwise life would become unlivable and science unthinkable.[9] Or take the thirst for truth so crucial to science. Why did Enlightenment scientists, for example, hate superstition? Doesn't that presuppose the metaphysical/moral principle that truth is better than superstition? Indeed doesn't it presuppose objective truth, that there's more than what's "true" for me?

Science proceeds by assumptions, by imaginative leaps, by a complex framework of stories. It depends on them. So do ethics and religion . . . and life.

And there's nothing wrong with that. Except that we don't acknowledge it.

Which makes our presuppositions invisible. And gives us a false sense of objectivity. People who don't agree with us aren't objective: they have presuppositions that aren't rationally supported!

But so do we. Except our presuppositions are shared by our whole secular culture; they're the new common sense that everyone accepts and so no one notices or feels a need to defend. They're the water the fish can't see because they've never been in anything else.

So when people are accused of having presuppositions, that only means they believe something their critics don't. A presupposition turns out to be anything not believed by the culture at large, anything removed by the secular lobotomy, anything contrary to what even the critics of secularism accept unthinkingly.

But in fact all knowledge is presuppositional. Or so I'm arguing.

Imaginative Constructs

So our worldviews are less objective than we imagine. They're not impersonal collections of facts but interpretive constructs through which we see "facts," and so the boundary between fact and interpretations isn't nearly as precise as we suppose. We may imagine that facts determine our worldview in a strict manner, but I suggest that our worldviews are stories, imaginative leaps by which we hang together what we then take to be facts, leaps that don't lead to predictions nearly as precise as Popper would like.

We imagine we should set aside our assumptions and look at everything afresh. Well, we can't. We can only look at things with our own eyes, our own set of assumptions and constructs, our own story. We want proof of a position before we believe it.[10] But that's backwards. What we must do, and what we in fact do, is step into a story and see if it helps us understand more of the world.[11] When we accept a new story, things get a new look; old facts are seen in new light. It's like getting a new pair of glasses. We put them on and discover that trees aren't just a green and gray blur but that they have distinct branches and leaves.

This is so different from what we're taught that it sounds complicated. But it's simple. If we start with the assumption that everything is matter, then we tend to never see things that aren't matter; but if we start with the assumption that some things are spiritual, then we see reality that way. We like the line "Seeing is believing," but it's at least as true that "believing is seeing."[12]

If a psychologist flashes normal playing cards before people, the people identify them with confidence, accuracy and speed. If the psychologist then starts flashing a few cards that don't exist in a normal deck (like a black four of hearts), the people continue to identify them with confidence and speed. Only not accurately. At that point, the people (who are all of us) see what they assume they'll see—either a red four of hearts or a black four of spades.[13] That's what we see because that's what our intellectual construct about cards leads us to expect. What we experience is determined to a substantial degree by what we expect to experience, by what our story leads us to experience.

Until Lavoisier proposed the oxygen theory of combustion, no one realized air was a mixture of different gases; evidence for it was available, but people didn't know how to interpret it. Before Wilhelm Roentgen came along, there was evidence for x-rays, but no one was paying attention to it because it didn't fit their paradigms.[14] Or to use a more mundane example, I had never "seen" a shortwave aerial until as a kid I became interested in getting a ham operator's license. Then I saw shortwave aerials everywhere. Even our next-door neighbor had one—and I suspect had had it all along.

We don't see what's there; we see what we're trained to see, what our framework points to.

Believing is seeing.

A Blind Leap?

But that doesn't mean we're locked into the presuppositions we start with. This isn't a blind, irrational leap.[15] Our experiences set limits on what theories are possible. After all, Lavoisier worked his way out of Becher's phlogiston theory, and more to the point, Jesus proposed a test for his presuppositional story. It's just that the test isn't the sort proposed by Descartes and Bacon, and it's not quite the sort proposed by Popper. It's a test of the whole rather than of the parts. In the case of the story of Jah, you don't try to discover a logical proof that redemption comes through the crucified God; you try to discover whether life comes by submitting to the crucified God.

By contrast, the rationalistic process is highly atomistic. You build knowledge in pieces, from the bottom up. As in building a house, you get your tools, then you build the foundation and go on to the wall supports and the roof and the plumbing; only after that do you put up plasterboard and decorate the interior. That is, you subject each part to tests of rationality and observability, and you believe in them only in proportion to the evidence.

So to find out whether a television set works, you don't turn it on to see if you get a satisfactory picture; you test each transistor, chip and switch independently. This has the peculiar result that if each part tests out, the set is said to work—even if you get no picture because certain parts are missing. Similarly, people accept the secular story because they think its parts test out—even though it has so many missing parts that when you turn the set on, you have only hollowness and soup cans.

But Jesus starts with God and morality and suggests testing the whole thing by seeing whether it produces a satisfactory picture. He tells a story and says, Now try it out, and you will see that it produces love. Try it out and see that it fills the void. This is a prediction, not one with the mathematical precision Popper wants, but it has all the precision needed.[16]

Christian Evidences

But I'm ahead of myself. Many conservative Christians accept the Descartes/Bacon model of epistemology. They point out, correctly, that besides being an itinerant storyteller, Jesus went around giving another sort of evidence for his stories: he performed miracles.

> Then [Jesus] began to reproach the cities in which most of his deeds of power had been done, because they did not repent. "Woe to you, Chorazin! Woe to you, Bethsaida! For if the deeds of power done in you had been done in Tyre and Sidon, they would have repented long ago in sackcloth and ashes. (Mt 11:20-21)
>
> Now Jesus did many other signs in the presence of the disciples, which are not written in this book. But these are written so that you may come to believe that Jesus is the Messiah, the Son of God, and that through believing you may have life in his name. (Jn 20:30-31)[17]

This sounds like Descartes and Bacon's style of evidence. Since Jesus performed miracles and rose from the dead, he must have been God and not just an ordinary man.[18]

But many people aren't moved by this sort of factual evidence (and I'm often one of them). Maybe the difference here is merely between left-brained and right-brained people (or whatever language you prefer to make the distinction). Maybe I'm right-brained and presuppositional and so these arguments don't reach me, but Bacon and factual evidence are fine for left-brained people.

I'm sure there's some truth to that, but it's not the whole story. In fact, the value of miracles as evidence for Christianity is severely limited, and the reason is precisely the presuppositional nature of knowledge. Modern people are far from impressed by the evidence for miracles in the New Testament; in practice, those miracles are a serious hindrance to their acceptance of Christianity—precisely because miracles don't fit the modern presuppositional structure. Thomas Jefferson, for example, "believed in Christianity" but rewrote the New Testament removing all miracles because he found them deeply offensive![19] (What we need is some way to get at people's presuppostions.)

Our story determines what we think the facts are. Part of the reason miracles should have worked as evidence for the Jews is that Jesus and the Jews had that part of their story in common. But people won't be impressed by accounts of miracles if their story disallows them.

Besides, Jesus offered more than miracles: he also offered profound moral teaching and a profound life, and if he hadn't, he'd have had little claim to being God. Let me put it this way: suppose Jesus performed the miracles the Gospels say he did but that he performed them only for the rich and powerful, and suppose he rose from the dead but when he came back he slowly tortured to death all who had opposed him. And suppose he taught exterminating the weak and getting even with your enemies—while claiming he was God and performing miracles of amazing power.[20]

Would his miracles then count as evidence that he was God, or would they suggest he had a demon (as the Pharisees charged)? The interconnections between stories and facts is more complex than a Baconian or even Popperian model leads us to believe. The power of Jesus' miracles alone is not enough to authenticate his claims; the power of his life and ethics is also required, especially if you're right-brained. To put it differently, miracles don't interpret themselves (and neither does anything else); their meaning depends on an overall interpretive construct, on a story, a set of presuppositions.

By the same token, factual evidence isn't irrelevant. The story of Jah claims to have taken place in space and time, and therefore the facts matter. If we somehow found Jesus' body, we would know that the story of Jah was false. We must hold the two halves together: the left brain and the right, the facts and the heart.

Jesus and Noncontradiction

If knowledge is a story, a presuppositional construct, then a lot of things change, and we need to look again at logic and feeling. They have a different role than before, though still an absolutely crucial one.

Now obviously Jesus didn't take a stand on presuppositionalism or foundationalism. But it's significant that he seems to have had a healthy respect for logic without having a need to "prove" what he said. That is, he never offered logical proofs for his teachings, but he frequently criticized the Pharisees for their inconsistencies.

Within a presuppositional approach, this makes a lot of sense. Logical *proof* is misplaced, a misunderstanding, but logical *consistency* plays a crucial role. The function of logic is to tell us whether what we say and do is consistent with our presuppositions. It's a way of unfolding the meaning and significance of the story we presuppose, a way of checking whether our story is internally coherent and of checking whether we practice what our story preaches. In other words, critical thinking is possible (and in fact essential).

The law of noncontradiction is valid (at least within the story I accept): a thing can't both be and not be the same thing at the same time in the same way. That's all logic amounts to: not contradicting yourself, not being inconsistent, not talking out of both sides of your mouth. And as such it's tremendously important. So it's a serious mistake to say, "Consistency is the hobgoblin of little minds."[21] No, inconsistency is the sign of little minds, a sign of talking gibberish.

And that's important—mammothly important. But it doesn't prove much. All it proves is that you're consistent *with the presuppositions you start with.* It doesn't prove that your presuppositions are right. (To put it differently, logic can disprove a story, but it can't prove it.) Being consistent isn't terribly hard. Many stories, many systems, are internally consistent or can get that way with minor adjustments.[22]

At least on a theoretical level. But not in life. A consistent theory is easy. A consistent life isn't. The real power of logic lies not in proving or disproving systems but in revealing lives for what they are. That's how Jesus used logic. He assailed the Pharisees not so much for inconsistent systems as for inconsistent lives—for lives that did not measure up to their own stories. So when they were outraged over his healing on the sabbath, he said: "Which of you, if your sheep falls into a pit on the Sabbath, won't lift it out?" (see Mt 12:11). And he railed at them for tithing mint and dill and cummin while neglecting the weightier things in the law: justice, mercy and peace (Mt 23:23).

Where logic has its greatest power is not in abstractions but in revealing people for who they are, especially to . . . themselves. How this applies to religious people is painfully obvious, but applying it to secular people and romantics is equally devastating. Some secular people may claim they don't believe in absolute values (such a position is internally coherent), but they can't possibly live it. They keep acting as if values were real. And romantics claim people should follow their feelings, but they don't believe it when someone else lives out feelings that violate them. They can't possibly live it.

Notice that this is almost the opposite of the existentialist claim that logic applies to science (Nothings) but not to the important things. *Logic applies particularly to life,* to the things that matter, to feelings. I'm claiming (and I think Jesus practiced) that logic applies to everything.

No one should suppose that passion justifies irrationality. Being passionate can never make it right to be inconsistent and stupid. (As being logical can never justify coldness and indifference.) If it's lethal to build up reason at the expense of feeling, it's also lethal to attack reason in order to save feeling.

Those who object to logic often do so out of disgust at those who try

to force life into neat little categories or into vast abstract systems that chop
bits and pieces off. And I agree. Western logic is dichotomous. In Western
logic, something is either true or false; there's no room for half true or
deliberately ambiguous. So a naive application of it encourages us to think
that a person is either wonderful or terrible. People and things are on a
pedestal till they fall off . . . and then they're filthy rotten. But even in
Western logic, if a thing isn't black, it doesn't follow that it's white; it might
be any one of an infinite variety of grays, not to mention of greens, blues,
yellows, browns and reds.

And stories naturally convey this infinite variety. Without falling into
self-contradiction, they can present complexity and dialectic and vagueness and paradox in a way that systems and neat categories don't. You can
require stories to be coherent, but you can't require them to be linear or
bipolar or to answer every question with the mathematical precision of
measurable categories. Stories have a way of presenting multiple facets of
life that are in dialectical tension in a way that systems never match and
rationalistic logicians rarely attempt.

The pursuit of logic chopping has been a Siren (a male one, I suspect)
luring the Western world into shallow waters, and the abandonment of
logic has been a Charybdis sucking us into an orgy of gobbledygook. We've
been caught between a seducer and a whirlpool. But Jesus found a way
through. Stories. Stories we live. Or rather *a* story—a story we authenticate
by experiencing love and grace when we live it consistently and passionately.

Jesus and Feelings

Which brings us to feelings. According to Descartes and Bacon, truth is
to be found without consulting our deepest hopes and fears. It's to be found
in the realm of reason and science; so passions, commitment, the imagination, the awesome, life even, have no role. (All by itself, this assumption
limits our choice of icons to varieties of soup cans.) Clearly in this approach, stories are not foundational to the pursuit of truth.[23]

In fact, Descartes was suspicious of feelings. That's an ancient thread,
going back at least to Plato. We Westerners have never been comfortable

with emotions. We believe they're dangerous and must be held in check.[24] But the worst of it is that a blanket condemnation of feelings is so odd that just noticing it has driven millions of sensitive people into the arms of passion. So romantics believe truth is found in passionate commitment, in following our bliss.

For them, feelings are all. In order to find out what to do, we get to know our self, and then we do what we think will fulfill the feelings of that self. In the process, feelings gain absolute control, the way proofs do for Descartes. At their frequent worst, romantics think they should do what their narcissistic selves feel like doing.

With this, Jesus shows less than no sympathy. (That's at least partly because of his belief in sin, which we'll get to later.) He doesn't act as if feelings were nothing, but neither does he act as if they were everything. He took a different route altogether: he focused on actions, not feelings. His story isn't authenticated when people *feel* loving; it's authenticated when they *act* lovingly.

That doesn't mean Jesus neglects feelings but that he puts them in a context. The Gospels often tell us that Jesus "was moved with compassion" (literally, "his heart contracted convulsively").[25] So feelings are important. But in each case, the feeling is the background for an action he's about to take: moved with compassion for a leper, Jesus stretched out his hand and said, "Be clean" (see Mk 1:41).

Something there is about feeling that goes bad if you focus on it. (The same, of course, is true with logic and everything else except God.) So rather than fall into that touchy-feely morass, Jesus focused on actions joined to feelings (joined to ideas?). It would be only a slight overstatement to say that Jesus' approach was: Take care of the actions and the feelings will take care of themselves. (Notice that this is quite different from saying, Take care of the *ideas* and the feelings will take care of themselves. Which seems to be accepted by everyone from Plato to in a sense Freud.)

But all of this misses the question of the epistemological role of feelings. What sort of guide to knowledge are they? Well, to start with, there are good feelings and there are bad feelings. Good feelings are a guide to life, and bad feelings are a guide to death. Jesus tells us that where you find self-sacrificing love and graciousness, you're near the warm spot at the center of the universe. But where you find hatred and resentment and greed, you're near a quite different warm spot. Clearly (at least given the presuppositions of the story of Jah), some passions and commitments are horrifyingly awful, cloaks for the worst in personal and international evil.

Failure to make this distinction is fatal. Descartes's failure to make it made him suspicious of all feelings when he needed to be suspicious only of the bad ones. (Which do indeed need to be held in check, Freud notwithstanding.) Oddly, romantics also fail to make the distinction; so their rhetoric fails to distinguish between sadism and love that seeks not its own. Jesus didn't make that mistake.

Paul comes close to giving us an anatomy of feeling when he talks about flesh and spirit, the old nature and the new nature.[26] Lust, hatred, jealousy, anger, greed, arrogance—they're desires of the old nature (bad feelings joined with bad actions). Love, joy, peace, humility, mercy—they're desires of the new nature (good feelings joined with good actions). So from the point of view of the story of Jah, we indeed need to get to know our self, our feelings and actions, but the trick is to know both our old nature and the new one . . . and to distinguish between them.

Then we find life.

This reveals the abyss of so much New Age spirituality. Old spiritual traditions usually provide some way to help the seeker identify what feelings and what parts of the self are problems,[27] but much of modern spirituality has people meditating and learning about themselves on their own without any recognition that much of who we are is problematic. Such people, spiritual though they may be, are almost certain to wind up celebrating their own twistedness.

Our hollowness is in the shape of Jah.[28] Once our biological needs are met, the basic human drive is to fill that feeling of hollowness. But the human predicament is that we try to fill it with all sorts of unrealities and half realities, all sorts of bent feeling and twisted desires and actions. So we are left profoundly dissatisfied. "Our heart knows no rest until it finds its rest in God."[29]

This feeling of dissatisfaction is intended to drive us into the arms of

Jah. Suppose you've lived the story of individualistic economic success until you're forty. You've made a lot of money, but you nonetheless feel terribly empty. At that point, you should know that your story is empty (and many people do). Of course, you may respond by throwing everything over for an affair, but at least that shows that you know you've been serving a false god. Then when your affair also reveals itself as hollow, perhaps your next fling will be with Jah.

To put it another way, exploring feelings of hollowness gives us a clue to the shape and texture of the void within and therefore of the ultimate reality that can fill it. And whatever brings a sense of fullness also gives a clue to the shape and texture of reality. We get a sense of who God is by what makes us feel cold and empty—and by what brings rest.[30]

The Depth of Stories

But I am understating the wonder of Jesus' epistemology. It's not just something about being logical or doing what you feel like. It's situated in life. For unlike any other epistemology since the Greeks enthroned reason, it's based on stories . . . and therefore it reaches life on an elemental level not imaginable in standard philosophy. For stories are as deep as the hollow places within and as true, or as false, as scientific equations—and nearly as testable.

Stories embody cultural ideals and deep, commonly felt emotions—the primary yearnings and convictions of a people, their unconscious hopes and fears, their elemental joys and awes and aversions. (Stuff like the Promised Land, on one hand, and Golgotha, on the other; Christmas and Nazi concentration camps.) They reach down to imagination, dreams, mystical states, emotion, ritual, history, sensation, the unconscious, intuition . . . as well as to logic and observation.

So stories pull together all that it is to be human (which is more than feelings and logic). They address our primal selves, both the darkness within and the hope without. They reach down to our yearning to see the defeat of the Dark Lord and to find the promised land. They empower us to continue the struggle against all odds. They give us rituals to encourage us when all seems lost.

Conclusion

Throughout this book I've been arguing that secularism closes us into the one-dimensional world of true and false exams and excludes us from painting ourselves crucifying God. And secularism's Siamese twin, romanticism, only makes us one-dimensional in a different direction. My claim has been that the central intellectual task of our age is to find an epistemology that can bring together our heads and our hearts, the whole person. We must find a way to address the great questions without falling into irrationality and self-indulgence—and a way to be rational without falling into dryness and irrelevance.

Well, here it is. All that and a lot more.

8

A Cross with Nails:
If the World Hasn't
Changed, the
Messiah Hasn't Come

Jah's story is authenticated when groups of people go to the cross for each other.[1] That's how to get beyond soup cans. As Francis Schaeffer used to say, "Love is the final apologetic."[2]

But we have a little problem here—the dismal record of the folks who tell Jesus' story. Any remotely impartial examination has to leave doubt that the followers of Jesus bear good fruit. How about Jim and Tammy Bakker's escapades or Oral Roberts's vision that God will take him unless the audience gives enough millions? And it gets worse: Christians sponsored the Crusades, the Inquisition and the drowning of heretics. While claiming to spread enlightenment, the church opposed Galileo and the rights of women. Christians say they support racial justice, but neither the Nazis nor the Klan has ever had any shortage of chaplains, and we all know the piety of slave owners.

Worse, it's not overwhelmingly obvious that ordinary Christians bear a whole lot better fruit than secular people. Pews simply aren't filled with selfless, loving people—or even with those trying to be. What Jesus was describing was a wonder, and while our lives may be a little better than the lives of non-Christians, it's hard to see how anyone could think that our self-sacrificing love is a wonder to behold. For every St. Francis or Mother Teresa, you can find a thousand Christians not at all interested in going to the cross for each other.

Which is serious even without Jesus' test. But given Jesus' test, it's almost fatal. Not to put too fine a point on it, the church fails to authenticate the story of Jah.

Now I realize that this sounds harsh and judgmental and perhaps arrogant, but remember, I didn't make up the test. Jesus did. And he clearly gave it as a test he intended us to use to sort out who were false prophets. It comes only a few verses after "Do not judge, so that you may not be judged" (Mt 7:1); so apparently deciding that someone's fruit suggests they're a false prophet isn't judging in the sense Jesus condemned.

Now I will eventually offer a more charitable analysis of the church than this. But the bottom line will not change: the church has failed. We have no excuse. Given the evidence of our lives, secular people *should* reject our story.

And they have. Our world is going to hell, in every sense of that word, and the reason is not finally some complicated history about the rise of science or the reaction of romanticism; the reason is that Christians don't go to the cross for each other.

The solution is obvious. We must repent . . . of not breaking down walls with our own bodies. We must authenticate the story of Jah in our lives. By becoming a people who go to the cross for each other.

So this book is a call to churches to repent. A call to Christians to become people who as an everyday fact of life break down walls between each other. Until then secularism, or some other evil, will reign triumphant. The only thing that can change that is your and my repenting and learning to love each other.

On Pretending to Follow Jesus

But things aren't quite as bleak as I've painted them. Remember, Jesus never said that everyone who claimed to be his disciple was. In fact, that's the point of his test: People all over the place will claim to be my disciples, but many of them won't be. So here's a test for whether they are (Mt 7:13-23 paraphrased).

Spectacular evils are exactly what we should expect. Wicked television evangelists, corrupt cardinals and Klan chaplains are going to be par for the course. After all, the story of Jah offers no magic to prevent evil and foolish people from pretending to be Christian. Evil rarely parades itself as bad and ugly; it claims to be beautiful and pious. Remember the serpent in the Garden (Gen 3:1-5) and Judah before Babylon conquered it (Is 1:10-17; 3:16-24), remember the Pharisees and Sadducees, and remember Judas when Mary put expensive perfume on Jesus' feet (Jn 12:1-8).

Those who commit horrors aren't followers of Jah—they only pretend to be. It's as simple as that. They're frauds, wolves in sheep's clothing, using Jesus for their own purposes. "On that day many will say to me, 'Lord, Lord, did we not prophesy in your name, and cast out demons in your name, and do many deeds of power in your name?' Then I will declare to them, 'I never knew you; go away from me, you evildoers' " (Mt 7:22-23).

If the story of Jah is true, half the charlatans and vipers that come along are going to wrap themselves in it. (The sheer number of crooks who claim to be Christian is a testimony of sorts to the power of the story of Jah!)

50-Percent Churches
But the more serious problem is the ordinary folks sitting in the pews.

Our summers used to be spent down South, where our profoundly dyslexic son went to a special school. The teachers were paid little more than minimum wage for work as hard as I ever saw teachers do. Over the years we gained real respect for some of them. One we especially respected invited us to her large fundamentalist church, and one Sunday we went.

It was the Fourth of July.

After being asked to pledge allegiance to the flag and listen to special music about the Statue of Liberty, I was considering walking out. I probably would have except we'd arrived late and were sitting in the very front row. If ever I've seen a church with mixed allegiance, this was it.

Then the preacher stood up to preach . . . from the Sermon on the Mount. And I soon forgot everything else. He preached up a wonder. He actually imagined Jesus might have meant what he said.

We had to leave through the back door because our friend didn't want to go past the preacher. ("He kisses the ladies.") As we left, we kept meeting the teachers we respected. They were all in that church. All of them. Going out the back door.

Now this was a church toying with apostasy. That pledged its allegiance to something other than God . . . during worship! And where members left through the back door to avoid the preacher. Quite a few, I gathered.

And yet a lot was happening there.

For me, that church is a parable for almost all the churches I've ever known. Its confusion of allegiance, its mixture of good and bad, its self-sacrifice and its lack of reconciliation. Probably the contrasts that morning were starker than usual, better and worse. But all churches spread some death. And almost all spread some life. A confounding of holiness and evil. That church was about half and half, I figure. They were a long way short of the Sermon on the Mount, but they were also a long way ahead of most folks.

Perhaps that's all we can expect of an endeavor involving human beings. The truth is, Christians do pretty well, all things considered. I'm not going to try to argue the point, but I suspect that if you leave out the inevitable wolves, we're a *little* better than other people. I've worked at a lot of offices and construction sites and schools, and I'm confident that the average person there is in worse shape than the average church member. Church members tend to care for each other at least a little more than do members of the Odd Fellows[3] or of a Wall Street brokerage firm.

Besides, Christian relief and development agencies channel billions of dollars to hungry people (secular groups aren't even in their ballpark financially). Many Third World hospitals and schools have Christian roots, and the same can be said for orphanages, skid-row missions, leprosy work, food pantries. As for peace and justice, many Christians have been in the forefront (with many others in the rear guard) fighting for everything from abolition to civil rights to getting out of Vietnam. And the stand of fundamentalists against alcohol, tobacco, gambling and extramarital sex eventually will be recognized as right even if they do often forget the point themselves. Only prejudice allows overlooking such things while endlessly recalling the Crusades and Galileo.

I tend to see things as either good or bad, but in practice all human beings combine the angelic and the demonic. It's not that a church either spreads life or spreads death but that it spreads some of each. It's tragic that ecumenical churches ask little by way of personal discipleship (even tithing is a rarity), but it's good that they tend to care about social justice. It's tragic that evangelicals have a hard time seeing structural injustice, but at least they give billions to social service.

Insofar as a church accepts the story of Jah, it spreads abundant life, and insofar as it rejects the story of Jah, it spreads death abundant. Following Jesus makes life flourish; not following him makes it shrivel. But most churches do a little of each. To reject a church because it isn't perfect is foolishness. (If for no other reason, then because it would stop being perfect as soon as you or I joined it.)

Sometimes I play a little game with myself. When I'm at a church, I wonder what percentage of the teachings of Jesus that church lives by and what percentage of the teachings of the dominion of Darkness. Churches like the one we visited that July 4 I call 50-percent churches. Now in light of the distance we all are from the Sermon on the Mount or from the grand vision of the church in Ephesians, that's probably generous, but I rather arbitrarily take that church as my average church, the one at the midpoint of discipleship. I don't play the game to sort out how good or bad a church actually is, but to remind myself that it isn't all or nothing.

The Test: Breaking Down Walls with Our Bodies

So 50-percent churches are Christian.[4] But that doesn't mean they're any help authenticating the story of Jah. They're not what Jesus said about how to tell who his disciples were.

The place Jesus talks about judging prophets by their fruit is near the end of the Sermon on the Mount. So when he says, "You'll know them by their fruit," he means, "You'll know that someone is a false prophet if they don't have the fruit of the Sermon on the Mount." Jesus has just taught that we shouldn't resist wrong, that we shouldn't be any more concerned about where our next meal will come from than a bird is, that we should cooperate with our oppressors. That's quite a test.

The book of John makes the same point. There Jesus says, "Love one another. Just as I have loved you, you also should love one another. By this everyone will know that you are my disciples" (13:34-35).[5] And when you remember how Jesus loved his disciples, that's as demanding as the Sermon on the Mount: "We know love by this, that he laid down his life for us—and we ought to lay down our lives for one another" (1 Jn 3:16). Another part of love is unity: Jesus prays "that they may all be one . . . so that the world may believe that you have sent me" (Jn 17:21).[6]

Jesus' test is whether a people live together in love: whether they live in peace and reconciliation, whether they go to the cross for one another. In short, the test is whether a people let their own bodies break down walls, the walls between rivals, between black and white, between God and people, between people and creation, and above all between each other.

We must take Jesus seriously. And he doesn't say, "Here's how everyone will know that you are my disciples: that you do a little better than the Odd Fellows." If we're only a little better, that means our story is only a little better than other stories—and a little better won't do. Being a little more loving is not what Jesus was about.

On Not Bowdlerizing Jesus

Christians may seem OK if we bowdlerize Jesus' test (reduce it to whether we're a little better than the Odd Fellows), but we don't do so well if we use Jesus' actual test. The idea is to lay down our lives for each other to the point of death the way Jesus did. And you know we rarely inconvenience ourselves for each other of a Saturday. Let alone Good Friday.

Be clear. I'm not saying we're all bad. I'm not saying that 50-percent churches aren't churches. I'm not saying that people in 50-percent churches aren't Christians. I'm not saying that God isn't working in 50-percent churches.

But I *am* saying that Jesus described a wonder. A wonder where we live lives of deep unity and self-sacrifice. We, however, aren't overflowing with unity and love in that way—in a way that makes the world wonder. Jesus was talking about a quality of life so abundant that the world would believe. And whatever our strengths may be, our life is not that abundant, not abundant enough to make the world feel wonder.

And when I say that, I'm not saying something controversial. I'm only repeating the general wisdom of Christendom. I don't know how often I've heard Christians say, "Don't judge the gospel by the church; judge it by Jesus." That is, we Christians openly acknowledge that our lives aren't a compelling witness for Christ.

It's not just that Christians gossip and tell white lies when convenient. Nor is it the stories anyone can tell who has been around churches for long: stories about pastors having affairs with young mothers they are counseling and ransacking the church treasury to finance it. Criticism like that leaves little room for the vast, unfathomable grace of Jah. Is Jah really unable to forgive a pastor who has an affair? Don't misunderstand me. That is deep evil . . . but God's grace is even deeper. David did worse than that, and God forgave him (2 Sam 11—12). Remember, in the story of Jah artists paint themselves crucifying Jah. Which is a good deal worse than adultery and robbery.

Such criticisms judge Christians according to a legal understanding of morality rather than according to the story of Jah. Jesus' test is not "By this everyone will know that you are my disciples: that you are sinless" or "that your pastors never have affairs." What he said was "By this everyone will know that you are my disciples, if you have love for one another." That leaves lots of room for sin—and grace and repentance and growth.

The question, then, isn't whether you find individual sins in a church, even serious ones, but whether a people live in peace, going to the cross for one another. What's at issue here is a quality of life, a pattern of being, what and who we are at the deepest level.

But a reconciled, gracious, sacrificial quality of life is precisely what's not common in churches. Some churches have kept their theology orthodox, some have devised wonderful liturgies, and some have a passion for justice, but somehow few have the sacrificial, reconciling love that is the heart of the matter.

Instead, an underlying quality of life in many churches is factionalism.

Otherwise, we wouldn't have so many church members who avoid each other, so many churches that split. Nor would we have so many denominations: Catholics, Presbyterians, Anglicans, Methodists, Baptists (Southern Baptists, American Baptists, National Baptists, Progressive National Baptists, Conservative Baptists, Freewill Baptists, General Association of Regular Baptists), Lutherans (Missouri Synod, Wisconsin Synod, American Lutherans), etc., etc., etc., ad nauseam.

Which is why secularism is triumphing. And why I sometimes skate on the edge of despair. And why our world is lost. An underlying pattern of lovelessness.

A Remnant

What are we to make of the failure of Christians to live Jesus' story in this radical sense? How do we stand it? I don't ask this casually or as a rhetorical device. This is the biggest intellectual problem of my entire life and one of my biggest emotional problems. In the end, all I can say is that we must repent and go to the cross for one another.

But before I get to that, what's happening has an easy explanation—at least on an intellectual level. Most people who call themselves Christian don't accept much of the story of Jah. We are selective. We protect ourselves from the parts that challenge us too deeply. We overlook anything suggesting that *our* bodies should break down walls; we prefer to think that Jesus will make us prosperous.

Which should be no surprise.

Half the story of the Old Testament is how the children of Israel didn't accept the story of Jah. Normally all but a handful were up to something else. Not that they officially rejected Jah: they might still attend the temple faithfully or at least sacrifice to Jah at the high places. So they rarely felt the need to announce their apostasy (and given the human talent for self-deception, they presumably rarely even realized their apostasy). But they were nonetheless apostate.

And that's a way of understanding the appalling state even of ordinary people in the church. We're as commonly and as deeply apostate as were the children of Israel.

Much of the problem is established religion. One thing we can be sure of is that Jesus wasn't too sympathetic with established religion. Established religion (especially its leaders) opposed Jesus at every turn and finally got him killed. Jesus spent almost as much time attacking the Pharisees as he did materialism.

So the fact that established religion today doesn't live up to Jesus' standards is hardly interesting. And the fact that the established religion in question uses Jesus' name doesn't change anything. The simple truth is that throughout biblical history, the religion officially serving Jah never stayed faithful long. And when we look at history since then, the corruption of established religion is one of its most obvious features.

One of the fastest corruptions ever was Aaron. He had only been leading Israel for a few weeks before he was sacrificing to a golden calf (Ex 32:1-6). One of the saddest was Joash. His life was saved from his murderous grandmother by Jehoiada, but no sooner had Jehoiada died than Joash was busy murdering Jehoiada's son (2 Chron 24:2, 17-22). When the children of Israel could first have entered Canaan, only Moses and Aaron, Joshua and Caleb were prepared to do it (Num 13—14). And history tells us that the Pharisees were good people to start with (Jesus may have adapted the "Golden Rule" from a Pharisaical saying), but within a few years they had become corrupt enough to arrange Jesus' crucifixion.

Faithfulness rarely endures. The most we should expect is a remnant.[7] That doesn't mean that everyone is corrupt except me and two of my friends. We need to remember Elijah when he was feeling alone. God told him that seven thousand remained whose mouths hadn't kissed Baal. They weren't vocal about it, clearly, but at least seven thousand people were refusing to serve Baal. Now out of all the population of Israel, that's not many, but it's a lot more than one. It's a remnant.

And in Jesus' time, the picture was about the same. He was popular with people as long as it didn't cost. I mean, getting healed and fed is a good deal. But when Jesus said hard things, the crowds thinned out (Jn 6), and when it came to trial and the cross, he was virtually alone.

It looks similar in apostolic times. Paul started many churches, but his letters show that they quickly deteriorated. When he was in prison, he wrote that all those in Asia had abandoned him (2 Tim 1:15). And of the seven churches in Revelation, John says five had problems serious enough to threaten their status as churches, though four had remnants (Rev 2:1—3:22).

Which is the normal picture. Tragically. When it comes to the cross, Jesus is virtually alone.

But if the story of Jah is true, there will be a faithful few. Scattered among all the official churches, I suspect. Pilgrims and sojourners. Resident aliens. Those in such a minority that they don't feel at home. "The gate is wide and the road is easy that leads to destruction, and there are many who take it. For the gate is narrow and the road is hard that leads to life, and there are few who find it" (Mt 7:13-14).

The Second Law of Thermodynamics

The truth is, we can understand this from our own lives. At least in my case, I begin forgetting important lessons within hours of learning them. The second law of thermodynamics seems to apply dramatically to the spiritual realm. (According to the second law of thermodynamics, the disorder in a system either increases or stays the same; so the heat in a system tends to dissipate.) Spiritual cooling is automatic, while remaining healthy requires heroic measures and outside energy. We are fallen. Even if by the grace of Jah we turn from our sin, over time we slowly drift back to it.

Look at the history of the church. Periodically, reformers arise, and a few generations later (if not a few minutes later) the groups they create are as corrupt as the old ones, sometimes in the very ways the reform was aimed at. So Methodists no longer know what Wesley stood for, Catholic orders make a mockery of their vows of poverty, some Mennonites are indistinguishable from Baptists, Churches of Christ are often sectarian in the very way Alexander Campbell opposed, and on and on.

If an organization were formed to sponsor bingo, it would continue to do so for generations. So why is it that if a religious organization were formed to oppose bingo, within a couple of years it would finance itself by Saturday-night bingo? The same reason, I suppose, that crabgrass is easier to grow than tulips—something about nature's preference for disorder and the second law of thermodynamics . . . and the Fall.

On Domesticating Jesus

But for established religion, the problem goes beyond that. As soon as a church becomes official, the pressure toward corruption increases exponentially. If the state supports and helps finance a religion, it expects support in return. It expects the religion to support its wars, its crusades against what it defines as evil, its policies toward the poor. So on perfectly reasonable grounds, well-meaning leaders responsible to keep churches afloat are likely to see things the way the state does. (It's called self-deception, but never mind.)

Of all Ahab's court prophets, not one would tell him the truth; Jehoshaphat had to go get an outsider who was not in Ahab's pay to find out what God had to say (1 Kings 22). And it was Jeroboam's high priest who ordered Amos to be silent: "Never again prophesy [here], for it is the king's sanctuary, and it is a temple of the kingdom" (Amos 7:13). And the high priest was right: it was a temple of the kingdom, not the temple of God. The temple of the king rarely is the temple of God.

Of course, officially established religions are less common than they used to be. "Established" means authorized by the state and supported by the civil authority, but a church can play the role of established religion without being officially established. When a church normally agrees with the policies of the government, it's established whether the financial arrangements are official or not.

On the deepest level, a church is established when it accepts the practices and beliefs of the culture or subculture it's part of. Kind of like the king in *The Little Prince:* even the sun obeys him, as long as he commands it to come up when it was going to anyway.[8]

Notice that a church can do that whether its subculture is Sandinista or fascist, Republican or Democrat, Victorian or libertarian. And not only *can* churches do it, they do. In fact, the normal function of religion (whether Buddhist, Christian or Muslim) seems to be to baptize the story of its culture: to reinforce its culture's views, to train its children to be culturally acceptable, to censure cultural deviants. By contrast, the New Testament calls people to turn their culture's stories upside down—to repent and begin serving in the kingdom of light.

Meanwhile in South Africa, Afrikaner churches advocated apartheid until the subculture began to realize that apartheid was not going to last. In the United States, churches that condemned Reagan usually managed to swallow the Sandinistas, and vice versa. In North Carolina, even some fundamentalist churches manage not to condemn smoking. And it's amazing how many churches manage to accommodate the sexual revolution and divorce. And in this day of self-fulfillment psychology, you hear in churches of every stripe more sermons on self-fulfillment than on going to the cross.

Why is it that in Marxist countries Jesus is seen as a communist, and in capitalist countries as a capitalist? Why is it that rich and middle-class people never admit how hard Jesus is on wealth? Why is it that almost no one actually believes that Jesus intends us to turn the other cheek when wronged?

Clearly, this sort of tame religion has little to do with Jesus or the story of Jah. So when people who practice it fail to live up to Jesus' test, it's hardly interesting. If anything, it confirms the myth of Jah. It's a moral outrage that official religion uses Jesus' name, but it is also entirely predictable. Establishment corrupts; absolute establishment corrupts absolutely.

When Christianity starts to behave like the successful, deodorized household pet of a subculture, it has ceased to be Christianity and become religion.

But a little band of geese will be left. A remnant.

As usual.

The Cross as Imperial Battle Standard

In A.D. 312, the Roman Empire was in the midst of one of its wars between competing emperors. One of them, Constantine, had a vision of a cross with the words "By this sign you will conquer."[9] So he designed an imperial battle standard that was a gold-covered cross with a heraldic device combining the first two Greek letters of *Christ*.

Soon after, at the battle of Milvian Bridge outside Rome, Constantine's soldiers had shields with this monogram for Christ, and they rallied around a standard in the form of a cross. Vastly outnumbered, they nonetheless slaughtered the troops of the rival emperor and "won a great victory for Jesus."

Christians had been severely persecuted under Diocletian (the emperor whose abdication eventually led to the imperial war Constantine won); so they welcomed this new emperor who halted the persecution and restored their property.

Perhaps they never noticed a certain change of symbolism. Which was to lead to Europe's becoming Christian. Christian in the sense of Constantine's heraldry.

Now one of the indications of Western spiritual poverty is that we don't see much importance in symbols. But as is often the case, this symbol mattered. The meaning of the cross was clear in the Roman Empire. It was not a symbol; it was a reality. Crucifixion was how Rome tortured to death aliens who committed offenses against the state.

So when Christians used a cross as their symbol, they were dramatically turning that symbol of death into a symbol of life. They were making a clear statement—about the empire and about themselves and about the sources of life and death.

It was not exactly a high-status symbol, not like choosing a BMW or a popular Roman general. More like choosing a gas chamber in Nazi Germany. Or an electric cattle prod in Chile. They were identifying themselves as nobodies, as failed revolutionaries, as outsiders, as dissenting aliens, as rabble who had no truck with the empire.

You'd think they'd have chosen something attractive: Miss Roman Empire, the capitol, a beautiful cathedral, a wildflower or something of the sort. But no, they chose the empire's means of suppressing alien dissenters, those whose citizenship was elsewhere, those who had been caught. And they were telling everyone that that was real life, life abundant.

For all intents and purposes, it was an advertisement that the empire had tortured their founder to death and could do the same to them before they'd recant. For they had found real life, and the empire would only make it more real if it killed them. Consequently, they would accept death and torture gently, as their Lord had done, without hitting back or attempting to kill their enemies.

The cross was in fact the perfect symbol for a little band of unsuccessful geese dedicated to letting their own bodies break down walls. They were the crucified.

Then came the battle of Milvian Bridge—with the crucifier sporting a cross and *using it to beat his enemies to death!* In the greatest irony in history (and that is not hyperbole), the cross of Christ became *the imperial battle standard.* Had Constantine missed the Christian symbolism? Did he suppose Christians were using the cross the way the empire did, to threaten enemies with death?

And Constantine's cross was gold.

Something there is about a gold cross . . . It's an inner contradiction that tears a hole in the universe. It's obscene. Insane. It turns the story of Jah upside down. It tries to make it pretty. Or to cover up the real story. It makes the cross a piece of costume jewelry. Like saying, "Didn't Auschwitz have a pretty gas chamber? And what a lovely setting. Designed by a Christian Nazi, I'm sure."

An Orthopedically Designed Cross

When I say that Christians don't live up to Jesus' test, I'm not saying anything all that controversial. But when I say that we've turned the story of Jah on its head, then I *am* saying something controversial. Many Christians are sure that parts of my version of the story are not in the Bible. Neither Constantine nor I care for the lines "Here and there little bands of joyful geese, joined by an occasional lion or owl, have become a people without walls. They live in reconciliation with each other, servants giving their bodies to be broken against walls."

We do not care for the thought that churches are intended to be little bands of geese; we prefer to think that we have as many rich and clever members as we do poor and broken ones, as many Constantines as illiterate slaves. And we may accept talk of "servants," but we're not even going to talk of giving our bodies to be broken against walls. Since Constantine (and probably long before), Christians have rarely pictured themselves that way.

How that can be, I don't know. I would have thought that the Sermon on the Mount was so clear that even those gifted in self-deception would have a hard time getting around it.[10] There Jesus clearly teaches that we needn't defend ourselves when people wrong us. He not only gives generalities about not resisting evil people and turning the other cheek. He also gets specific. He says that if someone is getting ready to sue you, you should give them more than they're asking. And he insists on giving to beggars and making loans to whoever wants them. And through it all he doesn't say a word about checking with a lawyer first, about securing collateral or about making sure you give only to worthy beggars (you wouldn't want to help them buy wine).[11]

Peter is perhaps clearer, if that's possible. He tells slaves to be submissive to bad masters. The idea is outrageous to any right-thinking, freedom-loving American. He actually says God approves of suffering patiently, though to us it's clear that people have not just a right but a duty to defend themselves. Then he says that Christians are *called* to that sort of thing! And his evidence is that Jesus did it, and he's our example. Jesus didn't fight back when he suffered unjustly.[12] Sounds like letting our bodies be used to break down walls, offensive as that may be to Constantinians dedicated to fairness.

Suppressing these teachings is the root of the failure of the church. How can we authenticate the story of Jah when we reject it? We have no intention of laying down our lives the way Jesus did—suffering unjustly and forgiving it without trying to get even. And without that, we can't live in reconciliation. It's easy to be reconciled to people who never wrong you, but if those are the only people you are reconciled with . . . well, perfect people are pretty rare.

It's no accident that in Romans 12 Paul repeatedly puts living in peace side by side with not fighting for your rights, especially not the overblown view of our rights most of us have. Reconciliation depends on humbly accepting a limited view of your gifts and allowing yourself to be wronged.[13] In my experience, a church (or a marriage, for that matter) can never be at peace if the partners are concerned about their rights. You can only be reconciled if you accept the sins of others in your body, as Jesus did.

Everything else is talk. Peace is not benign intentions but a cross with nails.[14] That's the foundation of the reconciliation that can authenticate the story of Jah.

It's not that people set out to change the story of Jah into imperial religion. I doubt that even Constantine realized he was doing it.[15] People rarely consciously sell out their beliefs for ease and success. But crosses, after all, are not orthopedically designed by the folks at Birkenstock. They don't help fallen arches. Nor do they cure premature baldness, make your teeth whiter or in any other way increase sex appeal. In short, crosses have no intrinsic attraction. Consequently, we tend to overlook the presence of the cross in the Bible, and when that becomes impossible, we try (with remarkable success) to plate it with gold.

That's why we don't love one another in a way that causes wonder.

On Getting Along with Sacred Cows, Personal and Cultural

Besides, every culture considers certain things sacred, and we naturally tend to treat with respect those things our culture treats with respect. Unfortunately, that often means systematically deceiving ourselves into thinking that Jesus blesses those things. In our culture, it's things like happiness, riches, job success, nationalism, freedom, self-expression (including sexual expression), the right to defend ourselves from every little wrong. So Christians tend to overlook or reinterpret teachings that condemn their sacred cows—and if that dismantles the story of Jah . . .

We don't approve every sacred cow, of course. Most churches roundly condemn one or two national favorites. Evangelicals and fundamentalists defy the culture by attacking sexual promiscuity (so normal according to many of our culture's stories). Ecumenical churches do better at condemning nationalism (at least if it's Western nationalism). Mennonites condemn our commitment to defending ourselves (at least on a national level). But scarcely anyone condemns materialism or teaches members to turn the other cheek as an everyday practice, and few empower married couples to live together joyfully.

We should suspect we're Constantinian if we are comfortable in our cultural roles. If we feel comfortable as Americans, as middle class, as conservatives, as liberals, as Hispanics, as engineers, as Texans, as Roman emperors—as whatever we are—if we feel comfortable, we can be sure we've tamed the story of Jah. We're not worshiping Jah but cultural sacred cows.

And just as we have cultural sacred cows, we also maintain personal sacred cows. We want what we want, and we'll find a way of deceiving ourselves into justifying it from Scripture. We will not be changed personally. Presumably, that's why few churches in any culture condemn materialism as roundly as Jesus did. And why we hear so few sermons on turning the other cheek. (That's costly in any culture.)

I've spent much of my adult life around churches deep into "peace concerns," and one of the most distressing discoveries I've ever made is that those folks are not markedly more at peace *with one another* than are those in "war" churches. The rest of my life I've spent around fundamentalists and evangelicals whose faith centers on their sins' being forgiven, but they're not themselves a whole lot more forgiving of others than the average pagan. That despite Jesus' incredible words on forgiveness. (See, for example, Mt 6:9-15.)

When I'm feeling grim, it seems to me that average Christians are about as likely to join the Mafia as to commit themselves seriously to living out the radical nature of Jesus' teaching.

This Constantinian turn is a mitigating factor for our age. At least it's a mitigating factor for those in the pews. Church members aren't taught that they're to go to the cross for each other. And how can you expect folks to do it if they aren't taught it?

The Secular Lobotomy

A second mitigating factor for this age is that secularism has undercut spiritual resources, and that makes it even more difficult to take the story of Jah seriously. We're trained to believe only what we can see. Everything not as practical and sensible as a refrigerator tends to get left out. Spiritual realities, like prayer or contemplation, have become invisible. Love is reduced to sex plus feeling for our own families; so it's unintelligible to love others to the point of going to the cross for them. And not just because of sin and selfishness but also because we've lost sight of any reality not observable under a microscope. As a result, our lives and our conversation leave little room for anything beyond refrigerators, shopping, football scores and work.

In *Glamorous Powers*, Susan Howatch portrays the reentry shock of a monk returning to the world after many years of seclusion. He encounters a woman who says how nice it must be to get out of the monastery where "you can't do any of the *real* things, like going to the shops or listening to the wireless or chatting with neighbors about the weather." That's reality? (In our culture it very nearly is.) "Talking about everything but actually saying nothing, . . . trapped in the world of appearances when I longed for the world of reality, the reality that lay beyond time and space and the puny perceptions of the five senses."[16]

Then the woman showed him around her expensive home:

It was clear the refrigerator interested her greatly. . . . I stood and listened in courteous silence and thought how baffling the scene was. If she had said to me, "I have this serious difficulty which is disrupting my life," I would have known exactly what questions to ask. But to be told the virtues of a refrigerator and to be expected to make an intelligent comment was a trial indeed.[17]

In a home where a refrigerator was treated with reverence, no doubt all the occupants would be seriously out of touch with reality.[18]

Now don't misunderstand me. In any age, people can find ways of not laying down their lives, but laying down your life is even less likely in an age so dedicated to illusion that it imagines refrigerators have something to do with reality.

Success Produces Failure?
A third mitigating factor in the United States is that here the church has in some sense "succeeded." It's a major power block, big money. And almost as soon as anything prospers or threatens to become respectable, the rot sets in. When we start feeling at home, it's almost over: "When the LORD your God has brought you into the land that he swore to your ancestors . . . a land with fine, large cities that you did not build . . . and

when you have eaten your fill, take care that you do not forget the LORD"
(Deut 6:10-12).

We stay more faithful if we're a little hungry—if we feel ourselves
strangers, a remnant. As Hosea said, "The more they increased, the more
they sinned against me" (Hos 4:7; see also 10:1). "When they had fed to
the full, they were filled, and their heart was lifted up; therefore they forgot
me" (Hos 13:6 RSV).

On Avoiding Triumphalism by Sinning
A final mitigating factor is that Christians have been taught to abandon the
idea that they can live like Christians. We think that means we're humble.

But churches are to be places that prompt outsiders to say, "See how
these Christians love one another."[19] They're to be places of wonder. Of
course, it seems humbler to say, "Don't judge Christianity by the church,
but by its Lord." So we say, "We readily admit what rotters we are. And
since we admit it, we're humble. No one can accuse *us* of triumphalism.
We're changing and growing, but the change in us is inner and invisible
and won't come to fruition till the Second Coming. So take your eyes off
Jesus' followers, and look to the Master himself."

That has a nice spiritual ring. Trouble is, Jesus said otherwise. He said,
"Look at those who claim to be my followers and believe them only if they
love each other."

Early Jewish opponents of Christianity put it succinctly: "If the world
hasn't changed, the Messiah hasn't come."[20] That's what Jesus was saying.
Only he narrowed it. If his people haven't changed, then the Messiah
hasn't come.

And early Christians took up the challenge. They agreed: if nothing is
happening, nothing happened. But they argued that something *was* happening, that the world *had* changed, that pagans weren't as good as Christians! Origen, for example, said, "The evidences of Jesus' divinity are the
churches of people who have been helped."[21] Or as Athenagoras said,

> But among us you will find uneducated persons, and artisans, and old
> women, who if they are unable in words to prove the benefit of our
> doctrine, yet by their deeds exhibit the benefit arising from their per-

suasion of its truth: they do not rehearse speeches but exhibit good works; when struck, they do not strike again; when robbed they do not go to law; they give to those who ask of them, and love their neighbors as themselves.[22]

But we can hardly claim that in established churches.

Christians must believe Jesus' call. He called us to love one another in a way that would cause others to wonder—or at least to notice. He said that that would authenticate his story. Everyone would know. Here's how *everyone* will know, he said. Even the principalities and powers will believe (Eph 3:10).

We call that utopian. We've given up. We say we can never do it. But Jesus told us we can. Anything less is defeatism. We must believe Jesus and set out to do it. So that the world may believe the story of Jah.

The Church of the Servant King

We don't need to show that the churches with gold crosses meet Jesus' test. Our task is to find a remnant who accept a cross with nails in it and to determine the quality of their lives together. Does love grow there and bring a life of depth and truth? A life beyond Campbell's Soup cans?

Some years ago, my family and I were struggling. I had quit a job of nineteen years under traumatic circumstances and had found nothing satisfactory to replace it. We weren't doing well with each other, and our tiny little church was not at peace. So we asked help from a group called the Church of the Servant King, and they sent a couple of people to be with us.

We talked. We recited our stories to each other. We played forty-two. They comforted us. They confronted us. (Boy, did they confront us.) We worshiped together. We prayed together.

In the end, they stayed for six weeks. They were people with families, with jobs, and we had no money to give them; but they suspended their lives for us—for brothers and sisters they hardly knew. From them we learned what it means to lay down your life for one another as Christ laid down his life for us.

We were so impressed by what they had done that practically our whole church moved down to become part of them. When we got there, we found not only that they lay down their lives for each other but that they live together in peace. They have serious conflicts (huge ones on occasion), but they're at peace in the midst of their fights (though often it takes several sundowns).

They pass Jesus' test.

That doesn't mean they're sinless. In fact, we saw things there that we think are wrong—importantly wrong. We saw what we consider individual and corporate sin. But we don't question whether these people are Jesus' disciples, because we continue to experience their reconciliation and their sacrificial love. On some points they're wrong (unless of course, it's us that are wrong!), but that's no big deal. In fact, it's not even interesting. After all, Jesus never said, "Here's how everyone will know that you are my disciples: that you're right about everything." The important thing is that they are reconciled.

An impressive thing about the place is that some of the biggest jerks I ever met in my life are there. But they're growing up, because what the church sees as sin, they confront and deal with. Their underlying quality of life (in the midst of all sorts of sins) is tough love, and that is what Jesus was talking about. That's the test for the myth of Jah. They live in grace and truth.

The Confessing Church

During the reign of Nazism, the majority of German Christians pledged allegiance to Hitler (of course), but there was a significant remnant—a small band of faithful people choosing to live on the margins of empire, giving their bodies to Nazis and confounding their persecutors.

Dietrich Bonhoeffer, Martin Niemöller and the Confessing Church of Germany became the only major organized German group to resist Hitler. They defended fellow church members and pastors who were ethnically Jewish. Hundreds of people in the Confessing Church were murdered, literally giving their bodies to break down walls between Jews and "Aryans."

A remnant of Catholics also gave themselves. Provost Bernhard Lichtenberg of Berlin Cathedral prayed publicly for Jews. For his efforts he was convicted of treason, and at his sentencing he asked to share the fate of Jews. In a boxcar on the way to Dachau, he died. The Nazis were sufficiently confounded by his behavior that they returned his body to Berlin, where several thousand attended his funeral.[23]

Father Maxmillian Kolbe, Auschwitz inmate #16670, volunteered to be starved to death in someone else's place. The SS guards, unable to bear his gentleness, shouted whenever they came to the cell, "Look at the ground, not us."[24]

Polish Catholics, perhaps fifteen thousand of them, though raised to believe Jews were Christ-killers, hid Jews in their homes all through the war.[25]

Eberhard Arnold and the entire Bruderhof refused to say "Heil Hitler" because they thought it meant "Salvation from Hitler." They had to leave Germany.[26]

This is not the one-dimensional behavior so obvious in most of us. No, it grows out of a story of depth. A story of love and power and wisdom, which tells of a cross with nails.

Authenticating the Story of Jah

Those stories are how I authenticated the story of Jah for myself. But for you to authenticate the story of Jah, you need to experience it yourself. You can't get it from any book, including this one. You need to experience a people of God on the margins of empire where folks lay down their lives for each other. You need to experience a little band of geese who live in reconciliation with each other, servants giving their bodies to be broken against walls.

The proof of the pudding is in the eating, as they say. What is needed is not an intellectual defense of the history of a remnant in the church but encountering such a remnant.

But that's a problem. So far as I can tell, there aren't millions of such churches to encounter. Thanks to Constantine and our own hardness of heart, not many accept enough of the story of Jah for it to reach critical mass.

The answer is simple. In a way. Christians must see to it that the remnant grows till it's not so hard to find. We must have better churches, churches that confound the empire and strike wonder. So if there's no remnant where you are, you have to help bring one into being. Jesus said that the world would know us by our love. That's the final apologetic. The sign of real life. Or at least that's what Jesus said. If we intend to take him seriously. Without love for each other, everything else is noisy gongs and clanging cymbals.

Some Comments

Now I said the solution was simple. We need better churches. Well, isn't that brilliant!

First, I said that Jesus gave us a way to authenticate the story of Jah. Then I said it doesn't work with the established church because all you can expect is a remnant. Then I said the remnant is so small that instead of expecting to find a ready-made remnant, you may have to make one yourself.[27]

Miserable. I have this feeling that I've formulated grounds for despair. And I have no quickie answers. All I have is some comments.

First comment. Focusing on churches that will go to the cross at least points to the right problem. If such churches are impossible—and I don't for a moment think they are—but if they are, then we *ought* to despair. And soon thereafter we ought to abandon the story of Jah and get on with something more sensible.

Second comment. Focusing on reconciled churches tells us that a lot of other things we have focused on are distractions. If the failure of churches is what messed things up, we can scarcely sort things out by getting prayer back in public schools or by brilliant intellectual apologetics showing that the secular emperor has no clothes. The solution has to be churches where people live together well, with love and grace. Anything else is a distraction.

Everywhere I go I meet clergy in despair over their churches. Then they tell me that if they taught what Jesus actually said they'd lose their jobs and have no way to earn a living. Which is exactly what Jesus told us would happen. So what's the problem?

Earning a living is a distraction, and until we accept that, we're secular

people and ought not to blame God for the lack of real churches. For almost
all of us, our job is more important than our church. Often we call it a
vocation and think nothing of moving to advance it. But how many people
do you know who have moved for a better church? If our jobs are more
important to us than our churches, how can we expect our churches to
live in a depth of grace and truth?

Everywhere I go I get a list of what is missing from churches: inward
journey, concern about justice, biblical theology, good music. Meanwhile,
I don't believe anyone has ever told me that the problem at their church
was that people didn't love one another. Isn't that odd?

Apparently we've lost our focus, and we shouldn't blame God for that.
Perhaps that's why so few churches have crosses with nails. Why secularism has triumphed.

Final comment. The situation is not all that surprising, really. Since the
cross is not orthopedically designed and human giftedness at self-deception is great, the number of churches that will teach a cross with nails is
going to be small.

The Bible taught us a long time ago about sin and failure; that's what
the Fall is all about. The remnant in the days of Elijah or Jeremiah or Paul
was no smaller than the one today. In that respect, Christianity delivers
what it promises. (And that's important.) Jesus was almost alone at the
cross.

Perhaps George Bernard Shaw gave the answer to all this in "Why Not
Give Christianity a Trial?"

The question seems a hopeless one after 2000 years of resolute adher-
ence to the old cry of "Not this man, but Barabbas." Yet it is beginning
to look as if Barabbas was a failure, in spite of his strong right hand,
his victory, his empire, his millions of money, and his moralities and
churches and political constitutions. "This man" has not been a failure
yet; for nobody has ever been sane enough to try his way. But he has
had one quaint triumph. Barabbas has stolen his name and taken his
cross as a standard. There is a sort of compliment in that.[28]

So perhaps it's always going to be that people of God will have to work
at calling together a remnant to be part of. Few are going to do it for you.

Strait is the gate, and hard the way that leads to life, and few there be that find it.

Until we do it, we're lost. So let's do it.

Jesus has told us that we must do it. He has told us we can do it. He has told us he will be with us while we do it. He has told us we will do it.

So let's do it. Let's love each other to the point of breaking down the walls between each other with our own bodies.

That the world may believe.

9

Two Plans of Salvation: Arnold Schwarzenegger vs. Julia Roberts

Pretty Woman is a stupid movie, a really stupid movie. I hate to say that because it's one of my favorites. When the video got down to $9.95, my wife and I bought it, and I bet we've watched it twenty times. And enjoyed it just as much each time.

Now that's embarrassing for someone who despises dumb movies. And is this one ever dumb. It's about a beautiful hooker with a heart of gold (Julia Roberts) who gets picked up by a guy with a billion dollars (Richard Gere), and they figure out that they have the same problem: they sell themselves for money. The solution is simple. She inspires him to quit using his cellular telephone, and they walk barefoot in the grass ever after.

Dumb. Really dumb.

But it's a nice plan of salvation. Really nice. No cost. A lot of stories have a plan of salvation, of course, but they're not all this nice. The popular ones tend to be nice (and make those who tell them rich), but they're dumb. The more plausible ones aren't so nice. Because life isn't so nice.

At least, mine isn't.

Plans of Salvation

Which brings us to the one important question. How do we get saved? That's what stories are about, a lot of them anyway. They tell us how to get saved. Which is a large part of the reason we go to movies and read novels. To learn about salvation. Not to be entertained. Though of course a nice plan of salvation is the main thing that makes a story entertaining. And if your life is hard (and whose isn't?), you need a little entertainment, especially if it promises you salvation.

Because down deep we all know that something is wrong, badly wrong, and we want a way out. We desperately want to believe that no matter how badly we've messed up, no matter how messed up the universe is, no matter how many kids are starving, no matter how many marriages are flying apart—everything will be all right in the end. There is a Holy Grail. Usually, that's what stories deal with.[1] Whether they're literature or pulp, philosophy or religion, politics or ethnic studies, they discuss plans of salvation (at least implicitly).

Plans of salvation have three parts: they have an account of what's good with the universe, an account of what's gone wrong, and an account of how to set things straight (now and perhaps hereafter as well). That is, they discuss creation, Fall and redemption. So when you're watching a movie or reading a book, you need to be asking yourself how it answers those questions. Because it usually does. And how the stories you encounter answer those questions will condition how you answer them.

Plan 1: Arnold Schwarzenegger

Basically, our culture has two plans of salvation. One stars Julia Roberts; the other Arnold Schwarzenegger.[2] The one starring Schwarzenegger is by far the more popular. It is *the* perennial story of stage and screen, Westerns and sci-fi, police programs and doctor programs, not to mention of science texts and history books.

In Schwarzenegger's plan of salvation, salvation comes from power. In modern Western culture, it's usually symbolized by strong white males and perhaps technology—Schwarzenegger, John Wayne, Matt Dillon, Robin Hood, Superman, the third little pig, Hulk Hogan, Jack Kennedy, Albert

Einstein and six-shooters of power. The list goes on and on and on.
Schwarzenegger's *Kindergarten Cop, Terminator 2, Total Recall,* and *Conan
the Barbarian* are among literally thousands of examples. (Did you ever
wonder why history books tell mostly about kings, presidents, generals and
a few other assorted white males? Oh, and battles.)

Typically, virtue is symbolized by a white woman (or perhaps a child)
abused by someone evil. She's weak and, of course, beautiful (but virtuous
and hardworking)—Cinderella, Maid Marian or the heroines of Harlequin
romances. In *Kindergarten Cop,* virtue is a beautiful, industrious, young,
blond schoolteacher and her sweet kindergarten son. (How innocent and
weak and white can you get?)

Evil is represented by anyone or anything the culture considers non-
standard. Typically that's a strong woman[3] or a person of color, although
an insane person and a homosexual are among numerous other possibilities.[4] Of course, sometimes the bad guy is a white man, but that's because
in this story the universe has few other real inhabitants. I mean, who but
a white man would be capable of playing a bad guy worthy of our hero's
attack? And if the bad guy is white, watch for a black hat, and don't be
surprised if he has a depraved woman somewhere in back of him (*Kindergarten Cop* and Kevin Costner's *Robin Hood*).[5]

This is the dominant plan of salvation in our culture, as you can tell by
our heroes and by the people who get elected to public office—note their
gender, their complexion and their proclivity to wage war and make themselves rich. This is the plan of salvation of political conservatives and
moderates, of fundamentalists and most evangelicals, of nationalists and
of almost all Marxists and kings and other dictators who have actually been
in power. In fact, this is the plan of salvation of all those who are patriotically correct.

Plan 2: Julia Roberts

Julia Roberts's plan is more or less the reverse and uses the reverse symbolism. The characters are the same, only now the strong man needs to
be saved and the savior is the weak woman. That is, the problem with the
universe is symbolized by powerful white males and cellular telephones,

and salvation by their opposite—by almost anyone who is somehow weak or "natural" or "different."

Typically in this story, a simple, unaffected woman saves a powerful white male from himself. So when Julia Roberts tries to eat a snail in a fancy restaurant, she sends it flying across the room (a salvific act?). Her very simplicity (she's never been to an opera either and doesn't know who all to tip) gives her clarity of vision, whereas Gere's sophistication and money leave him confused. So when he says he must go to work, she cuts through the silliness by a look: after all, he has no boss and he doesn't exactly need the money.

Love and friendship, beauty and walking barefoot in the grass are what's good in the universe. What's gone wrong is bad boyfriends and bad fathers, preoccupation with work, domination of others and love of money. Salvation is turning your back on all that and devoting yourself to love and beauty—walking barefoot in the grass instead of going to work to get richer, going free and letting others go free.

The story gets told in many forms. Not handsome prince rescuing abused maiden (that's the other story), but abused maiden calling handsome prince out of the wasteland of male conquest. She promises a gentler, more feminine life. The classic, prefeminist form of this story is the noble savage as expounded by Jean-Jacques Rousseau's followers. So *Pretty Woman* encompasses *Walden*, most romantic poetry, much of the work of Ursula K. Le Guin,[6] *Being There*, a few TV programs like "The Rockford Files" and "All in the Family,"[7] and dozens of movies like *The Fisher King, Fried Green Tomatoes, Hook, Sleeping with the Enemy, Dying Young* and *Regarding Henry*.[8]

This is the plan of salvation of hippies, greens, many feminists and people of color, and some Anabaptists and radical Catholics. In short, this is the plan of salvation of those who are politically correct.

Choosing Between Stories

So our culture asks us to choose between Arnold Schwarzenegger and Julia Roberts. And we do. Without thinking about it. Without even feeling much about it. We choose one or the other. Why should we think or feel about *Kindergarten Cop* or *Pretty Woman*? They're just stories.

Stories we live by. Stories by which we work out our salvation . . . or our damnation. And that of others.

So we need to make our choice consciously, using both reason and feelings. Philosophers and scientists have made such choices seem hopelessly complicated: we can't accept a story unless we can find logical or scientific proof for it. And since that's impossible, we blindly and unconsciously accept whatever story has the best propaganda. Or if we're romantics, critical judgment is unnecessary and undesirable, and so we accept whatever story turns us on. That is, once again we blindly accept whatever story has the best propaganda.

But let's try Jesus' suggestion of testing a story by the lives of those who tell it. That test will get us someplace. It's complicated but not so complicated that we're incapable of doing it.

As you can perhaps tell, I'm not unduly fond of Arnold Schwarzenegger. I much prefer Julia Roberts. I try hard not to live Schwarzenegger's story, and so I can't claim to be judging it sympathetically, or from within, or after having tested it in my life. Which means that I violate our culture's presuppositional requirement for objectivity. And I even experience *Pretty Woman* from within the presuppositional framework of the story that has brought me life, the story of Jah. For that I have no apologies; it's the sort of circle we all need to be in.

Schwarzenegger's Lies

Still, I've tried to test these stories mostly by how I've seen them affect people's lives. And that's why I hate Schwarzenegger's plan of salvation. I hate the way I've seen it worked out on blacks, in international politics and in family life; I hate it with all my being. Those who are patriotically correct may not become rapists of logical necessity, but it sure is what happens in practice, sometimes literally.

That, at least, is one of the claims of *Pretty Woman*. (To a surprising degree, *Pretty Woman* and *Walden* are conscious critiques of Schwarzenegger's plan of salvation.) The attempted rape at the end of *Pretty Woman* is no accident, nor is it added for excitement: it's there because rape is a symbolic and literal portrayal of the spiritual outcome of domination.

That is what I've observed, and it's what I've lived when I've dominated others.

And cellular telephones are a symbolic and literal portrayal of the spiritual outcome of being emotionally unable to stop working. Industriousness may have gotten Cinderella a clean house and the third little pig a brick fort, but all Gere's hard work only cuts him off from human contact. It gets him a divorce, abandonment by girlfriends, artificial contacts at polo matches and the service of a dehumanized lawyer. His relationships are mediated by, and secondary to, plastic technology.

And prostitution is a symbolic and literal portrayal of the spiritual outcome of the pursuit of money and success. Roberts and Gere are both prostitutes who buy and sell illusion. Which is all there is to the world of money and success—illusion, stupidity. Such stuff can never fill the hollowness within. That's part of what Jesus meant by repentance: turning our backs on illusion. And it's the meaning of Warhol's soup cans: Schwarzenegger's ideals are so inadequate as icons as to be both tragic and comic. We need to repent of such shallowness.

Surely our century has proved once and for all that we can't be saved by technology and strong white males. The idea is at least as silly as the idea of the noble savage. For what can power save us from? What can it save us to? It can save us from the bad guy; it can let us kill our enemies, as Schwarzenegger and our presidents never tire of demonstrating. It can make us rich, and according to the movies and to news stories about presidential candidates, it can even get us pretty women.

But not many people really think that dead enemies, money and sex are salvific. With all that, we're still kind of empty.

In other words, Schwarzenegger tells a lot of lies.[9]

Julia Roberts's Truths

Whereas Julia Roberts tells a lot of truth, truth of depth and importance. Her story rightly rejects domination, compulsive work, power and perhaps wealth. Which is part of why *Pretty Woman* succeeded. (Not to mention some great dialogue, the size of Julia Roberts's smile and lots of sexual pandering.)

The *Pretty Woman* story is also at least half truthful in what it points toward. Love, beauty, fidelity, rest, having time for people—such things can sometimes fill the hollowness within, at least for a while. The *Regarding Henry* version puts the story even more clearly. In it, Henry gets brain-injured and is no longer able to be a high-powered, crooked, adulterous lawyer; he then becomes an honest simpleton devoted to his wife and daughter. In *The Fisher King*, the hero stops being an angry, insensitive drunk driving to make it big as a radio personality and becomes a loving boyfriend who cares for a schizophrenic street person.

Le Guin tells the same truths in *Always Coming Home*. There she contrasts two cultures. One is a male-dominated, warlike, racist, economically oppressive, urban society whose ruler has his opponents' intestines ripped out in front of the palace. (It's a picture of superpowers, who always follow Schwarzenegger's story.) The other culture is a gentle country people represented by a woman. They have plenty of internal problems, but they're in touch with nature at a spiritual level, and their idea of wealth is giving a lot to others.[10] (It's a compelling picture of the life advocated by greens, hippies and many feminists.[11])

Clearly this story is better than Schwarzenegger's, which is about soup cans. It comes close to parts of the Sermon on the Mount: peace, humility, meekness, mercy, love, generosity, unpossessiveness. (That's my excuse for loving a dumb movie like *Pretty Woman*.) And yet . . .

My Story Again: A Journey of Pain

Walking barefoot in the grass is a vast improvement on worshiping power and soup cans, and yet . . . it's pretty silly. And doesn't make it as an icon.

I know that from inside. For many years, I believed some form of it, a Christian form. But reality got me down. I think I had Jesus confused with romanticism, with Julia Roberts. Not completely, not by a long shot, but to a degree.

After long experience of the insensitivity of evangelicals, I had started looking elsewhere for the Holy Grail. Eventually I combined Kierkegaard and cummings (both of whom were Christian) with a nonviolent form of liberation theology, and the resulting romanticism felt a lot better than the dead orthodoxy of evangelicalism.[12]

Not that I rejected evangelical theology. I just put it away in the attic and never used it.[13] If anyone challenged my orthodoxy, I could get it out and show that I still had it. But that wasn't the engine of my life; it wasn't where I found meaning. (In fact, it's rarely the engine for anyone's life, evangelicals included.[14])

In the language of romanticism, I'd found who I was, or I thought I had. I was someone who felt passionately about the suffering of others, and I was dedicated to fighting that suffering, especially if the sufferers were poor and oppressed (simple prostitutes like Julia Roberts). I set out to be the opposite of Arnold Schwarzenegger. The thing wrong with the universe was that the powerful (mostly white males) dominated the weak (mostly women and people of color, but also the earth and weaker white males). Salvation lay in feeling the pain of the oppressed, in nurturing the way mothers do, in fighting nonviolently for freedom.

That is, salvation lay in walking barefoot in the grass. That became my icon. I found myself at home with people who shared that icon, no matter what they thought (or didn't think) of Jesus. And Christians who didn't share those views disgusted me. (In other words, I was politically correct and despised those who were patriotically correct; being politically correct was my real religion.)

But don't misunderstand me. I wasn't abandoning my faith. No doubt it helped that *Pretty Woman* was favored by the intellectuals of the era, but I wouldn't have bought it if it hadn't also been substantially biblical—at least as biblical as the other forms of Christianity kicking around. Jesus treated materialism and the desire to succeed as central human problems, and therefore it still seems to me that the Beatitudes are closer to Ursula K. Le Guin than to Jerry Falwell. From cover to cover, the Bible is clear that the children of God will be on the side of the oppressed and that power causes problems rather than solves them.

But all that is only a part of the biblical story. The Julia Roberts story has an inadequate notion of sin and therefore of freedom. And so it's inadequate as a plan of salvation. Eventually I began to suspect as much. This wasn't the Holy Grail at all. My problem with it wasn't theoretical or exegetical; it was practical. My plan of salvation wasn't working out in life—in my life. And as I've argued, that's the ultimate test of any story. Romanticism promised depth and compassion, but as far as I could tell, it didn't deliver. (The history of the lives of romantics should have taught me that before, but though I knew most of the facts, they didn't register with me till I experienced the disasters personally.[15])

Politically correct Christians, myself included, turned out to be as quarrelsome as the fundamentalists I was fleeing. We couldn't get along with each other, and we had as many ego collisions as if we'd been children. It just wasn't working. Even more serious, our marriages weren't working. Not that they were worse than average; in fact, I suspect they were better than most. But still, half the radical Christians I knew had unhappy marriages.

Was that normal? Was I just an idealist discovering that I didn't know as much as I thought? Young upstart that I was, was I now having to face that ideals are harder to live up to than I'd realized and that my life would therefore turn out as messy as the lives of those I'd criticized? Maybe there *was* no salvation on earth.

No doubt a lack of realism was part of my problem, but there was more to it than that: the story I was living was also inadequate.

Once again, don't misunderstand me. *Pretty Woman* has tremendous interpretive power. As a key to life, it fit a lot of doors (the oppression of blacks, the destruction of Native Americans, the servitude of women, the deadness of white males, the devastation of the earth, the violence of both gangs and presidents, a culture that worships soup cans). So while I concluded that I needed to get beyond *Pretty Woman*, that hasn't meant reverting to Arnold Schwarzenegger and *Total Recall*; getting beyond political correctness hasn't meant reverting to patriotic correctness.

But what's the point of understanding everything about neocolonialism, racism, sexism and every other ism if you then proceed to mess up the lives of those closest to you?

This was no Holy Grail. I had tried it, and it too was a lie.

Barefoot in the Grass?

The problem was that I'd accepted the stupid part of *Pretty Woman*. That's the bit about walking barefoot in the grass. Not that that isn't better than wearing leather shoes on concrete, but salvation is harder than taking off your high heels or wingtips and walking barefoot in the grass whenever you feel like it.

Walking in the grass is symbolic, of course, and maybe I'm pushing the symbolism too far. But I don't think so; walking in the grass is a bad symbol when it's serving as an icon.[16] A really bad symbol.

Walking in the grass? Didn't Jesus say something about taking up your cross?

And it was a cross with nails. Which is a rather different icon. One that doesn't put freedom at the center.

So now we see why *Pretty Woman* is so popular. And so sad. It's a plan of salvation with a lot of truth but no cross. It promises that things will end happily whether you take up the cross or not. And that's a lie. Pretty, but a lie.

Which is why the story of Jah isn't popular. Crosses aren't pretty. Not nearly as pretty as Julia Roberts's walking in the grass.

In back of Julia Roberts is the noble savage and all that. (Rousseau, *Walden*, the good old days, living in the country, back to nature.) We'd all be better off if we gave up civilization and went barefoot like primitive people. The thing wrong with us is sophistication and civilization, not sin and rebellion against God. All we need do is become more natural, less dominated by others, more fully and freely ourselves.

However, the fact is, savages aren't noticeably more noble than Greeks.

It's not at all obvious that being primitive makes people more compassionate or less inclined to dominate. For example, though some groups are less violent than others (just as some individuals are less violent than others), you just can't make the case that more primitive groups are typically less violent. Primitive tribes in New Guinea have quite as many wars as civilized tribes in Europe. Admittedly they kill fewer people, but that's only for want of technology. And while Native Americans from California weren't very warlike, neither are the present natives of Stockholm. The issue just isn't the degree of primitiveness or of civilization. (I suspect you could make a case that less powerful groups are less violent.)

Not that I'm unduly impressed by modern civilization. I much prefer the
Rockies to Disneyworld. God's creations are preferable to people's. Few
spots are more beautiful for having had people there, and those that are
(like palace grounds and cathedrals) often got that way at hideous human
cost. Nonetheless, we are the poorer if we prefer Formica to the materials
God made, the poorer if we no longer notice daffodils or hear little birds.
So other things being equal, I'd rather be close to nature (providing a bagel
store was nearby, and a major-league baseball team). But the basic human
problem isn't how far modern people are from nature but how far all people
are from God. The basic human problem is sin.

The noble savage as a plan of salvation should be understood as a reaction to the Arnold Schwarzenegger story, and both should be dismissed as
parallel spiritual and intellectual aberrations. Now I think most of us know
that, at least on a conscious level; we know that moving to Walden Pond
(or shooting your enemies) won't solve many problems. Once you get past
rhetoric, those who actually want to return to the good old days are as rare
as live cuckoo birds. (We're much too fond of penicillin and paperbacks.)

But for some reason, everyone from politically correct Christians to
Ursula K. Le Guin keeps relapsing into metaphors like walking barefoot in
the grass. We hear endlessly about the virtues of the good old days, the
purity of country life, the goodness of women and people of color, the
importance of total freedom. Perhaps we mean it only metaphorically, but
without our quite meaning it, our symbols turn to icons.

At least, without my quite noticing it, I came close to replacing Calvary
with Walden Pond. Renouncing domination and money and that stuff is
essential. But it isn't enough; it isn't anywhere like enough.

Problem 1: Evil and Me

It isn't enough because when I get to Walden Pond, I am there, and I screw
everything up—all by myself. When Julia Roberts marries her billionaire,
they won't live happily ever after; they'll start messing with each other, and
soon they'll hate each other ever after.

Walden Pond turns into a cesspool shortly after the first human being
arrives.

Garrison Keillor must have meant something like that when he said, "I learned about total depravity at my mother's knee, and nothing has happened in the thirty years since then to make me think otherwise."[17] We are so corrupt and selfish that we turn everything we touch into sewage.

So we have to die. That's central to Jah's plan of salvation. We need to die, just like Jesus died on the cross. And that part of the story gets left out of *Pretty Woman*. And *Walden*. (After all, it isn't very pretty.)

Let me put it this way. My marriage was unhappy because I didn't want to die. I was too selfish. Which is another word for sinful. There's really only one marital problem—sin, selfishness. And that's also why my radical Christian friends and I fought so much. Sin and selfishness. In fact, that's practically the only problem there is. Sin, selfishness. And it can only be dealt with by the cross. Which *Pretty Woman* and *Walden* leave out.

The central fault of *Pretty Woman* is that it minimizes this evil within. Stories like *Pretty Woman* either externalize evil, acting as if it came from somewhere else, from someone else, or else they act as if it's a relatively minor part of who we are. Evil doesn't have a home in me. (In the *Total Recall* stories, this is even more true. Evil is someone else in obvious, physical form; Schwarzenegger is without sin.)

So of course if we move to Walden Pond and get away from the evil of others (or if we kill the guy in the black hat), things will be OK. I am not the problem. Or things will be OK if we quit our evil jobs and get married to someone we're in love with. Or things would be OK if women ruled the world.[18]

But things wouldn't be OK . . . because when we move to Walden Pond, sin and selfishness come right along; they have a home in us. They won't just die off because we decide to adjust our values or because we kill the bad guys. No, they'll flourish in new and creative ways, bringing death wherever we go. It's like in a shooting gallery with pop-up criminals; no matter how many you hit, another one always pops up, and the most important one is you.

And be careful, because the essence of self-righteousness is imagining that the really serious sins are committed by people other than ourselves. And that's true whether we think the serious sinners are white males with cellular phones or unemployed blacks drinking cheap wine.

Problem 2: Happy Endings and Pain

A lot of critics said the same thing about *Pretty Woman*. Oh, they didn't complain about its inadequate view of sin, but they did complain about its happy ending. They scorned it as unrealistic. How many hookers do you know who married a john and lived happily ever after? For that matter, when was the last time anything miserable ended well?

There needs to be a sequel to *Pretty Woman*. And it wouldn't be about Richard Gere's dying tragically of leukemia and leaving his billion to Julia Roberts to start an orphanage for children whose parents had died of AIDS. *Pretty Woman II* would start with Gere's beating Roberts because he imagined she looked in the direction of another man, and it would end with her killing him because she had no other way out.[19]

Or so the film critics said. And I almost agree.

But that's not quite the point. After all, this story isn't about the happy marriage of the average hooker.[20] It's not even about a hooker and a billionaire who have screwed up their lives and find a way out. It's about you and me who have screwed up our lives, and it promises us a way out. *Pretty Woman* is about the possibility of *our* salvation; it's about hope. Which we don't find much on the daily news, so we're delighted when a story offers it.

But the critics find hope and salvation embarrassing. Such things aren't sophisticated.

Which is not my objection. When I complain about *Pretty Woman's* happy ending, I don't mean to endorse the cynicism and despair so deep in our culture that it's visible in everyone from the critics to the painter Francis Bacon to the average politician or TV evangelist. When my Julia Roberts plan of salvation wasn't working, I was close to that conclusion, but I now think I've found a way of salvation. Like Julia Roberts, I have hope.

But I doubt that Julia Roberts and company should . . . unless they're prepared to change their story. Tolkien can end *The Lord of the Rings* happily, because he emphasized the difficulty of the journey. So he can promise that human history will end in what he calls eucatastrophe—a sudden overturning for the good. "It denies (in the face of much evidence, if you will) universal, final defeat, . . . giving a glimpse of Joy."[21] After all, Jesus also promised a happy ending. We may get crucified along the way, but in the end, all will be well.

Which is my problem with *Pretty Woman*. Not that it has a happy ending but that it leaves out getting crucified along the way. It makes salvation too easy.

Laughing Gas

Now to be fair to myself and to others who are politically correct, we had some sense of this. But we hadn't grasped existentially (at least I hadn't) just how costly salvation was. Where sin was concerned, my systematic theology would have suited Calvin himself, but I had no idea of the pain sometimes involved in repentance. I thought that all I had to do was turn my back on money, power and adultery, be forgiven through the cross, and then I could walk barefoot in the grass. Oh, I knew I might be killed someday, like Gandhi or Martin Luther King Jr.

But I hadn't quite grasped that I'd have to agree to that death . . . and make it a daily event. That was too painful.

And be clear: *Pretty Woman* and the romantics aren't the only ones who leave out that part of the story—practically everyone does. Evangelicals included. All you have to do is accept Jesus as your Savior, and all the pain will go away. Some version of that is the nearly official stance of our culture.[22]

My dentist is typical. As soon as greetings are over, she puts earphones on me—tuned to the station of my choice (the sound of drilling must be drowned out, because the knowledge that it's coming from my own mouth might distress me). Then she gives me laughing gas, applies a topical painkiller and, after letting them have a chance to take effect (wouldn't want me to feel the needle), gives me a local anesthetic. And all during the visit, she tells me (earphones and all) what a good patient I am and how well I take care of my mouth.

She sees to it that I feel no pain. More than that, she sees to it that I feel good. Especially about myself. She would never ask me to repent of not flossing. By the time I leave, I'm in a state of euphoria and feel I've performed some remarkable feat on a level with slaying a dragon. All with no pain. I can walk barefoot in the grass even while killing dragons or having my teeth drilled!

Our culture is dedicated to helping us feel that way. It's essential for our self-esteem. Otherwise, we might get depressed and not fulfill our potential. So we must eliminate pain and feel good about ourselves.

With the natural result that we're all shriveled up into one dimension. And appallingly unhappy in our search for a more exciting soup can.

Take schools. They haven't been as successful as my dentist in getting their clients to feel good about themselves. For millions of kids, school isn't a positive experience. I know because I was one of the millions. But that's a problem our culture is working on. And I agree we need to do something about it. At least, I think I do.

But the standard solution is to try to make school as exciting as *Kindergarten Cop*. Figure out what kids want and give it to them, and above all take out the parts they don't like. Arguably, the primary thing taught in a typical (permissive) school today is that we have a right never to feel pain, never to fail and usually to do what we want. We'll be saved if we're free to be us, free from anyone trying to dominate us (or teach us).

Well, that just doesn't deal with the way sin has a home in us.

For my daughter's senior year in high school, some of her teachers took votes on what to study and how. That way, they reasoned, kids could educate themselves and enjoy it too.

Only they didn't. They hated it. And they learned almost nothing.

Human nature is strange. If someone is bored and unhappy, the obvious solution is to give them what they want. Only it has the opposite effect: they become more bored and unhappy.

The problem is that if you see pain as important to avoid, you spend all your time running from it. And eventually it catches you anyway. Then, feeling a little uncomfortable, you imagine you've experienced a tragedy and you dissolve into waves of misery, wailing about the unfairness of it all. The pursuit of happiness and the avoidance of pain cause permanent and unavoidable misery. And make growing up impossible. (The shallowness of our culture again.)

So we need to focus more on what people need and less on what they want. Pain just isn't important enough to merit extensive avoidance rituals. We often need to head into pain instead of avoid it. And that's what we need to teach our kids in school. Not that teachers should try to make school boring and meaningless. But we must learn to distinguish between teachers' teaching and teachers' dominating and being punitive.

Don't misunderstand me. If you can accomplish the same thing while taking a painkiller, take it by all means. But most worthwhile things can be accomplished only with discomfort or worse. So we'd better be clear that laughing gas is not always available. Is not always a good.

Because we have to die. And that's painful.

A Story About Marriage

Let me put it this way. My marriage was unhappy because I wanted my own way, because I made my happiness a priority. I didn't want to go through the pain of dealing with my selfishness. (No known laughing gas is effective during selfishness extraction.) When I wanted to walk barefoot in the grass, I wanted to walk barefoot in the grass. And when Judy got in the way, we had what are called marital problems. I don't mean we were infantile about it; we didn't scream and cry. We were very adult: we quietly resented each other.

One time we were crossing a desert that was going to take most of the day to drive through, and the only radio station we could pick up was country western. Now that was OK with me because I like country music, but Judy doesn't. So we made a suitable compromise (on some of the time, off some of the time), but it still meant quite a few hours of no radio. Before long, the desert began to seem terribly long. (In the end, it took the better part of a week for me to get through, though Judy and the car were through it late that night.)

Gradually, I worked myself up into a frenzy of blame, resentment and gloom. I fed my anger and it fed me. I loved it and nurtured it, and it brought me comfort and pleasure. I reveled in it. I enclosed myself in a tower of darkness; no white knight was going to rescue me. I was enjoying my misery at least as much as I would have the country music. Because evil has a home in me.

(Isn't being yourself fun?)

We left the main road and promptly got lost. It was immediately obvious to me that it was Judy's fault. She might have been asleep the whole time for all I knew, but it was clear that she had done it deliberately and with malice aforethought. Divorce seemed likely, Armageddon probable.

Somewhere along the way, we have to decide to kill off that evil, silly self. We have to send that person to the cross. Daily.

The Severity of Sin

But we don't see a need to do anything that drastic. Our failings aren't that serious. Getting angry and resentful the way I did is unfortunate, a weakness, but it's no big deal unless it happens a lot. And even then all you need to do is take a self-improvement course. Or if it's real serious, get psychoanalyzed.

Which is dangerous. Not just psychoanalysis, but all minimizing of evil. Watch out for talk about human potential and self-fulfillment that is quiet about sin and the cost of salvation.

And that spirit rules not just secular society but most contemporary religion as well. Whether it's evangelicals with their church-growth emphasis on making people feel good or the new spirituality with its focus on centering prayer without repentance, they're peddling cheap grace. Beware of religious people who think that the solution to our problems is merely speaking in tongues or fanning the spark of goodness within. When all is said and done, they all play down the Fall and play up letting ourselves blossom in the sunshine of God's good creation.

Beware, because that's not the way you blossom. You blossom in the sunshine of God's good creation only if you first face your selfishness and die. "Unless a grain of wheat falls into the earth and dies, it remains just a single grain; but if it dies, it bears much fruit" (Jn 12:24). It's not enough to decide to become a magical, mystical bear. You must choose to die before you can become a magical, mystical bear.

Hard, Little Choices

So you can see why I find walking barefoot in the grass an inadequate symbol for salvation. A cross with nails is more truthful. Though as Constantine taught us, the cross isn't hard to turn into laughing gas.

Which is what I did. I thought day-to-day salvation was as easy as walking barefoot in the grass; I didn't know it would feel more like being nailed barefoot to a cross. I thought Jah was a magic bullet, that he would snap his fingers and make everything OK. So I left out the tough steps; I left out the hard, little choices to die to myself.

For that is what the Holy Grail is. Hard choices, usually little ones. To give up my list of demands on the universe. Daily, hourly. Wrenching choices. Choices to kill my self, to kill my selfishness, to kill my insistence on having my own way. Choices to do the necessary things for which there is no laughing gas.

Little choices like washing the dishes or being the one to get up from dinner to refill the pitcher. Little choices like skipping the sports section that day so you can spend five extra minutes praying. Little choices like turning your mind away (twenty times a day if need be) from anger at the person who somehow shafted you, away from feeling sorry for yourself because you can't listen to country music. Choices not to gossip and judge. Choices to say something kind and gentle. Choices not to think only about how something will affect you.

And choices, sometimes big ones, not to pursue illusion. Not to pursue a job for the money. Not to buy a car for the status. Not to try to appear to be something you aren't to win friends.

If we are truly redeemed by the cross, we die along with Jah. On the other side of that, and only on the other side of that, do we find joy and fullness in our hollowness. Like the kids in my daughter's senior class we need to learn that if we pursue happiness and avoid the hard parts, we'll be miserable forever. But we can forget about happiness, head into hard things, and discover happiness while pursuing things that are real.

The heart of it is learning to give up our way. We all have lists of things we want, and we're angry when we don't get them. We think we'll be happy if and only if we have them. But it's only as we lay them down that we discover happiness. *Real* happiness.

From the story of Jesus in the garden we learn what we have to do and how it feels:

> They went to a place called Gethsemane; and . . . [Jesus] began to be distressed and agitated. And he said to [the disciples], "I am deeply grieved, even to death; remain here, and keep awake." And going a little farther, he threw himself on the ground and prayed that, if it were possible, the hour might pass from him. He said, "Abba, Father, for you all things are possible; remove this cup from me; yet, not what I want, but what you want." (Mk 14:32-36)

Not my will, but yours. That attitude is the Holy Grail. A lifetime of continuing to choose it daily, a lifetime of continuing to grow in fullness, love and grace. Not an overnight happening but a long journey in the same direction. We slowly learn that it's OK not to get to listen to country music and OK to be shafted at work. We slowly learn that we don't have to be angry and resentful and miserable when we don't get our way. Then we're freed to be happy, or perhaps I should say joyful.

"Not what I want, but what you want" is the road to wisdom and depth, to filling the hollowness within. That's the Holy Grail.

10

On Being Woody Allen: The Blood of Agamemnon or the Blood of the Crucified God?

've been writing about the importance of heading into the pain, and how *Pretty Woman* in particular leaves that out. But that makes it sound as if we could save ourselves by taking up the cross—by accepting the years of pain involved in growing up. And while that's the closest thing to a working plan of salvation that modern people can have, damnation lies on that route, too.

The trouble is that if we start trying to die to ourselves, we soon discover we can't. We need grace. And we aren't quite prepared for that. I mean, Arnold Schwarzenegger always succeeds, and so does Julia Roberts. The triumph of the individual is one thing they have in common. Neither story deals with failure. So if they decided to die to themselves, they'd die to themselves.

Did you ever notice how big Arnold Schwarzenegger is? He's not a loser. His part could never be played by Woody Allen or someone five feet tall. John Wayne, Matt Dillon, Perry Mason, Sylvester Stallone, Hulk Hogan,

Superman—they're all big. They're the sort of people who accomplish whatever they set out to do. In that story, salvation is a matter of size and strength. And in the movie version of the Julia Roberts story, it's beauty. That's not what that story is supposed to say, but you'll notice the movie wasn't named *Ugly Woman*. And couldn't be. Woody Allen couldn't play Julia Roberts's part either. He's too ugly. And fails too often. He probably couldn't even die right.

You see, in our culture's two main stories, you have to become either Arnold Schwarzenegger or Julia Roberts. Those are your choices. Otherwise, you can't be saved. Which is hard on all of us. Hard on women who aren't pretty and on men who aren't strong. We have no hope of salvation. Not even any hope of self-esteem (the ultimate tragedy for modern people).

Julia Roberts and Arnold Schwarzenegger are too competent to say anything about how Woody Allens like us get saved. We need grace.

Schwarzenegger's Plan of Universal Damnation

Our damnation is clearest in the Schwarzenegger story. The role of men is to be powerful, and the role of women is to be beautiful and helpless.

That doesn't mean the men have to be muscular; they can be rocket scientists or doctors, wily stockbrokers or fat Mafia dons; they can even be little (like the Karate Kid), providing they're great at martial arts. And in recent versions, it doesn't even mean the women have to be weak. Due to the influence of feminism, they can now be strong too, providing they're not strong enough to save themselves (Schwarzenegger still has to be the savior). And they still have to be beautiful. If they're ugly or "pushy," their function is to symbolize evil.

We're damned, all of us. The weak are damned because they have no role in life; the strong are damned because they have a false role.

The Woody Allens—those of us who are five-foot-tall nerds—either have no part in the story or have a bad part. We have to devote ourselves forever to striving vainly to become strong or beautiful. Something we will never achieve. For most of us are losers. And the Schwarzenegger story offers no forgiveness. No forgiveness for men who are weak or women who are plain; no forgiveness for losers like Woody.

Which is the point of most Woody Allen movies. They're about nerds who accept Schwarzenegger's plan of salvation. When you're choosing up sides at recess, Woody Allen is the one chosen last. His heroes are small and weak, anxious and fearful non-WASPs, wear glasses and have small biceps and gigantic neuroses. They have no hope of salvation here or hereafter. (How could they? They can't even remember their mantras.) They're the last word in losers. (This was written before his affair with his adopted daughter was known. That is sin, not just the sort of weakness I meant us to identify with.)

It's a life of eternal frustration, a life of eternal destruction of self-esteem. Sisyphus and Tantalus had easy lives compared to Woody Allen's. He has to lift weights all day, go to beauty parlors all night and diet for his entire life. And he'll still never be in a bathing-suit ad—not even for K Mart.

Of course, there's another possibility. Success. That's possible for a few. It's possible for the strong and the beautiful. Unfortunately. Unfortunately because those storybook roles are worse than failure.

Feminism has made the hollowness of success in those roles especially clear. A woman who accepts being beautiful and weak is damned. She spends her life at being beautiful: applying lotions, having liposuction, getting divorced to try another man, never being fulfilled and finally and inevitably reaching an age when no quantity of face-lifts can help. For Schwarzenegger is unforgiving.

And it's no different for a man. (Or for a woman who chooses the version of feminism that says women too can become Arnold Schwarzenegger; now both men and women are free to become Mafia dons?) Money, power, success, domination—at best they're drugs that keep us from noticing we're in hell.

The Dragon Within

In *Tehanu*, Le Guin gives us a plan of salvation that looks different. In it, the hero is a terribly deformed little girl who has been abused. And she saves the world. Which is healing for those of us who are short and ugly, healing for those who have been abused and hurt. We too are worthwhile even if we aren't as strong as Arnold Schwarzenegger or as pretty as Julia

Roberts. We count. The Woody Allens are OK. We too can save the world.

We can? I must admit I'd never noticed. In fact, I have grave doubts about my potential as savior. Tehanu (that's the little girl's name) is different from me. You see, on the outside, she's Woody Allen, but inside she's a dragon (literally). Whereas I'm Woody Allen both outside and in.

Her advantage is that when the bad guys get too bad, she can call an adult dragon to burn them right up. And when she grows up, she'll be Schwarzenegger with a built-in flamethrower.

In other words, *Tehanu* is a retelling of the Arnold Schwarzenegger story. Only the imagery is changed. Now good isn't represented by strong white men but by an ugly little girl who is a dragon inside. Salvation is by power.[1] This is the Superman story from a feminist perspective: Clark Kent looks like Woody Allen, but inside he's enormous. That makes the Superman story ever so much more attractive to normal people. He looks like us, which gives us hope that we too can save the world. It puts all of us on equal footing with Arnold.

Which is dangerous. Instead of deluding just the strong and the beautiful, it deludes us all. For most of us are not dragons inside. We're sinners who must die to ourselves. And an essential part of that death is dying to the dream of being a dragon inside. Or rather, we must face what the dragon inside us is like. It's a nasty, selfish, helpless little thing.

We cannot save ourselves. We need grace.

At least, that's been my experience. I can't save myself even from a temper tantrum over country music. I'm Woody Allen in spades. And so are we all.

Pretty Woman's Plan of Universal Damnation

Of course, *Pretty Woman* doesn't tell it that way. It has a plan of salvation fundamentally different from Schwarzenegger's: salvation lies not in power but in love. And I agree with that. The catch is that like Schwarzenegger's plan, this one has people saving themselves. Love is within your reach. All you have to do is quit using your cellular phone and start loving people.

Which is to say, you can save yourself.

Only I found that I couldn't. I tried hard, and it didn't work. Oh, I did

OK at not using a cellular phone, but I didn't start loving people. In fact, I didn't even like people. I fought with most everyone. Because I wanted my own way. Because I couldn't die to myself. I just couldn't stop being resentful when I imagined someone had violated my rights. I couldn't die to myself; I needed grace.

Actually, *Pretty Woman* makes the case for me. Without meaning to, it demonstrates how hard it is turn from illusion to love. The point of the story is that Roberts's simplicity is beautiful and Gere's compulsive work is ugly. While he labors with his stocks and his fax machine, she enjoys herself watching ancient reruns of "I Love Lucy." While he talks on his plastic telephone, she spontaneously sings a silly song in the bathtub. She may not know who and when to tip or which fork to use, but she knows how to live.

If we're spontaneous, all we need is reruns and silly songs? Maybe, but if so, why does she get off on a quarter-of-a-million-dollar necklace and Gere's penthouse suite? Why is it so exciting to go spend all you want on Rodeo Drive and get even with silly clerks who thought you were poor? In scene after scene, her happiness is dependent on his wealth and power. On his being the Arnold Schwarzenegger of financial markets.

She may be calling him to turn away from his compulsive work habits, but she does it from within the comfortable confines of the penthouse at the Regent Beverly Wilshire: she certainly isn't calling herself to turn away from the millions they'll lose if he obliges.

The power of *Pretty Woman* turns substantially on her beauty and his wealth—the very things the story claims to critique. *Pretty Woman* would have integrity only if Julia Roberts were missing a front tooth and Richard Gere lived in a flophouse. Stripped of the Hollywood tinsel, *Pretty Woman* would lose its attraction. And that's typical of our human attempts to save ourselves. Half lies.

For in *Pretty Woman* no one fails. The hero and heroine always triumph. The story ends with the hero's going after the heroine when she rightly walks out on him. And it has to end that way. It can't deal with the possibility (I should say, the near certainty) that the hero will settle for another girl and go back to his old work habits. That would turn the story into an unremitting tragedy, like the prince's marrying one of the stepsisters instead of Cinderella.

This story simply has no plan of salvation for those of us who fail. For Woody Allen (and that's all of us) it has only a plan of damnation. But real people need grace. We need a way to be forgiven for failure.

Sin and Self-Esteem

Or rather we need a way to be forgiven for sin. We don't need to be forgiven for being five feet tall or for being klutzes—those things aren't sin.[2] The idea that they're a big deal is merely a piece of silliness from the Schwarzenegger story.

People who can't distinguish between sin and failure are parables of our culture, ultimate signs of our shallowness. Because the difference between the nerdy and the demonic is immense. And confusing the two is death by silliness.

It sounds strange to modern people, but human beings can't live without a concept of sin. We can't live without a concept of sin because without it we can have no concept of forgiveness, no concept of grace. But talk of sin sounds strange to us, because sin is hard to see under a microscope, you'll recall. So how could we have concepts like forgiveness and grace? After all, they're hard to see under a microscope too.

But in another sense modern people have a concept of sin. What exactly would you call having Woody Allen's nose? What exactly is it when a man is a crybaby? Don't kid yourself. In the canons of theology of Arnold Schwarzenegger, being weak and ugly is sin. They're taboo as sure as incest is in *Oedipus Rex*. And so is failure in *Pretty Woman*. In both stories, if you fail, there is no salvation, no way back. Except to try, try again—and eventually that runs out. I mean, if Gere doesn't come running to get you back, you're not likely to bag the second billionaire either. The laws of life are strict and unforgiving.

And so modern people live under a constant burden of guilt: guilt for being short, guilt for not being athletic, guilt for being a failure. All without any possibility of forgiveness. (Guilt feelings, I suggest, arise at the gap between your actual story and your performance. So noticing what you really feel guilty about is a good way to tell what your story really is.)

Which makes one of the standard criticisms of the story of Jah odd. Self-esteem psychologists are always blasting Christianity for its notion of sin. Jah is too demanding. The concept of sin, they're always telling us, destroys self-esteem.

It does? I would have thought it was the theologies of Schwarzenegger and Roberts that destroy self-esteem. The demands they put on us are at least as extreme as those of Jah. I mean, who can look like either Schwarzenegger or Roberts? Rarely do we feel guilty about sin in the biblical sense. We don't lie awake nights worrying about not loving others. No, the things we do that we really worry about are nonmoral failures. (I will never get over one time in Nazareth spilling a cup of coffee on the dress of the Swedish ambassador's wife.)

But the story of Jah focuses on grace. It talks about sin in order to get to grace and forgiveness. If you sin (and in the story of Jah, you surely do), forgiveness awaits. You sin, you hurt those you care about most, you're nasty—and that's made OK because Jah loves you and was crucified for you. No loss of self-esteem here.

King David, one of Jah's favorites, saw a woman taking a bath, committed adultery with her, and had her husband murdered. And God forgave him, and he lived on in grace. And wrote half the Psalter.

But moderns can't do that; we're too confused. On the one hand, many of us live in angst because we don't measure up to our silly, demanding stories. On the other hand, we simultaneously insist we aren't serious sinners. Oh, we have little weaknesses, but nothing a self-help class . . .

Rape and the Need for an Accounting

But when those little weaknesses are sins, they're evil. The sort of thing I did crossing the desert—that stuff destroys the universe. Each time we give evil a cozy home in ourselves, we tear a hole in the universe. And through the hole, principalities and powers enter; light and goodness are sucked out of reality, leaving it darker, more one-dimensional and boring, more vicious.

If you raped a woman, you wouldn't just casually apologize to her and then invite her out for coffee, would you? And if you did and the woman accepted, you would both be doing something terrible. She and you would be treating rape as something minor, and it isn't. It isn't like forgetting to turn out the lights when you leave a room; it isn't like being the last person chosen at recess. Rape is violating a person, and for that, some kind of accounting is demanded. Some sort of redemption is required, some sort of atonement (which is different from either appeasement or revenge).

According to the story of Jah, even little evils are like that. They're a violation, a violation of the personal nature of reality, a rape. After you violate a person, you deserve to die. You can't just wave it off. God doesn't say, "Oh, it's OK. No big deal. Don't worry about it." You have viciously torn a hole in the universe, and things have to be put right; you and the universe somehow have to be cleansed, healed, exorcised.

And that's at the heart of what happened on the cross.

But it just doesn't fit the presuppositional structure of modern people (whether romantic or secular). We've almost lost notions like sin and evil and therefore notions like redemption and expiation. (They're hard to see under a microscope, you know.)

But remember rape?

Something mysterious happens in rape, something that can't quite be explained scientifically. Scientifically, it's a piece of matter entering another piece of matter, a lot like inserting an electrical plug into an outlet. And nothing about inserting a plug into an outlet seems like a violation. But when a man forces a woman to have sex, that *is* violation.

What's the difference? The difference is that one is a personal encounter, or at least it should be, and the other isn't. (Perhaps it would be more precise to say that rape is an impersonal encounter at the most personal level.) If the universe were only extension, mass and time, rape would be insignificant. But besides extension, mass and time is the personal, and the personal brings with it mana and taboo, the spiritual and the beautiful, depth . . . and violation. And the need for grace and redemption.

The Blood of Agamemnon
Primitive cultures have more sense of mana and taboo than we do. Accord-

ing to Aeschylus, when Atreus was king of Mycenae, his brother seduced his wife. So Atreus invited him over for lunch and served him three of his sons in a stew. Ancient Greeks knew that this had torn a hole in reality, that Atreus deserved to die. And they knew that something had to be done about it. Unfortunately, what was done about it was that Aegisthus, the only son who hadn't made it into the stew, killed Atreus.

For this charming behavior, the whole family was cursed. Later when Agamemnon, Atreus's son, became king, he decided to sack Troy because of another seduction, but due to the family curse, the wind wouldn't blow enough to move his fleet. So he sacrificed his daughter, Iphigenia, to make the wind blow. Again, the Greeks knew that this had torn a hole in reality, that Agamemnon deserved to die, and that something had to be done about it. Unfortunately, the sort of thing Greeks knew to do about it was done by Iphigenia's mother, Clytemnestra. She took Aegisthus as her lover, and together they murdered Agamemnon in the bath and made themselves rulers.

But such things aren't allowed; so that tore another hole in the universe: now Clytemnestra and Aegisthus deserved to die. Which had to have something done about it. So Electra and Orestes (Agamemnon and Clytemnestra's surviving children) had to cleanse the universe by killing Clytemnestra and Aegisthus. And all of this out of religious duty. (TV soap operas suddenly seem uneventful.)

Except for extreme conservatives, modern people find this joining of violence and religion in the old stories distasteful. One of the great advances of modernity is that our religions are no longer bloody. We have learned that God is nice[3] and doesn't require a bucket of blood. Psychoanalysis will do.

Well, I have news for you. God is not nice, and God does require a bucket of blood, and sinners do deserve to die. When the personal is violated, when a hole is torn in reality, when people sin, God doesn't laugh it off. Sin isn't just extension, mass and time interacting in unfortunate ways; it's a monstrous, vicious trampling on persons, which sets evil powers loose in the universe.

And for that there must be an accounting. Someone deserves to die.

The Costs of Child Abuse

The Greeks were wiser than we are in that they understood that evil has consequences. They knew that evil has a spiritual life of its own and multiplies through generations, choking the parents, the children, the grandchildren. Modern people are recovering some sense of this through studies of child abuse and slavery, but we haven't really understood. We don't finally see the cost of our violence, let alone of our promiscuity.[4]

An honest history of America, or of the world, would read a great deal like that of the house of Atreus. But because we deny that part of reality, the best modern people can do is Arnold Schwarzenegger movies. There the bad guy usually pays with his life, but the violence of the good guy doesn't come back in his face, doesn't undermine reality. (The movies of Martin Scorsese may be an exception, but even he is no Aeschylus.)

But since the Greeks grasped the consequences of evil better than we do, they knew its perpetrators had to be held to account, its power exorcised. When there's evil, a blood sacrifice has to be made. For the Greeks, the blood sacrifices were Atreus, Agamemnon, Clytemnestra, Aegisthus and on and on. The Greeks had no concept of forgiveness, and so for them atonement was a bloody mess (as it is for Schwarzenegger too, only not as bloody as it really would be—complaints about the level of violence notwithstanding).

So modern people dismiss all this as superstitious savagery. (While, however, continuing to love violent movies—a natural outcome of repressing our knowledge of the need for blood sacrifice? I wonder if a Martian anthropologist studying our movies and television might conclude that violence has a central religious role for us.) Getting beyond blood sacrifices is one of the presuppositions of secularism and has been accepted even by most romantics and by many religious people. For modern people, God is tolerant and loving—like the rape victim who says, "That's OK. It's no big deal. You couldn't help it: you had no other way to get what you wanted." Which is silly. Everyone has a right to what they want, and no one has to account for it, except maybe to a psychologist . . . ?

The Blood of Jah: Finally a Plan of Salvation

But Jah has a better story than Aeschylus's, Schwarzenegger's or Julia Roberts's. It's that evil requires a blood sacrifice and that God has paid it himself. So forgiveness is available free. You see, God isn't nice, but God is love. (The difference between niceness and love has escaped our culture.) And since God is love, the sacrifice lovingly offered was God's own son.

It's not that a strong white knight outfights evil and saves an innocent, weak maiden. Nor is it that a simple woman saves a strong man from himself by her simplicity. Nor is it that powerful people kill each other for their mutual sins. It's that all-powerful Jah limits himself to weak human form to save the bad guy. Through weakness unto death, Jah allows himself to be used as redemption and a model for life. Salvation came not by Jah's slaughtering the bad guy but by Jah's letting the bad guy slaughter him. That somehow plugs the holes in the universe. And makes salvation possible for anyone, no matter how short or ugly—or vicious. And releases mana.

Unfortunately, this story is not one of the standard myths like "Cinderella" or "The Three Little Pigs." Perhaps that's because it's beyond human invention, beyond even human comprehension. In the thousands of years people struggled with problems of propitiation and expiation and sacrifice (culminating in *Total Recall* where the bad guy dies in agony), no one ever dreamed that God would give himself as the sacrifice. But he did.

And even now we have a hard time retelling that story in any form other than the original one. We have dozens of variants of *Agamemnon*, hundreds of variants of *Pretty Woman* and tens of thousands of variants of *Total Recall*. But the story of Jah scarcely ever gets told except in church and perhaps synagogue, and then in its original form. Jah's incarnation and death seem too large to fit into human story form.

C. S. Lewis's *The Lion, the Witch and the Wardrobe* comes close. In it, God is in the form of a lion, Aslan, and he's betrayed by one of his subjects. Primordial law requires a death for treason, and Aslan gives himself to be executed. This cracks the stone on which the law is written.

Now that's grace—a story of redemption and forgiveness that cleanses and heals reality. And plugs the holes by releasing mana. But the Greeks didn't have a concept of forgiveness because their gods weren't love, and *Total Recall* doesn't need a story of forgiveness because Schwarzenegger can kill evil with a gun, and *Pretty Woman* doesn't need a story of forgiveness because evil isn't serious enough to require it and failure isn't considered.

So without the forgiveness in the story of Jah, we have a choice between endless violence on the one hand and on the other a nice god who doesn't much care if we violate persons. In the Aeschylus and the Schwarzenegger version there seems to be justice without love, and in the Julia Roberts version there seems to be love without justice. But in reality neither has either. The story of Jah, however, has both. It combines the strengths of Schwarzenegger and Aeschylus with the strengths of *Pretty Woman* but without their pitfalls. Evil is taken seriously, and love is preserved—tough love.

You can have your evil accounted for and washed away. Whether it's rape or a temper tantrum over country music, it's done. And you're empowered to change. But in the other stories it's never done. You're five feet tall till you die. And you can't even be forgiven for it.

You're trapped in a vicious cycle. For the Greeks (and in reality, for Schwarzenegger), the cycle is that evil requires a blood sacrifice, which itself requires another blood sacrifice, which itself requires another blood sacrifice . . . For romantics, the cycle is that I can't say I'm a sinner, because that would damage my self-esteem; so I have to deceive myself about who I am, which damages my self-esteem and leaves me unable to deal with my problems, which further damages my self-esteem and leaves me less able to say I'm a sinner; so I have to deceive myself about who I am, which . . .

But the mana in forgiveness gets us out of those traps. And makes it possible for us to make an accounting for our sin.

A Sacramental Metaphysic

However, our metaphysic makes all this hard to understand. When all is said and done, most of us believe that the universe is matter only. We may not believe that in theory, but in practice we have no idea what spirit or taboo might be, mana or grace. Consequently, sin and forgiveness are unintelligible to us and being held to account is unacceptable.

But we haven't managed completely to repress our sense of the spiritual or of taboo; so we know that things like rape are terrible beyond what could happen to a machine. However, within our framework of practical materialism we've got no way to understand them, no vocabulary to talk about them, and therefore we resort to a physical metaphor: sickness. A rapist can't have a spiritual problem because there isn't such a thing: he isn't a sinner; he's sick. Or maybe he's a failure.

Folks in the ecological movement have found a way out of this trap: they want us to go back before secularism. One reason people exploit the environment is our secular metaphysic. If the earth is just matter, then why not exploit it? If nature has no spiritual aspect, then it isn't sacred, and neither spotted owls nor anything else has an intrinsic claim to protection. By contrast, one of the strengths of primitive people is their sense of the sacredness of the earth. If they kill a buffalo or cut a rice stalk, many primitive people talk to its spirit; they say a prayer. Consequently, they rarely degrade their environment the way secularized, modern people do. They live uncontaminated by Anaxagoras, with the earth still a thou.

Understanding this, the romantic wing of the environmental movement sensibly calls for a sense of the sacredness of the earth: they want us to change our metaphysic. They want us to take care of the earth because she is our mother, not because it pays. To preserve the spotted owl not because it might turn out someday to be valuable to us, but because it's sacred. Within the presuppositions of such a metaphysic, the degradation of nature is taboo (quite apart from its consequences on human beings) and its preservation is mana.

This same insight, this same presuppositional framework, restores the intelligibility of sin. (That's part of the package of being primitive and presecular.) Sexual promiscuity isn't wrong just because of its physical consequences. It's also wrong because sex is sacred and any use of it outside the context God made it for is taboo. That also explains why rape is terrible: it is extreme profanation of the sacred.[5]

So romantics set out to break down the distinction between nature and God. They see the spotted owl as part of God. God and nature are one. Mother Earth is our God, or rather our Goddess—Gaia.

Rembrandt and the Hebrews

Primitive Hebrews accomplished the same thing while leaving nature separate from God. They believed that God was a person and that nature was therefore the creation of a person. A person made the universe and made it in such a way that it reflects that person's being. It is therefore personal and sacred. It's not a thou, but it's made by a thou into the image of a thou and therefore possesses mana.

Rather like a painting by Rembrandt. A painting by Rembrandt is separate from Rembrandt, but it's his creation, and with his great talent he was able to make his paintings an extension of his person (something most of us can't do). So we take care of a Rembrandt creation: we treat it with a certain awe. We have a sense of its power, its mana.

And all the more if the creation is God's. We should stand before a spotted owl with at least the awe we do before Rembrandt's *Night Watch*. We should sense its mana. All reality has a sacramental quality because it's made by God. All reality is personal, sacramental. For the Hebrews, the earth was not their possession; it belonged to God and was only on loan to them for as long as they kept covenant.

Some years ago, a man slashed *Night Watch* repeatedly. He did great economic damage, but that's not the point. The point is that something as great as *Night Watch* deserves respect and that the man was so spiritually blind that he didn't grant it that respect. He violated the person of Rembrandt and the person of all those who stand in awe before Rembrandt's work. Although arguably all he did was rearrange some molecules, he actually committed rape. And for that he can't just say "Sorry" and take Rembrandt out for coffee. He violated the sacred and must be redeemed. Otherwise, the good will leak out of the hole he made in the universe. And more evil powers will enter.

Which gets us back to the point. When we violate persons created by God, we must be redeemed and forgiven. Or all hell breaks loose.

God and Grace
And there's not much we can do about that by ourselves.

Let me put it another way. Woody Allen can be saved if he accepts that he's Woody Allen and needs help. Evil is defeated when we recognize that we're too weak to defeat it ourselves. It's defeated when we recognize our need for God. Our need for grace.

But that's a major understatement. It's not just that we aren't strong enough to do the saving. It's not just that we're Woody Allens. It's that we're the bad guy (which Woody Allen is too, but that's not admitted in his movies). We're the one from whom others have to be saved.

We have here a profound paradigm shift, perhaps the most profound of all. We are the bad guy. In the Schwarzenegger story, a hero saves an innocent victim from a bad guy, and if we can't identify with Schwarzenegger, we can identify with the innocent victim. But in the story of Jah, the hero doesn't save an innocent victim: he saves the bad guy—who is us. There is no innocent victim for us to identify with, because the only innocent victim is God. So insulting as it is, in the story of Jah we're supposed to identify with the bad guy. So Rembrandt once painted himself crucifying God. Rembrandt and you and I. We are the bad guys. But Jah loves us anyway.

Now that's grace.

And the opposite of the Schwarzenegger story. This perspective, this grace, has an odd cost. It transforms me as good guy deserving salvation into me as bad guy deserving death. And that hurts. It's hateful, humiliating. We want to be the hero ourselves, and at the least we want to deserve being saved by a dashing hero. We *won't* be the ugly, wicked stepsister.

But Jesus didn't marry Cinderella; he married the stepsister. Cinderella was too self-righteous. "I have come to call not the righteous but sinners to repentance" (Lk 5:32).

Now perhaps we can go so far as to admit that we bumble our way through life. Perhaps we can come to terms with that. We can't save ourselves; we're too weak; we need a helping hand from God. That's a healthy revision of the Schwarzenegger story.

But it's still not the story of Jah. And it's not grace. Weakness is a sin only in the Schwarzenegger story. In the story of Jah, being weak doesn't make you a sinner; it only makes you a nerd. A Cinderella who steps on the prince's toes during the dance. And that's not sin, not in the story of Jah. In the story of Jah, that's fine. What's not fine in the story of Jah is being nasty and vicious, like the stepsisters. That punches holes in the universe.

When we see that we're Cinderella's stepsisters, when we see we're the house of Atreus, then we're eligible for God's grace. Then God gives us mana to begin dying to ourselves, and we become the bride of Christ.

Gollum

In the story of Schwarzenegger, salvation comes through strength. In the story of Jah, it comes through weakness. Which seems odd to those of us who have had Schwarzenegger pounded into our souls since infancy. But the crucial event in world history wasn't Jah slaying Satan with a sword; it was Jah loving us so much that he let Satan crucify him as a human being.

Which is obscured in *The Lion, the Witch and the Wardrobe*. In it, Aslan is a monarch and a powerful lion, rather like Schwarzenegger. It would have been closer to the story of Jah if he had been someone weak, like a carpenter's son in a backwater of the empire or a baker whom no one much notices.[6]

Lewis obscures the importance of weakness in another way too. Like most conservative Christians, he seems to have not quite grasped that the way Aslan died indicates how his followers should live. It's part of how we're saved on earth. By not needing to defend our rights. By not letting it ruin our day when someone wrongs us. That's mana. And sometimes those who wrong us are so amazed by our response that they're saved too. That's grace and truth now.

But Lewis tends to have the good guys slaughter the bad guys. To be fair, he symbolizes the importance of weakness by having the heroes be children. And the most insightful of them is the youngest, the weakest—a little girl. But they don't allow themselves to be injured to exorcise evil. And as the stories progress, the children become stronger, more adult. And by the end, they're using the sword on evil with nearly the verve of Conan the Barbarian.

Lewis's story seems to reduce the cross to saving us in eternity; it has little to do with salvation in day-to-day life with friends and enemies. Aslan died; so we don't have to. But near the heart of the story of Jah lies accepting the evil of others in your own person. In weakness, not strength. Aslan died; so we should too. That helps fill the holes.

That part of the story is told better in *Lord of the Rings*.[7] It includes lots of violence, but the violence isn't glorified and never saves anyone. Salvation comes from Frodo, a silly little hobbit, who has to choose daily to do the hard things. (He's about as muscular as Woody Allen.) It also comes from a depraved former hobbit, Gollum. Gollum is evil and has done terrible wrong, but Frodo spares his life. And in the end, Frodo doesn't accomplish his mission; Gollum does.

Furthermore, the dark lord knows an attack is coming on his stronghold, and so he watches the people of power. (Dark lords invented the Arnold Schwarzenegger story and can't imagine anything else.) It never occurs to him to watch out for silly little hobbits. And so when the crucial attack comes, he's looking the wrong way and is defeated by weakness. Which is the only way to defeat evil.[8]

Because evil isn't the sort of thing you can defeat with a six-shooter of power. Especially not your own evil. Which is the main kind. And especially not since evil is selfishness. If you're trying to deal with your own selfishness, what do you do with a six-shooter? Blow your brains out?[9]

No, dealing with evil requires the crucified God. Who gives us the power to be weak. To die to ourselves.

A True Story

It also requires a story of truth, truth in the broadest and deepest sense of the word. Stories like *The Lion, the Witch and the Wardrobe* and *Lord of the Rings* come close. They are far truer than *Total Recall* or *Pretty Woman*, but they still aren't true enough. And I don't just mean that neither of them manages to get in the whole of the story of Jah. I mean rather that neither of those stories actually happened in space and time.

That of course is not a fashionable concern for religious intellectuals. It's merely a factual matter, something of no importance—what I called a Nothing in earlier chapters. All that matters is the meaning in back of the facts, the meaning for me. So it doesn't matter whether the story really happened; it doesn't matter whether Jesus rose from the dead physically— that's just a question of fact. What matters is the story in back of the story, which is that goodness lives on and will ultimately conquer despite much suffering. That's all the resurrection story is meant to teach.

This answer (it's the existential answer) has been influential in theology, and with good reason. Who cares what the capital of Oregon is? Who cares how many blind men Jesus healed outside Jericho? What matters is that Jesus cared about the blind and the sick. Nothing matters except the personal. So read the Bible and other stories for their meaning for I-thou relationships and forget everything else. That's the natural conclusion to the kind of thing I've been arguing. Right?

Wrong. Remember Tolkien's definition of eucatastrophe? "It denies (in the face of much evidence, if you will) universal, final defeat."[10] That's exactly what *Pretty Woman* does. Julia Roberts and her roommate say outright that prostitutes never marry johns. In other words, the story is factually mistaken. So how can it give us hope? How can we get hope from a story with a fake ending?

By self-deception, that's how.

You see, sometimes the facts do matter. All creation is God's. And at the least the facts matter when they impinge on the personal. It may be merely factual whether people with AIDS live longer when they take an experimental drug, but it matters—it matters to people with AIDS. Similarly, it matters to prostitutes whether they sometimes marry their johns and live happily ever after. And if we are to take *Pretty Woman* as our story to live by, it matters to us. At least it should. How can you take hope from something that has never happened, could never happen?

Which is one reason the story of Jah is so much better than other stories. It actually happened. Jesus *was* resurrected. It's really true. And that gives us hope for the defeat of evil, hope for forgiveness and grace, hope that isn't based on self-deception, hope that isn't based on silliness about Schwarzenegger's muscles or a prostitute's ability to reform a billionaire.

The crucified God actually came and lived and died among us. And rose from the dead in space and time. And as a matter of actual fact, forgave us. Now that's grounds for hope.

Conclusion: Lives of Grace and Truth

Perhaps we could construct a view of the world without ideals and without taboos. A few secularists try to. But in that world, our lives would degenerate into terror and madness even more quickly than our civilization already has. At least, that's what I argued earlier in the book.

Or we can accept a view of the world with strong taboos and high ideals but no grace. That's the world of Schwarzenegger, of most secularists, though they often hide it from themselves. And while that's probably better than a world with no ideals, it's a world of fear and legalism that doesn't encourage lives of growth and joy. This is the petty world of the Pharisees or the tragic world of Aeschylus. In it, we're forever losing sight of love, of what matters. Life shrivels into self-righteousness and vengeance, into striving for success and belittling others' successes to make our failures seem better.

Or we can accept a romantic view of the world starring Julia Roberts. This one has high ideals and endless (usually unrecognized) taboos. But it doesn't take sin seriously; it doesn't recognize how much pleasure people take in smashing the mana, especially in someone else. And by middle age its optimism turns to cynicism and defeat. With no concept of sin, it can have no concept of forgiving sin, and so bitterness is the only recourse. The universe is a hostile, sick place.

Unless, of course, you're gifted at self-deception. In which case you can continue telling yourself that you're growing in grace and truth while walking barefoot in the grass and trying to get your own way. But you grow only in selfishness and shallowness.

Or we can accept a view of the world with strong taboos and high ideals and endless grace. This is a world in which sin matters, in which we all deserve to die. In which Jah has done it for us, and we can relax and thrive in grace and truth. In the knowledge of our sin and of Jah's love for us sinners, life can burgeon and we can grow in depth. We grow not to avert God's wrath but to please the one who loves us and brings us joy.

The taboos and the ideals might even be the same, but in a gracious world our approach to them is different. *Pretty Woman* illustrates this (it has some truncated grace): Richard Gere changes not out of legalistic obligation but because he loves Julia Roberts, and together they are transformed. To change the metaphor, we run fast not because the coach will make us do extra laps if we don't but because Julia Roberts is waiting for us at the end of the course and we hurry to be with her. Running still hurts, but we try harder. That's how grace motivates. We die to ourselves not out of legalism but because the crucified God in infinite wisdom wants us to, and we love him as much as Julia Roberts loves Richard Gere in *Pretty Woman*.

What will it be? Soup cans in various colors or the grace of the crucified God?

11

Playing with FIRE: Or, Narcissism as Sacred Duty

My wife, Judy, teaches severely retarded high-school students. Most of her kids can't speak, and those who can tend to repeat themselves a lot. But Vicki (not her real name) was an exception. A bright-eyed sixteen-year-old with a wonderful smile, Vicki spoke fluently and could even read a little. Her records suggested mild retardation and severe emotional disturbance caused by neglect or worse.

Professionals recommended therapy, but instead she kept being sent to the next "lower" level because of behavior problems. Finally, she wound up with kids who were severely retarded. There they had a staff person for every two or three kids and were more or less able to control her. Never mind that they couldn't offer her the academic or therapeutic help she needed, and never mind the trauma of being classed with severely retarded kids, beautiful though many of them are.

I don't mean to say that the school's problem was easy. It was drastically underfunded, and Vicki was impossible. She wanted her own way, right away, all the time, and when she didn't get it, she was liable to run away or throw a tantrum.

In any case, while Judy was trying to get her a more appropriate placement, Vicki began to threaten to run out in front of a car and was hospitalized. When she was released, it was clear she was being neglected; so early in 1991, we made room for her in our family.[1]

Vicki was indeed impossible. A simple request (like "Time to eat") could result in a stream of abuse like I haven't heard since I quit working at a ready-mix plant. When she wasn't hiding in her room, she had to be the center of attention or she'd cause a crisis. She'd run away or slap someone or refuse to go to school. Or all of the above. In addition to active aggression, she had a black belt in passive aggression. She seldom answered questions, and asking her to hurry guaranteed a long stall. In more clinical terms, her narcissism left her profoundly dysfunctional.

We had expected hassles from Vicki, though not as dramatic as we got, but we hadn't expected hassles from bureaucrats. First, we were told that teachers can't have students in their homes, because if the child is injured the school is liable. After Judy persuaded the authorities that Vicki's placement was wrong, they removed her from class . . . but didn't give her a new class; so for an extended period, Vicki languished at home. Even after much effort, we were unable to get her access to her social security payments. Then to top it off, her social worker reported us for running an unlicensed home for the retarded, and it looked as if we were going to be fined two hundred dollars a day unless we let them warehouse Vicki in a group home.

We figured she didn't need that trauma on top of everything else; so we went to an organization that provides free legal services for kids. Within days, things began to change: "This is Vicki X's attorney, and I want to know why she doesn't have a school placement." That sort of one-minute call, made to several agencies, got a response. Which our extended efforts hadn't.

Soon concerned social workers began to arrive in droves. After the formalities, their first question was some version of "Vicki, where do you want to live?" They went on with "Vicki, where do you want to go to school?" and "Vicki, do you like John and Judy?" Eventually we became Vicki's guardians, and she got into a school for emotionally disturbed adolescents where they do their best to give her what she wants. She continues to be impossible. And for a time her social security payments were lowered because she receives free food and lodging (you'd never guess from our bills that they're free), and they tried to deduct from her check money she was defrauded of when she first came to live with us. However, she gets nearly enough money for living expenses, she hasn't run away for months, she usually goes to school (often on time), and she doesn't slap us too often.

A Parable of Our Culture

For me, all this has become a parable for our culture: a nation that cares deeply about child abuse—but that has no idea what to do with abused kids except spend money. Large amounts of money (in a cheap year, the state spends thirty thousand dollars on Vicki[2]), but little benefit. A child so desperate to get her way that she can't function in normal society, and social workers and teachers who think they're helping by giving her her way. Rules designed to protect kids, and impersonal bureaucrats who enforce them even when it hurts the kids. One school more concerned about control than the good of the child, and another school (especially designed for kids like her) imagining it would be untherapeutic to control her. A bureaucracy more responsive to the whisper of a lawsuit than to the prolonged cry of a child and her new family.

For me, the key to this parable came from Vicki's lawyer (who was excellent). At our first interview, she told me: "You understand, we're not here to get what's good for Vicki. We're here to fight for her rights, to get her what she wants. Sometimes that won't be good for her, but that's our job. We're lawyers, and she's our client."

We're not here to get what's good for Vicki. We're here to fight for her rights, to get her what she wants. Sometimes that won't be good for her, but that's our job. Enmeshed in that statement is a whole story system, a story system that resides at the heart of modern culture and is common to both Arnold Schwarzenegger and Julia Roberts. A culture that understands little more than lawsuits and what people want.

But the accomplishments of this story system have been unprecedented.

We have gone from a world of near universal tyranny and poverty to a world where substantial segments of the population are prosperous and free. And real, if not huge, steps have been taken toward racial equality and the liberation of women. If a story is judged by its consequences, this one must be taken seriously.

But then come its failures. Vicki and its inability to cope with Vicki. And the fact that all modern people are Vickis. For the modern story feeds the Vicki in all of is. She is simply the modern story writ large and truthfully. Which story is revealed as shallow and ineffectual when confronted by Vicki. Who is all of us.

"We're not here to get what's good for Vicki. We're here to fight for her rights, to get her what she wants . . ."

Here we have a child so disturbed that some mornings she can't choose her own clothes. It's unusual for her to know what she wants—about anything. Her feelings are so chaotic and undisciplined that they confuse her. And when she does know what she wants, it's often bad. In almost any culture but our own, it would be obvious that Vicki should be given what she needs, not what she wants. And what she needs is to be enveloped in goodness, not handed her rights. But if any public institution tried to envelop Vicki in goodness, it would get sued by the ACLU. In our pluralistic culture, we hold in common so few stories about goodness that the ACLU would probably be right.

Perhaps a fallen society can't be organized any better than that. As soon as officials have the power to tell people what they need, they are corrupted by that power and tell them the wrong things. Consequently the power of government needs to be limited. That is a great insight of modernity (perhaps *the* great insight of modernity).[3]

Without such limits on the government, we would be told who to worship, and Vicki and other "troublemakers" (like people who criticize the government) would soon be jailed or worse. Where government is concerned, we need a bill of rights, a legislature and administration independent of each other, and courts that oversee them both. In governing, checks and balances are good—or at least they're necessary evils in a fallen society.

But as government gets involved in more and more aspects of life, we are checked and balanced right out of morality, if not sanity. Since government has taken over education and welfare, teachers and social workers are silenced about what matters. Anything they might tell Vicki authoritatively about goodness, anything they might insist she *needs* to do, could violate her rights; so public employees are very nearly limited to giving her what she wants. Anything else verges on unconstitutionality.

But the problem is only partly constitutional. The courts don't require social workers and teachers to be quite as silly with Vicki as some are. There is a deeper problem: the same stories that shaped the Constitution also shaped the rest of the Western spirit. So we obsess over things like rights and freedom, even when we're dealing with our own children: so in a typically permissive home, parents ask young adolescents to decide for themselves about attending church or using birth control. And we naturally make the same mistakes when dealing with people who have emotional or developmental disabilities.

Hence that part of the parable. We are a culture committed to helping people become so narcissistic that neither they nor the culture can long endure.

Once beyond the sort of morality that all societies have to accept to survive (don't commit murder; don't steal), we have few stories in common about morality, and those we have are about things like rights and freedom. But as modern people understand them, rights and freedom are oddly independent of notions like goodness. A person who violates the rights or freedom of others is bad, but other than that, rights and freedom are almost empty concepts.

They are negative concepts, value-free values. Freedom is the right *not* to obey the lord of the manor. It's noncoercion, and as such offers no positive sense of what we're to do or who we're to be; freedom *from*, not freedom *to*.[4] So we're clearer about the need for kids to decide for themselves than on who they should decide to be.

John Locke founded modern political thought by talking about "the right to life, liberty, and property." In saying that, he was setting negative limits on what the government and others might do to the individual; he wasn't giving a moral theory on how we could be fully human. The right to life meant that the government and others *weren't* to take your life arbitrarily; it didn't tell you what was good to do with the life they weren't to take. None of these rights helps with what is worth doing. We have the right to choose for ourselves, but no help on what's worth choosing. If we want help with what to choose, we need some added framework, some larger story.

Which added framework our culture as a whole doesn't have. This is partly because goodness and worthwhileness aren't the sorts of things you can measure; so both secularists and romantics tend to reduce them to feelings, to what you want. It's also because we're a pluralistic society, and people with stories about goodness are perceived as special interest groups who mustn't violate others' rights by imposing their views on them. We are, after all, a free society.

Remember Vicki? She's the one who usually doesn't know what she feels and the rest of the time feels like blowing up half the world. The one the social workers and therapists are always asking what she wants. "Follow your bliss," they tell her in effect. "Do what you want." They have no story to enable them to say the obvious: "What you want is confused and not good; so let's help you find what's worth wanting." Even the tough-minded person in the "helping professions" can do little more than help her "clarify her values." They can't just point her toward real values, toward salvation.

As a culture, we are fixated to the point of illness on individuals' right to what they want. Which has produced a billion free and prosperous people. Who have nothing to say to empty people confused about what they want (which is all of us), who have nothing to say to empty people who sometimes want bad things (which is all of us). Which is to say, our culture has produced a billion free and prosperous people as empty as Andy Warhol's soup cans.

The Human Predicament
The problem is that modern people have misdiagnosed the human predicament. We believe that our predicament is that we don't get what we want often enough, that we aren't free, that our rights are violated, that life isn't fair. If only we were free and our wills weren't thwarted, we'd be happy.

On some level we may know that this isn't true, but we come pretty close to living as if we thought it were. We talk endlessly about rights and fairness, and we churn inwardly when others keep us from getting our way. And we imagine we'll be happy when we at last get the house or computer or spouse we want.

We've turned a sensible approach to politics into a silly approach to life. The Enlightenment story puts it pretty explicitly: the power of rulers and the superstition of priests are what make us unhappy. We need to fight for our rights by replacing monarchy with democracy and superstition with reason. Then we'll be free, and we'll live happily ever after. In the romantic version, our predicament is not rulers and priests but rulers and reason. We need to fight for our rights by escaping the confines of civilization and doing what comes naturally. When we're both politically and personally liberated, we'll live happily ever after.

In both of these stories (which have become closely intertwined over the centuries), the human predicament is that we aren't free, which violates our rights. So the positive parts of modern history can be written substantially in terms of liberation movements/rights movements: the American Revolution, the French Revolution, the freeing of slaves, the Marxist revolutions, the right to labor unions, wars to liberate colonies (expressed today mostly as wars to liberate ethnic groups), the civil rights movement, the Free Speech Movement, the women's rights movement, gay liberation.

Although Christianity played a major role in shaping these movements, the final articulations came from people implacably opposed to Jah, people like Rousseau and Locke, Mill and Kant, Freud and Marcuse, Friedan and Millett. They were profoundly influenced by the story of Jah and lived in part off their fading memory of it, but as they wove their stories, they added a twist profoundly contrary to the story of Jah. They dedicated themselves to the self, to its Freedom, its Individualism, its Rights and its Equality: FIRE. Their ultimate commitment was not to Jah but to the self and its FIRE. In an otherwise vaguely Judeo-Christian context.

Jefferson gave the classic statement of it, at least for Americans: "We hold these Truths to be self-evident, that all Men are created equal, that they are endowed by their Creator with certain unalienable Rights, that among these are Life, Liberty, and the pursuit of Happiness." The first official American flag put it more succinctly: "Don't tread on me"—emblazoned below a rattlesnake.[5]

And what Jefferson wrote in the Declaration of Independence and what the colonies had on their first flag, John Wayne lived in Westerns—and the rest of us live in life. We're all Vickis. We believe it to be our right, our moral duty, to fight when we don't get our own way.

Don't tread on us.

At the center of the Enlightenment and romanticism are freedom and individualism, rights and equality. And at the center of each of those things, only slightly hidden, is the self. What's at the center isn't rights but *my* rights, *my* individualism, *my* freedom, *my* equality.

This FIRE is burning us up. The modern story encourages us to go around constantly checking on our rights and freedom. It encourages us to do battle with anyone who treads on them. If a monarch taxes your tea, that's quite sufficient grounds to kill tens of thousands of people in a war of liberation; if your spouse limits your freedom, that's quite sufficient grounds for divorce. We're blocked at every corner by monarchs and reason, spouses and colleagues. The human predicament is that we don't get our rights often enough; none of it is our fault.

And we have not only a right to free ourselves of those oppressions but a duty. The person who doesn't is a wimp, unhealthily passive. While rights is an oddly negative concept, it does imply a sort of duty. If we have a right to life, liberty and the pursuit of happiness, we also have some sort of duty to defend those rights, an obligation to fight for them. So the Declaration of Independence says that when a people are governed by a despot, "it is their Right, it is their Duty," to get rid of him.

So Americans are morally obliged to liberate themselves from the king, and slaves are obliged to liberate themselves from their masters. And in time students are obliged to liberate themselves from teachers, children from parents, parents from children and individuals from the community. We should fight anyone and anything that thwarts our happiness—and in the process, make *ourselves* king.

Narcissism is a right; in fact, it's a sacred duty.

Well, we won't be happy till we take up the cross, and neither will Vicki. But I've already told that story.

Equality

Equality is an important and valid moral concept. I must understand that I'm no better than the average street person or Pharisee, that I'm no better than Vicki or other people I help. Any other attitude destroys I-thou relationships.[6]

But the way modern people understand equality is another matter. We confuse moral equality with equality of gifts and equality of effort.[7] So in progressive schools, classes are held in a circle to dramatize the essential equality of student and teacher—who is known as the coordinator since *teacher* implies superiority. Students are likely to be more concerned with their own ideas than with the ideas of Plato or Jesus, and classes become bull sessions where students share their ignorance. After all, self-expression is more important than grasping the wisdom of the ages.[8]

It makes no difference if some people have searched for truth for a lifetime and others don't care. It makes no difference if some people think more clearly than others. Everyone's opinion is as good as everyone else's. No matter how little I may have worked at it, no matter how wise or experienced others may be, my opinion is as good as theirs.

So "sensitive" religious people don't proclaim the truth the way Jesus and Isaiah did. That would open them to charges of authoritarianism (even if dealing with a Vicki). But Jesus didn't "coordinate" bull sessions with the Pharisees, or even with his disciples, because they had little to offer.

"All men are equal" progresses along a line something like this: "I'm as good as you. No one is better than me. I don't have to listen to anyone. I won't learn from anyone. Don't you tell me what to do." In the pursuit of the modern notion of equality, we become unteachable. Or perhaps we're able to be taught by our peers, but if they share such views, they have little to teach.

This is inefficient (it means we have to reinvent the wheel), but it's worse than inefficient. It's a spiritual issue as well. A fundamental issue of the heart. Those who can't submit to others will forever be midgets. For the logic keeps progressing: "Since no one is better than me, I don't have to respect anyone. I can't revere anyone. I don't know how to be loyal to anyone. I won't bend the knee to anyone, not even to God." Once we learned not to bend the knee to George III, it became hard to bend the knee at all.[9]

The result is that in our culture we have little left that we think deserves loyalty and almost nothing left that we think deserves reverence. Which leaves us poor and flat. What do we revere? Perhaps the flag or movie stars or other things that don't deserve it. (And perhaps that's inevitable: if people reject what merits reverence, their hollowness makes them seek a substitute, and so they put trash in its place.) We're better at dragging things down to a lower level than at building them up, better at debunking than at exalting (an oddly archaic word, which is interesting).

And so we are spiritually impoverished. For at the heart of spirituality is reverence, awe. The awareness of something beyond our reach. A sense of mystery at what surpasses comprehension. Contact with the numinous. But we have lost almost all sense of that reality. In the Bible, at moments of such contact, here's the typical reaction: "And Joshua fell on his face to the earth and worshiped, and he said to him, 'What do you command your servant, my lord?'"[10] My lord? Command? Your servant? Not very democratic.

But in Joshua, wonder and humility go together. Wonder before God who exceeds our grasp and therefore humility at being so small. I doubt that we can learn much worthwhile without this dual experience of wonder and humility. Wonder and humility before the facts, wonder and humility before others, wonder and humility before God.

But such a thing is almost unthinkable today. More's the pity.

Naboth and Vineyard Rights

At the center of all of this is rights. A notion not found in the Bible or elsewhere in the ancient world. (Neither Greek nor Hebrew even has a word for it.[11]) It's a modern idea that arose alongside science and secularism. Rights were cast in their modern form in the second half of the 1600s by the English philosophers Thomas Hobbes and John Locke.[12]

But the notion of rights is foreign to the story of Jah. Remember Naboth's vineyard (1 Kings 21)? King Ahab wanted Naboth's vineyard (it was next to the palace) and made him an offer he couldn't refuse. But he did. Naboth refused because way back at the conquest of Canaan, that particular piece of land had been assigned to his family by God. Naboth's refusal made Ahab angry and sullen; so Jezebel, his wife, arranged Naboth's murder, allowing Ahab to seize the vineyard.

Modern people would denounce Ahab for violating Naboth's right to life and property, but Elijah denounced him for selling himself "to do what is evil in the sight of the LORD" (1 Kings 21:20-21). Elijah thundered at Ahab as resoundingly as Locke or Jefferson would have, but he used different words. And as is often the case, different words carry a different message because they come from a different story.

Within the story of the children of Israel, individuals don't have property rights as we understand them.[13] The land is God's, on loan to a family for as long as they keep covenant (Lev 25:23; 26:15, 32-35). Land is God's gracious gift, neither natural nor inalienable nor individual. So as long as Israelites have land, they owe it to God, and if someone seizes it from them, they're not being wronged as much as God is.

We have here contrasting stories. Stealing land is intelligible in both of them and wrong in both of them, but one expresses this by talking about "violating rights" and the other by talking about "working evil in the sight of the Lord." These two stories have a lot in common, but they have even more not in common.

What we have here is a paradigm shift.

A titanic one. The most obvious result is the shift from God to Naboth. We shift from a story centered on God to a story centered on the self. Naboth isn't irrelevant in the story of Jah, far from it, but neither is he the center. He plays a major role, but Elijah's denunciation doesn't even mention him. After all, Naboth is merely the tenant of the land; God is the owner. Which puts Naboth in his proper place, nowhere near the center. Here, and only here, can he be fulfilled. The story of Jah is odd by modern standards because it says that individuals are complete only when they aren't center stage.

Meanwhile, in the modern story Naboth is the beginning, the middle and the end. His rights have been violated—full stop. He has only himself and his rights with which to fill his hollowness. He will spiral into himself in an infinite, lost regress. Like Vicki.

But goodness, not to mention health and sanity, can come only as we allow someone else to be at the center. Putting ourselves at the center distorts us hideously, pushing out everything else. Pushing out God, the only one who can fill our hollowness.

The idea of finding fullness this way troubles modern people, including Christians. We may believe in God, but we're so secular we can't picture God having so large a role. But Jah is not just the one who started the mechanism going, nor is he some distant, vaguely benign figure; he's king. That's the story of Jah. Of course, we prefer the modern story, which supposedly rejects kings altogether—because that leaves the self king . . . beyond possibility of challenge.

The issue is simple: Who will be king, you or Jah? Earlier, I've asked various forms of the basic human question: Why is it that life goes wrong? Why do people do horrible things to each other? Why do we often feel empty even when things are going well? Why does life seem so one-dimensional? Now we have that question in its ultimate form: Who will be king, George III, you or Jah? It's a question of sovereignty.

And unlike the other forms of the question, this one is easy to answer. It takes no philosopher to understand the difference between "Don't tread on me" and Joshua's "What do you command your servant, my lord?"

And it's not just that the Bible doesn't have a notion of rights; it's that it has close to the opposite. When Jah was on earth, he wasn't exactly fighting for his rights. At least, if he was, we have to think he wasn't very bright. He went to the cross without a struggle.

And told his followers to do the same: "If any want to become my followers, let them deny themselves and take up their cross daily and follow me. For those who want to save their life will lose it, and those who lose their life for my sake will save it" (Lk 9:23-24; see also Mt 16:24-25; Mk 8:34-35).

As I recall it, Jah didn't exactly say, "Blessed are those who fight for their rights, for they shall succeed. Blessed are those who kill their oppressors, for they shall inherit the earth" (Mt 5:4-5, Revised Standard Perversion).

Remember what Peter said to slaves being treated unjustly? It wasn't "Slaves, stand up for your rights, not only to kind and gentle masters, but also to the harsh, for it is a credit to you if you daringly defend yourself while enduring pain. But what credit is it to you if you suffer unjustly and don't rebel? For to this you have been called, because Christ also fought for his rights, leaving you an example that you should follow in his steps. When he was abused, he returned abuse; when he suffered, he fought back; he didn't simply entrust himself to the one who judges justly. By his rights campaign you have been healed" (1 Pet 2:18-24, same translation).

Or how about this from Isaiah: "He was oppressed and he was afflicted, and he shrieked about his rights being violated; he fought back like a gladiator led into the arena, he charged like a bull before a matador" (see Is 53:7).

Jah taught that the human predicament is that the self has made itself king; it's a usurping murderer who crucifies God. That's the source of our emptiness. What we need to do is to throw the self out, put it to death.

Which is about as far as you can get from modern stories, whether it's secularism or romanticism, Thomas Jefferson or Karl Marx, Arnold Schwarzenegger or Julia Roberts.

Individualism

Alongside this shift from a paradigm of God-centeredness to a paradigm of self-centeredness is another shift that cuts deep. It's the shift from the group to the individual.[14] The focus on Naboth not only takes the focus off God; it also takes it off the people of Naboth, their land and history. Hard as it may be for modern people to imagine, almost everyone but ourselves takes the group rather than the self as primary.[15] The group, their history, their land, their God.

In some substantial sense, Naboth wasn't the tenant of God's land; his family was. So Ahab's sin was in part against the family to whom God had given the land four hundreds years before. In Ahab's action, Naboth's family was being scorned, as were all his ancestors to whom the land had been given, and all the land given by God, and all the history of the children of Israel.

To put it differently, the community of Israel had covenanted with God to live together in a certain way on a certain piece of land; they had been solemnly agreeing to this in elaborate ceremonies since the time of Abraham. And now Ahab was breaking covenant, betraying the relationships, polluting the land, despising his community and abandoning a way of life gravely agreed to by his family and Naboth's, his tribe and Naboth's.

But in the modern version of the story, Naboth stands alone within a violation of his inalienable, natural rights. It's Naboth and Elijah against Ahab and Jezebel: a struggle of individualistic heroes, finally won by that great individual, Elijah. Left out entirely are the social, historical, divine, territorial, ancestral and tribal contexts. Such things are irrelevant because it's a question of rights, and rights have nothing to do with such things. Rights are private, had by all and can't be lost; so what could context matter?

It's a thin story, the modern one. Not nearly enough to guide social workers in helping Vicki back to wholeness. Because Vicki doesn't need her rights; she needs a family, the family of God, stretching from Abraham to Ruth to Naboth to Jesus to Luther—to Judy and me.

Victims, Resentment and Adversaries
Out of all this grows a victim mindset.

If things aren't going well, it's more than likely not your fault; someone is violating your rights. You're a victim, and you can do little about it except fight, preferably by filing a lawsuit. If that fails, you have few options beyond self-pity and resentment.

I have a right to be as rich as anyone else, and if I'm not, I resent it. A politics of ingratitude and self-pity grows inevitably out of such story.[16] No matter how wonderful things are, they're only what I deserve, and I resent it that I don't have more, much more.

You can hear the whine a mile away. Not to mention the obsession with self.

But in the story of Jah, Naboth's land is the gift of God. Naboth's having it is God's grace, and if he remembers his story right (which Israel rarely did), he'll be grateful. Such a story provides a foundation for gratitude and thankfulness, for through it you see the graciousness of God in everything good that happens. A life of grace and joy opens out instead of a life of resentment and narrowness.

And as is often the case, when we aren't busy blaming someone else, it turns out that we can do at least a little about our situation. We may well have been wronged (Vicki certainly has been, terribly) or we may only be imagining it (she often does now), but in either case, feeling sorry for ourselves and hating those who wronged us does no good. We're responsible before Jah for what we do in the situation we've been given, and all of us can begin taking little steps to get on with life.

Jesus never treated people as victims, even poor people. He didn't lecture the poor on how terribly oppressed they were; instead, he called on them to repent of *their* sins. He denounced oppressors—but it was when he was talking to oppressors, not when he was talking to the oppressed. What's the point of talking to people about the sins of others? Talk to people about their own sins. Any other approach breeds feelings of resentment and self-righteousness, victimization and paralysis.

Killing all the grace and joy in life.

A Depersonalized Culture

What we are left with is a squabbling collection of individuals organized into impersonal corporations and impersonal bureaucracies, an adversarial society governed by a faceless legalism that tends toward litigation and force. Ours is one of the most litigious societies in history, and except for Marxist countries, one of the least personal.

Our individualism and our stress on rights and freedom have dissolved community and the personal in school, at work, in the family, everywhere. If what I want is primary, the group is secondary and probably tertiary, and if freedom and rights are paramount, the group is almost irrelevant. It would be a violation of my rights for the group to ask me to make a personal sacrifice for the sake of others.

Which in time affects the family. If my spouse won't do what I want,

I have a right to a divorce, and if I don't enjoy child care, it would be silly not to dispense with children by using my right to an abortion; after all, children limit their parents' freedom. And if a family is started, in no time they all have their own interests, and home becomes a motel with eating privileges.

One time in a gas station off an interstate, I saw the ideal American family. Mother, father, son, daughter, dog. In a Mercedes. Each listening to his or her own Walkman—except the dog. I suppose they didn't like each other's taste in music or didn't like the sense of someone else's controlling what they heard. At least they didn't have to talk to each other. In their Mercedes.

Rights and freedom and individualism, not to mention plain selfishness, are centrifugal forces weakening any group with a personal basis. By definition, the personal requires at least one I-thou relationship, and I-thou relationships only develop as people sacrifice for each other, as they give up their rights and freedom and individuality. And in a culture like ours, the very idea is unconstitutional.

But individuals can't function without each other; we need substitutes for community—impersonal substitutes, of course. So we invent depersonalized corporations to replace family businesses, and impersonal bureaucracies to replace town councils and village elders. It's no accident that modern corporations arose about the same time as modern rights: they were invented to be impersonal enough to protect owners accused of violating rights. And they had the added advantage of freeing those involved in them from feelings of responsibility and loyalty. And how about bureaucracies? When people don't know each other, how are we going to help the poor without a vast, impersonal bureaucracy to catch the cheaters?

So FIRE replaces God with narcissism; it feeds individualism; it's court-oriented, adversarial and legalistic; it encourages self-pity and resentment. As a result, a FIRE-based culture is impersonal and has little chance of meeting Vicki's needs even on a physical level, let alone on the level of the hollowness within. Such a culture will spend more time whining than serving and in time will tear itself apart, leaving a series of disintegrating self-interest groups.

FIRE acts as a solvent. It disconnects the person from history, from ancestry, from tribe, from locale, from religion, from loyalty, from family, from the call to sacrifice for others, from God. We are free, isolated . . . and empty. For we need a context in which to be filled, something larger than ourselves.

Real Freedom

That context can be found only in the biblical notion of freedom. For freedom, unlike rights and individualism, is a biblical notion. But the Bible's notion of freedom is fundamentally different from that of Vicki's social workers. As I've said, the modern notion is negative. It's the freedom not to obey George III so that you can do as you please.

So when slavery ended in the United States, former slaves got only negative freedom. Lincoln asked for forty acres and a mule for them, but Congress wouldn't agree. Not only would it have cost too much, but the Enlightenment's notion of freedom was negative. So negative freedom is all they got, leaving them free of a way to support themselves.

It would be like Moses leading the children of Israel into the wilderness—and abandoning them there. But that isn't what happened in the biblical story. There, getting the Israelites out of Egypt was only step one. God then led them to Canaan, where each family got land. God's freedom includes positive economics as well as negative politics.

But before God gave land to Israel, he did something even more important. Having gotten them out of Egypt, God didn't say, "You're free; so go do what you want." (Like social workers do with Vicki.) No, he gave them the Law; he said, "Now go do as I tell you." In the modern story, that would be bondage, but God was telling Israel how to live well, and in the biblical story, pointing people toward a life of joy and fulfillment is true freedom.

And God didn't stop even there. He also gave the children of Israel a people to live their story out with. That's almost unintelligible to us, but they were not left as a series of individuals in large impersonal cities nor as rugged individualists alone on the frontier. They were surrounded by others who shared support, defense and worship. People can't make it on their own.

But being with Vicki has made me aware that it's more than a support group we need. It's true, of course, that even if Vicki had an economic base and instructions on how to live, she would be lost without people to support her, but that understates it. Words like *family* and *mother* are key because they reach down to something deeper than consciousness, something archetypal. Vicki has been betrayed and abandoned by family and mother; perhaps she can never be whole now. But God gave Israel family and mother, husband and child, a tribe and a people. We all need that, or we're as hollow as soup cans. We can't be truly free without the family of God.

As part of this, God also gave Israel a history, a story. Modern people are becoming vaguely aware of the importance of history as we notice its role in the identity of blacks and other minorities. But in the biblical story, its importance was always known. The children of Israel aren't just given Ten Commandments without a context; the commandments start with "I am the LORD your God, who brought you out of the land of Egypt, out of the house of slavery" (Ex 20:2). The Israelites are constantly reminded of how God liberated them from Egypt and of their ancestry in Abraham, Isaac and Jacob. Their book of life, their Bible, was little more than a history. There they got the Law, not as an isolated list of rules, but as a way of life in a family that belonged to a tribe that had a land and a history.

And a God. The Ten Commandments, the history of Israel, the land— these things weren't brought into being by Israel, nor did they just happen by themselves. Rather they were brought into being by God. God guided the children of Israel, protected them, threatened them, taught them, nurtured them. And knew them each by name. An I-thou relationship. And God was someone they could revere. Someone they could look up to and trust and be loyal to. That is true freedom.[17] Our dignity isn't found in individualism or political freedom but in our dependence on God.

That's the only thing that can help Vicki with her narcissistic emptiness.

Liberty as Slavery
But that's not the basic difference between the modern idea of liberty and the biblical one. The basic difference is that, again unlike Vicki's social

workers, Jah wasn't trying to arrange things so the Israelites could do as they pleased, but so they could do as *Jah* pleased. In the Bible, *freedom* doesn't mean serving no one, and even less does it mean serving yourself. It means serving Jah.

When we read the story of the exodus, we naturally read it with modern glasses; we read it as the history of a liberation movement. But astonishingly, words like *freedom* and *liberty* don't even appear in the exodus story.[18] The famous line "Let my people go" doesn't end there. It continues, "Let my people go that they may *serve* me."[19] You see, the Israelites weren't being freed as we understand it—their master was being changed, that's all. They were going from Pharaoh as their lord and master to Jah as their lord and master.

Now when we read that the Israelites wanted to serve God, we're liable to understand that as no more than their wanting to perform religious ceremonies.[20] And the Hebrew word for *serve* can mean that, but the very same word is used throughout the story for *being a slave*. So when the children of Israel asked Pharaoh for permission to serve God, they can be understood as asking to be the slaves of God—and not the slaves of Pharaoh.

And I think that's probably how they and Pharaoh understood it. When the children of Israel got frightened, they said to Moses, "Let us alone and let us *serve* [be slaves of] the Egyptians" (Ex 14:12). They didn't want to serve God anymore. And when Pharaoh regretted having released his slaves, he said: "What have we done, letting Israel leave our *service?*" (Ex 14:5).[21]

So the essence of freedom in the Old Testament is being free to be God's slave, which of course is hard to do if you're Pharaoh's slave.

So it should be no great surprise that Moses, the great liberator, is referred to as the slave of God so often that it almost becomes a title for him.[22]

And in Leviticus 25, everyone in Israel is said to be God's slave. After limiting slavery among the children of Israel, God says the reason is that "the people of Israel are slaves to me; they are my slaves whom I brought out of Egypt: I am the Lord your God" (Lev 25:55, my translation). And again, "For they are my slaves whom I brought out of Egypt; they shall not be sold as slaves" (Lev 25:42, my translation).

In a fundamental sense, the modern notion of freedom is an illusion according to the biblical account. Human beings are never without a master. The only question is who that master is. Will we serve Pharaoh or Jahweh or ourselves? The solution isn't to strangle all the masters, as Diderot imagined—for then we would have to strangle ourselves as well. (I suspect Vicki understands this better than most of us.) The solution is to get the right master. That's what the Vicki within all of us needs. Nothing else can fill the hollowness within.

Freedom in the New Testament
The New Testament has a similar notion of freedom. Jesus says, "You cannot serve God and wealth" (Mt 6:24), implying that you are either a slave to God or to someone else. And Paul is proud of being a slave—a slave of God—and so were James, Peter, Jude and Timothy.[23] Almost all English versions translate this as "servant,"[24] but the standard dictionary of New Testament Greek says that this translation is largely confined to Bible translators![25] In other words, it's a euphemism, if not a bowdlerism: everyone else knows perfectly well that *slave* is meant here, but Bible translators can't bring themselves to say so because of our revulsion at slavery.

But in the New Testament being a slave is not a disgrace, nor is it of ultimate concern. The question of importance is who your inner master is. How to overthrow Pharaoh is not given coverage, for sin and selfishness are the lords and masters that must be overthrown.

In the Enlightenment (and in classical thought too) the tyranny of sin and self is not recognized. Human beings are basically good and can free themselves by using reason. And according to romantics, we free ourselves by following our bliss. But according to the New Testament, human beings are in such fundamental bondage that we can't get ourselves loose. We have no possibility of taking ourselves in hand because we are always going to be tripped up by sin and self. We are enslaved to sin, death, the law and principalities.[26]

But we don't need to fight our way out of bondage: our freedom has been given to us by Jesus Christ. Not that we're free in the Western sense but in the sense that we now have a good master. "You, having once been slaves of sin, . . . have become slaves of righteousness" (Rom 6:17-18). Often Paul puts it paradoxically: "You were called to freedom, brothers and sisters; only . . . through love become slaves to one another" (Gal 5:13). In the enigma of the gospel, we're free so that we'll enslave ourselves to our brothers and sisters, to righteousness, to God.[27]

We don't have to be Vickis. The one who came "to proclaim freedom to the captives" freed us by showing us how to die on a cross with nails.

How Important Is the Right to Screw Up Your Own Life?

My argument is a strange one, I acknowledge. I say we should judge a story by the lives of those who believe it. Then I say the idea of FIRE has brought liberation throughout the world, while the Christian church has done no such thing. I then proceed to reject that notion of equality and promote the story of Jah.

How can I criticize a story that has had such wonderful effects? Because that story liberated people only to leave them enslaved to self. Twice as much the children of hell as before. It left people ultimately isolated and unable to function together.

Of course, it's better for women to control their own lives than for their husbands and fathers to do it, and it's better for India to govern itself than for Britain to do it. It's better for me to govern myself than for a dictator to do it. But it may not be a whole lot better if I then think it's *good* for me to be my own king and that any claim God may make to rule me is unjust. For all the oppression the modern story has ended, it has also come as close as it's possible to come to justifying the fundamental human rebellion named sin.

I'm not suggesting a return to monarchies and other forms of white male domination. They too are usurping the role of God, just as the self wants to do. The failure of liberalism doesn't justify conservatism. But neither liberalism nor conservatism, secularism nor romanticism touches the fundamental human predicament. All they do is vary who is screwing up our lives for us.

Leaving the wrong monarch enthroned in our hearts.

Bureaucracy vs. Church

White male domination needs to be attacked, but FIRE is not a great alternative. Remember the problems over what class Vicki would be in? The difficulty was not so much viciousness or stupidity as it was the inevitable outcome of modernity.

How does a school bureaucracy deal with a Vicki? Well, the teacher has to fill out forms for the department head, who has to decide whether to pass them on to the principal, who has to decide whether to order testing by the school psychologist, who of course only comes in two days a week and has to service nine hundred kids in that time. Then comes a meeting with half a dozen expensive professionals, who send a recommendation "downtown."

Which has a problem. No money. So nothing happens till your lawyer (whom you don't know personally) calls to inquire about rights from people neither you nor she has ever met. Then "downtown" will act, because even an expensive placement costs less than a lawsuit. All completely impersonal.

That's what impersonal modernity is like. And some version of it recurs whenever we face serious health problems,[28] mental illness, institutional racism, crime or pollution. It's like talking to the wall till you threaten to sue.

But it doesn't have to be this way. People *can* form communities, what the New Testament calls churches. We can choose to worship Jah rather than ourselves. But it means giving up freedom and individuality, rights and equality. In return we get I-thou relationships. Where we know each other and care about each other. Where we rejoice with each other, cry with each other and help each other (not to mention sin against each other!). If some among us are poor, we care for them without stacks of forms and endless interviews with social workers.

To use different language, Jah's alternative to the bureaucracies of modernity is a loving, caring body, a body that takes care of its parts. In this body, "there is no longer Jew or Greek, there is no longer slave or free, there is no longer male or female; for all of you are one in Christ Jesus" (Gal 3:28). A faithful remnant. The family of God.

"All men are equal" (except for its sexism) may not seem all that different from "There is neither Jew nor Greek . . ." But it's fundamentally different in that modern people gave it a deadly twist by taking it out of its context in God. As happens so often, something good became a monster out of its proper place.

In the modern story, slaves are taught that no one has the right to be their master. But Paul approaches slavery differently. He teaches that both master and slave "have the same Master in heaven" (Eph 6:9). It's not that no one should be a master, but that God is the master of us all. And that's different.

Paul's story reaches down to the fundamental human problem of who will be master. Modern people (like most people) have answered clearly, "I am the master of my fate; I am the captain of my soul."[29] That's where we go wrong. The only answer that doesn't leave us one-dimensional is "God is the master of my fate, the captain of my soul."

The modern story goes wrong another place, too. It tends to confuse equality with sameness. In the Bible's story, Christians "are all one in Christ," but the picture is all of us being part of a body. In a body, the parts are different. A hand is not a knee is not a brain is not a muscle. This means that the parts can recognize those who are wise and can give them authority; they can recognize those who nourish the body and can enable them to pastor. The parts won't revere someone just because he claims to be a patriarch, but they will submit to righteousness they see in people's lives.

But according to the modern story, this would be dangerous and destructive.

To put it more strongly, in a body every part serves every other part, and questions of equality hardly make sense. What the Bible is teaching is mutual servanthood; what modernity is teaching is individual selfishness.

In a soup can.

I've told you the history of ideas that brought us to this point. Now let me tell you the theological story that explains why we were so willing to buy the silly, wicked ideas of modernity.

12

Castles
of Darkness,
Castles
of Wonder

n parts of this book I've probably made it sound as if our basic
problems were epistemological. Our scientific view of reason got us
entangled in secularism, which dumbed us down so much we react-
ed with various forms of romantic gibberish. So what we need is a story
that relates reason and feeling in a better way. If we do that, we'll be freed
to worship God and to become a people of depth.

Fat chance.

Our most basic problem is not our view of reason or our view of feeling,
nor is it how we relate the two. Our most basic problem is sin. Our
problems with reason and feeling are real, but they simply reflect a far more
basic problem: human beings are fallen. We have chosen darkness and
messed up all of life, even what and how we know.

According to Jesus, truth is found by turning away from our bad instincts
and our fallen self. The human predicament is simple. It's not that we aren't
rational enough or that we're too rational. It's not that we don't feel enough
or that we feel too much. It's that we have things we value more than truth.
Our predicament is that knowing the truth would require us to abandon

something we love more. Neither Descartes nor Rousseau could understand the human predicament (including the problem of knowledge) because they didn't understand the depth and severity of human sin and rebellion.

According to the story of Jah, God made a great and wonderful universe and taught us how to live in it in joy and wonder. But it meant having God as our master; so we rebelled because we wanted to be gods ourselves. We chose to serve our silly little selves (FIRE) rather than the mighty God. That's the ultimate reason we're shallow and the ultimate reason the world is a mess.

We want to be heroes, masters of our fate and of the universe. In charge. Not that we have to be anything grand, but we're sure not going to be anybody's slave. Being a good mother, succeeding in a career, finishing a book—almost anything will do as long as it gives us a sense of importance, of freedom, individualism, rights and equality.

We have a small problem, of course. We're rather flimsy creatures, neither terribly powerful nor terribly bright. A tree falling on us, a bad marriage, losing our job, the approach of old age, a silence which allows us time to think—almost anything can put an end to our dream of mastery and remind us irrevocably of our creaturely, servile status. Defeat is always just around the corner. As is death. Opus, the penguin in "Bloom County," once commented, "Men fear solitude as they fear silence because both give them a glimpse of the terror of life's nothingness."[1]

So to keep going, we lie to ourselves. Not only random lies that we develop on the spot to avoid particular unpleasant truths but vast, carefully structured lies around which we build our lives. And we do that not only as individuals but as cultures. Individually and culturally, we build our lives on lies and self-deception. On false stories. On bad faith. Imaginative intellectual constructs. Lying life projects. Life lies. Culture lies. Lies with which we can blind ourselves to the obvious truths that mock our pretensions.

Among these culture lies are rationalism, romanticism, FIRE, *Pretty Woman*, *Kindergarten Cop*, career, family, capitalism, communism and all the other stories by which we hide from Jah. Our basic problem is not any particular story or our reaction to any particular story; rather our problem is our preference for lying stories.

As Graham Greene commented on Mexican communists many years ago, "The supporters of the proletarian revolution have staked their lives on a philosophy. . . . You cannot expect them to admit even to themselves that Russia has proved them wrong—or Mexico—without the conversion to some other faith. Nobody can endure existence without a philosophy."[2] The question is, what philosophy will we accept: the truth of Jah or some silly lie?

If we're to think straight and live deeply, we need better stories than rationalism and romanticism and *Pretty Woman*. But the lying stories aren't the main problem; they're merely among the forms the problem shows itself in, among the darknesses we hide behind. If we show rationally (or romantically) that one story is a lie, most people just adopt another lie. Since the lie of communism became clear in the Eastern bloc, most of the population seems to have bought into capitalism or nationalism.

We have chosen castles of darkness. We love these castles, and we protect them with whatever lies and darkness are necessary.[3]

Culture Lies

When I was just out of high school, the Soviets claimed they had shot down an American spy plane. President Eisenhower dismissed it as nonsense. When the Soviets proceeded to say that the pilot had been supposed to swallow poison if captured, I thought they had hyperactive imaginations. It was a silly story and Ike wouldn't lie, I knew that much.

Then the Soviets produced the pilot and the plane.

Ike was a liar. Within a few years it became obvious to me and to most Americans that our foreign affairs depend on lying. Thirty years later, when an American correspondent was arrested in the Soviet Union for spying, people didn't know what to believe. Washington denied that he was a spy, but by then we'd read John Le Carré and knew that was what Washington would say whether it was true or not. If we decided he was innocent, it wasn't because Washington (or Moscow or London or New Delhi) said so. All of which is to say that lying is a matter of government policy.

(Meanwhile, Christians argue whether the state is obligated to follow the

Sermon on the Mount as if we were arguing a real question. But in fact even the best governments don't follow the Ten Commandments or the most rudimentary moral standards, let alone the Sermon on the Mount.)

Lies infect our very language. One of the oldest stories around is the story of Babel (Gen 11), and part of its point is that language can be used to confound communication. That has been said best for our culture in George Orwell's novel *1984*. There the Ministry of Truth devises new words and forbids old ones in the hope of making it impossible even to say certain things. It's called Newspeak.

Our government's language is not yet Newspeak, but neither is it noted for its ability to reveal truth. Making fun of the language of bureaucrats is a standard form of radical chic. However, the usual implication is that bureaucrats are nearly illiterate, and that's radically naive.[4] The problem is not so much that they speak English badly but that they speak the language of deceit well. Gobbledygook is not just the language of turkeys but also of those who crave darkness because their deeds are evil. The language of you and me, not to mention of the politicians we elect.

I don't mean that people who know the truth speak the language of Babel to keep others in the dark. Lying is worse than that; we lie mainly to keep ourselves in the dark. Those who babble usually don't know what they mean themselves. Which breeds utter darkness and makes it impossible even for the babblers to find the way.

That's why one of the marks of evil is its dull stupidity. Evil people blind themselves so they will never have to see the light. Watergate was at least as stupid as it was evil. Which I say not to excuse the evil but to explain the stupidity. To read the transcripts of the Watergate tapes is to read the conversation of morons. And yet they were brilliant men—who had built a castle of darkness that confounded them: "They became futile in their thinking, and their senseless minds were darkened. Claiming to be wise, they became fools" (Rom 1:21-22).

C. S. Lewis portrays this beautifully and terribly in *The Last Battle*. As the world ends, a group of dwarfs are thrown into a stable that turns out to be paradise. But the dwarfs find this unbelievable and continue to experience it as a stable. Like the men of the Enlightenment, they're not going to be taken in by any humbug.

And so they are in darkness. When Lucy gives one of them wild violets to smell, he thinks she's rubbing stable litter in his face. And on, and on. "They are so afraid of being taken in that they cannot be taken out."[5] We see what we want to see, what we presuppose, what we've blinded our eyes to allow in.

We often think of evil as beautiful, but in *Perelandra* Lewis portrays its ugliness and folly. In it, the evil one goes around torturing frogs for the sake of torturing them. He doesn't even enjoy it; it's just a way of passing time. On the surface he has great designs, a plan for the universe on the scale of God's, but deep within there is nothing but dark "puerility, an aimless, empty spitefulness, content to sate itself with the tiniest cruelties."[6]

The Song of Roland

The Song of Roland is one of the classic stories of medieval chivalry.[7] It was a primary lie by which the military class of that culture was indoctrinated into putting glory and honor above safety and compassion. Dying honorably in combat was so glorious that men were willing to fight against any odds without regard for the justice of the cause, the wisdom of the battle or the effect of their death on their loved ones.

In the story, Charlemagne is retreating from the Saracens, and he puts Roland in charge of the rear guard. When a large force attacks the rear, Roland refuses to blow the trumpet for help, because he wants the glory of battle even if it means death for himself and his men. At the end, defeated and bleeding, Roland heroically blows the trumpet to warn the main army, and just as he finishes, his dearest friend, Oliver, accidentally strikes him down.

Or so the story goes.

Graham Greene offers another version, one that has the ring of truth. He suggests that when the Saracens were spotted, Oliver tried to persuade Roland to blow the trumpet, but Roland was a big, boasting fool and refused because he was more concerned about his own glory than about the lives of his men or the victory of his faith. Outraged by the needless slaughter and risk of the faith, Oliver deliberately killed him at the end.[8]

But this version of the story didn't fly in the courts of the barons where the minstrels sang. The barons didn't give a rip about the faith and often wanted their knights to fight recklessly. So the truth was tidied up, and a silly, evil lie was elevated to a central cultural role to prop up the darkness of violence and exploitation so loved by Charlemagne and his barons (not to mention by the Arnold Schwarzeneggers of modernity).

It happens all the time. Julia Ward Howe's Mother's Day Against War was tidied up into Mother's Day for Hallmark Cards. Failure at work is tidied up into persecution by the boss. The Bible's clear commitment to the poor is tidied up into a defense of the status quo. Fear caused by a deep sense of separation from ultimate reality is tidied up into any number of phobias and neuroses treatable by pills and therapists. A job needed to keep food on the table is tidied up into a heroic career to give us meaning and importance so we won't have to face the emptiness of life. Insane hatred of Jews is tidied up into a holy cause to save the Aryan people. A midlife crisis, when we're about to notice the truth about ourselves and reality, is tidied up into a psychological event that we need to be sheltered from.

We build our lives on lies.

Jesus
At least, that's what Jesus said.

Most of us admit to some self-deception, of course, but we think that most mistaken opinion is just that—a mistake. If someone accepts a false story, it isn't a deliberate choice, but an accident, an error, maybe a misunderstanding. So according to rationalists, truth is calculated rather the way a computer calculates its answers, only we human beings aren't very good computers and sometimes miscalculate. Or according to romantics, truth is intuited or felt, and sometimes we intuit wrong.

But for Jesus, truth isn't so much calculated or miscalculated, intuited or misintuited. For him, as for any prophet, truth is accepted or rejected. If people don't accept the truth, they're willfully rejecting it—refusing it because it threatens them and their interests. It's their choice. That doesn't mean that calculating and feeling are unimportant in the pursuit of truth, but it does mean that it's rare for failure at either of them to be the heart of the problem. The heart of the problem is that we don't want to know the truth; we prefer our lying life projects, personal and cultural. So we refuse. We refuse to calculate well. We refuse to feel deeply.[9]

One time when Jesus was talking about truth, the Pharisees started to argue with him. He didn't engage them in a philosophical discussion about the nature of truth. This is not Plato debating his opponents. No, Jesus said, "Why do you not understand what I say? It is because you cannot bear to hear my word" (Jn 8:43 RSV). The reason people are ignorant of truth is that it costs too much.

But Jesus doesn't stop there. He locates the problem in deceit: "You belong to your father, the devil, and you want to carry out your father's desire. . . . There is no truth in him. When he lies, he speaks his native language, for he is a liar and the father of lies" (Jn 8:44 NIV). For Jesus, the opposite of truth isn't falsehood or miscalculation; it's lying. And those who reject truth aren't just mistaken; they're liars. They're deceiving themselves—not by accident but so that they won't have to hear the truth. So that they can be free individuals with rights and equality. Gods. Whose native language is lying.

According to Jesus anyway.

"*Because* I tell the truth, you do not believe me" (Jn 8:45 RSV).

Paul says that God's "eternal power and divine nature" are plain "because God has made it plain." If people don't know the truth, it's because they "suppress the truth by their wickedness" (Rom 1:18-20 NIV). He even says that Gentiles who are without the law have it "written on their hearts" (Rom 2:14-15). According to Paul anyway.

And in both John and Paul, truth is regularly connected with light, which is readily available, and falsehood with darkness (which is presumably also readily available). It's light that makes things plain, and Jesus came as the light of the world to make plain the truth of God. If we don't know the truth, it's because we choose darkness and refuse to walk in the light; it's because we love darkness rather than light.[10]

When Paul says that what may be known about God is plain (Rom 1:19), the word for "plain" comes from the word for "light." It could almost be translated, "What is known about God is in the light because God has put it in the light."

What we need to know, God has put in the light. Our job is not so much to figure it out as to stop running from it. As the psalmist asked, "How long will you love vain words, and seek after lies?" (Ps 4:2). The path to truth is not as much reasoning better or feeling better as softening our hearts so that we can receive truth better. Our task is to stop following our lying life projects so that we can follow truth wherever it leads. Until then, there's not much point in hearing the truth.[11]

The soil of our hearts is not ready.

Kristallnacht

But if someone is wrong about something, isn't it normally just a mistake, an accidental miscalculation? For those of us educated in Campbell's Soup cans and romanticist feelings, Jesus is profoundly offensive here. Whatever happened to modern liberal tolerance?[12] Jesus sounds like those heartless fundamentalists who think that anyone who disagrees with a single word they say is of the devil.

But remember the tired question of whether average Germans knew what was happening to Jews during World War II? It makes Jesus' meaning intelligible. Of course, the average German didn't know the details of how many Jews were being killed or the full horrors of how they were being tortured. However, everyone knew how Jews were mistreated on *Kristall-nacht*, that Jews were being deported, that the government spewed out an idiotic mythology of anti-Semitism, that Hitler had written about a final solution. Which is enough.

Suppose that the grand vizier of the Ku Klux Klan were elected president of the United States, that he had clearly written what he intended to do, that the possessions of blacks were thrown out into the streets and that blacks were sent away in cattle cars. Could white Americans then say, "But we didn't know he was *killing* them"?

No, if we don't know it, it's because we *refuse* to put together the evidence, not because we *fail* to put it together. We are self-deceivers.

And even if we were to allow that a few people might with integrity fail to put the pieces together, it would be irrelevant. Irrelevant because what they did know would be enough. I can hear it now: "Well, I thought the Klan was just taking their possessions, stirring up hatred and herding them off like animals. I didn't know they were doing anything serious . . ."

That is lying. Self-deception.

To change the example, it may be true that on average, privileged people don't know about the forty thousand poor kids dying daily. But that's not the question. The question is, *why* don't we know? We don't know because we don't want to know: if we knew we'd have to change how we live.

Which would be inconvenient. Knowing is contrary to our perceived self-interest. We lie so we can feel free to sit in front of the TV gobbling up garbage and saying, "How was I supposed to know about the forty thousand?"

Enough Is Enough

Jesus told a story about a rich man in hell who looked into paradise and saw a beggar named Lazarus. Now the rich man had known Lazarus in life and refused to help him. That's apparently the reason he was in hell. So the rich man asked Abraham to send Lazarus to warn his brothers of the importance of helping the poor, but Abraham refused: " 'They have Moses and the prophets; they should listen to them.' [The rich man] said, 'No, father Abraham; but if someone goes to them from the dead, they will repent.' [Abraham] said to him, 'If they do not listen to Moses and the prophets, neither will they be convinced even if someone rises from the dead' " (Lk 16:29-31).

Abraham is saying that the brothers have all the evidence they need, and if they still don't believe, no amount of further evidence will help. Enough is enough.

At some point we have the evidence we need to make the necessary connections and take the necessary actions. To demand more evidence then is a game, a delaying tactic called self-deception. What is needed is to own the sin that is keeping us from changing our intellectual constructs.

I frequently speak in middle-class churches on Third World poverty and Jesus' teaching about money. The response is, uh, interesting. Even allowing that much of what I say may be wrong, I don't get the feeling that people are hungering for truth: they're defending how they live.

If I were advocating bottled rats' breath as a cure for colds, my message would sell better. In that case what I was saying would be obviously false, but it would be acceptable because the cost would be slight. Which is what we want. People don't like crosses.

In all the years I've gone around lecturing on such topics, I've only encountered one person with the guts to say, "I think you're right about what Jesus says about money, but I like my possessions a lot; so I reject you and Jesus." I liked that person. I suspect she was closer to the kingdom than many who consider themselves Christians. She at least was not a liar.

When confronted by truth that we don't like, we rarely face it openly. We don't say, "I don't like that truth, but I'll follow it anyway." We don't even say, "I don't like that truth, and I'm not going to do it." Instead we rationalize; we say, "That's not true, so I won't do it." Which is to say, we lie—to ourselves and to anyone who will listen. We are liars who serve the father of lies. While imagining we're free, we have in fact chosen a cruel and lying master.

Jesus' analysis is harsh, but if you know anything about human nature, including your own, you know it's not far from right. I think it was Eugene O'Neill who said, "As the history of humanity shows, the truth has absolutely nothing to do with anything."

Freud, Marx and Jesus

And remember that psychology, sociology and existentialism have come to the same conclusion as Jesus. Bad faith is a central category for Sartre and other existentialists,[13] and Freud had names for the ways we try to fend off truth—rationalizing, projecting, sublimating, compartmentalizing, and on and on. He called them ego-defense mechanisms. They are forms of self-deception that we use to defend ourselves against truth.

And Marx suggested that we develop whole ideologies (story systems) to persuade ourselves that reality fits our class interests. And even now that Marx is largely discredited, sociology still has as one of its fundamental presuppositions that he was right on this topic. Lying to suit our class interests has become a whole area of study called the sociology of knowledge.[14]

But a couple of thousand years before Sartre and Freud and Marx, Jesus knew all about it. He called it lying. It's as simple as that. And as difficult. I know it's offensive, but the biblical teaching is that people believe whoever their master is, and those who don't believe Jesus have the father of lies as their master.

The truth of Jah we cannot bear.

Ultimately, that's why things like Campbell's Soup cans are the icons of our culture rather than Rembrandt's portrait of himself crucifying Jesus. We can't bear the truth about how we keep choosing to crucify God. We'd rather be hollow.

And pretend we're God.

A Wonderful Corollary
All this may seem depressing, but it's really anything but.

If self-deception is what keeps us from truth, then it follows that we can have the truth simply by stopping lying to ourselves. Truth is accessible to anyone who wants it badly enough. Ignorance and low IQ aren't the problem; self-created illusion is. We know as much as we need to know—but we hide it from ourselves so we can hold on to the pathetic lies we live by, our favorite bits of garbage.

In almost all epistemologies, truth is accessible only to experts. Rationalists think finding truth requires intelligence, education and advanced technology; romantics think it requires an artist's soul capable of maintaining passionate feelings. In either case, it's the province of specially gifted people whose almost occult skills go beyond what ordinary people can dream of. But according to Jesus, truth is there for anyone who genuinely wants it: "Search, and you will find" (Mt 7:7).

Of course, it's not that Mandarin and quantum mechanics become easy if you seek them. They're not the sort of thing Jesus was talking about. He was talking about wisdom. But wisdom is accessible to us all.

In Proverbs, wisdom is portrayed as standing in a busy street loudly calling everyone to come, but people don't listen because they "love being simple" and "hate knowledge" (see Prov 1:20-33). God "stores up sound wisdom for the upright" (Prov 2:7), and to get it, all you have to do is "seek it like silver" (Prov 2:4).

I think it was Mark Twain who said, "It's not the parts of the Bible I don't understand that bother me; it's the parts I do understand." And there you have it. We all understand a lot of things—a lot of things we don't act on. All we have to do is live what we already know, and we'll find wisdom. That's the key. That's how we stop lying to ourselves. We don't know everything, maybe we don't even know much, but as we do as much as we know, we're given all the wisdom we need. As we put truth into practice in our lives, more and more truth comes into the light.

In the Western tradition, truth is the kind of thing you know intellectually. But in the Bible, it's also the kind of thing you do. If you don't do it, you soon don't know it even intellectually, and if you do do it, wisdom increases.[15] Truth isn't just in the head; it's also in the feet, in the choices we make, in the lives we lead.

And so are lies and soup cans.

The Offered Choice

Here we arrive at one of the central issues in modern thought. It's another version of the old debate between rationalists and romantics, a version with immense consequences. We're usually given two choices: Is truth the sort of thing that corresponds to reality and that we can figure out rationally and store in our heads? Or is it a matter of the heart in which questions of "objective" reality are irrelevant as long as our hearts are passionate?

That's the topic for the next chapter.

13

The Wild Truth:
Thomas Jefferson,
Malcolm X & Jesus
the Servant King

A few years ago, I was teaching arithmetic to welfare mothers in Watts. In order to complete my certification in adult education, I took a course at UCLA. In one session, the teacher asked us to choose partners and close our eyes. He then went around and put a rock in each person's hands. With our eyes still closed, we were supposed to describe the rock to our partner and then tell how the whole experience made us feel. The idea was that this would be a good icebreaker for us to use in the classes we taught.

I was laughing so hard I was unable to describe the rock to my partner (she taught massage), but I *was* able to tell her how the experience made me feel. I told her that at first it made me angry because I didn't see how it was going to help me teach arithmetic to welfare mothers, but I wasn't angry any longer because I realized that the experience would save me thousands in medical bills: anytime I got anxious, I could snap myself out of it merely by contemplating passing out rocks to my students.

I learned nothing in that class that helped me teach adults who lived anywhere but the Beverly Hillses of this world (UCLA is a short drive by

Porsche from Rodeo Drive), but it was an invaluable lesson on modernity, or at least on Southern California. It doesn't matter what you have in your hands; it only matters how it makes you feel. Objective reality is insignificant.

Battleships or Ocean Beaches?

In another session, the teacher asked us to come up one at a time to his desk, where he showed us a large picture with all but one small part covered up. We were then asked to write down what we thought the whole picture was. Each of us was shown a different part of the picture, and we wrote down quite a number of different things we thought it was. One person thought it was the beach, another a broadcasting antenna, another a forest. It was in fact a picture of a battleship close to a wooded shore.

The teacher didn't use this to argue that you're silly to jump to factual conclusions with little evidence, or that you should be humble in presenting your views because you may not have the whole picture, or that disagreements are natural since we see from different points of view. And he most certainly didn't say that through dialogue we could come closer to truth. All of that I would have agreed with, at least to some extent.

But no, he used his object lesson to assert that all truth is relative (or perhaps that there is no such thing as truth; he seemed not to distinguish those two statements, and on that he was perhaps right). He said that truth is not Truth, only truth for me and truth for you. He proceeded to tell us in no uncertain terms that we must not imagine we have the answers, that real education is a dialogue of equals and not indoctrination by a teacher, that education is not a matter of the intellect but of the gut. We were to be delighted if students had a wide range of views: it would produce interesting discussions and might open minds.

Jesus and Rodeo Drive

I asked him whether that meant I should have a dialogue of equals with a student who said two plus two equaled five. He assured me that it didn't but that it did mean I should treat all students with respect. I agreed but suggested he was also saying that "two plus two equals four" was true for me and perhaps for him, but not necessarily for all my students. He laughed cheerfully and said that all truth is relative, even what he was saying; so it didn't bother him if it didn't apply to arithmetic, because he wasn't an arithmetic teacher.

I suppose he meant that he had the truth for him, teaching education a few minutes from Rodeo Drive; now I had to find truth for me, teaching arithmetic a few light-years away in Watts.

I didn't say it, but I couldn't help wondering if that wasn't exactly what Hitler had done. Found truth *for him*. Of course, that wasn't truth for Jews. But that's OK because truth is relative.

And I wonder if a few years ago George Bush wasn't finding truth for himself while Saddam Hussein was finding truth for himself. Unfortunately, it meant the people of Iraq had to start finding graves for themselves.

Truth as Correspondence vs. Truth for Me
We are caught here between two views of truth. The dictionary says, *"Truth is most commonly used to mean correspondence with facts or to what actually occurred."*[1] So for Western people (most of whom are probably still in the secular, rationalist tradition), truth is accurate statements of facts—like Columbus found the Americas in 1492 or Salem is the capital of Oregon.

How boring. How impoverished and impoverishing.

As usual, secular rationalism takes one legitimate dimension, focuses on it and makes us forget all other dimensions. In its imperialism, it squeezes everything else out of us, leaving us much the poorer.

Which almost requires the romantic reaction. For romantics, like my teacher at UCLA, truth is what you feel; it's truth *for you*, and there's no claim that it corresponds to anything out there. So if you're studying a text, what the author meant or what the words mean is an unimportant abstraction; all that matters is what it means to you. Reading is a tool for self-discovery, and what the author was trying to do with the writing is relatively unimportant.

It doesn't matter what you have in your hands; it only matters how it makes you feel.

I can see it now. Jesus meets a nice young man on Rodeo Drive, and they have a nice talk in which Jesus tells him to sell his possessions and move out of the Regent Beverly Wilshire. Afterward, the disciples ask Jesus what he meant by what he said, and he replies, "It doesn't matter what I meant as long as that nice young man got something out of it for himself. Your job is not to worry about my exact words but to get something out of it for yourselves."

If he had said that, the disciples would have been greatly relieved and would doubtless have doubled their contributions to the Jewish United Way. And in doing so they would have abandoned all Jesus was about.

Jesus' exact meaning matters.

That meaning, however, can't rightly be reduced to an intellectual abstraction or a list of facts. That's what romantics hate: getting stuck on the level of abstractions and information (correspondence) and never getting to personal meaning. And they're right. If we don't get to meaning for us, we haven't gotten anyplace. Their mistake is failing to grasp that sometimes facts (what corresponds to reality) have personal meaning, meaning for us. And if we get those facts wrong, we get the wrong meaning for us—and ruin our lives. Generally Jesus' exact meaning has a meaning for me; what he was trying to do with his words can be applied to me.

We don't have to choose between a rock and how it makes us feel, between truth as correspondence and truth for me. They're integrally connected, and we can keep both. In fact, we must.[2]

Minority Studies

This crass statement of the view by my teacher isn't respectable anymore, at least not in literary criticism or technical philosophy, but some version of it that amounts to nearly the same thing has been accepted by just about everyone in academia when it comes to ethics, aesthetics and religion. Even rationalists accept it in those areas. After all, values can't be measured objectively except as cultural customs; so anything more than that must just be feelings. Except as customs, right and wrong correspond only to what's in me.[3]

Anthropology and sociology have made it abundantly clear that different groups and tribes have different ethics. A group develops customs, and in order to protect its way of life it soon persuades itself that those customs are moral duties. Customs relative to a culture are soon seen as absolutes for everyone everywhere: short hair on men, bras on women, not eating dog meat, arriving at a precise time, not belching after a good meal, not having sex with someone else's spouse. So the belief that some things are universally wrong and that something independent of yourself corresponds to them is merely ethnocentric insistence on the customs of your particular culture.

And this view is often accepted in departments of minority studies in our universities. Which is natural because the works and customs of dead white European males (DWEMs) have been enshrined in education as absolute values, ethnocentric as that obviously is. Standard curriculums consist almost entirely of DWEM poems, DWEM battles, DWEM philosophies, DWEM achievements, DWEM music. The history and achievements of African-Americans, Latinos, women and everyone else not white and male are ignored. They are valueless.

White males control the curriculum; so they focus on Thomas Jefferson, Beethoven, Plato, Shakespeare, Rembrandt and Homer while overlooking Malcolm X, Duke Ellington, Buddha, Pablo Neruda, Hokusai and Native American mythology. And the majority who aren't white and male (called minorities, oddly enough) are supposed to like it.

Only they have rebelled. Hence, minority study programs. Not everything worthwhile was done by DWEMs. Soul music is as great as classical, and Indonesian shadow puppetry as great as Western drama, and African-American English is as good as white English, and it's all cultural. There is no truth, only truth for African-Americans, truth for women. Aesthetic and historical values are all relative.

Except relativity. Which is absolute. So ethnocentric art is absolutely bad. And that means literature assuming unliberated women is bad (which is all DWEM literature, from Moses and Homer on). And it means that Wagner's anti-Semitism makes not only the man bad but also his music. And since standard history is DWEM history (in its ethnocentrism it deals mostly with white rulers and their battles), it too is bad.

Liberal Tolerance in a Diverse Culture

Accepting this sort of relativity is a moral duty in a free society, or so tolerant liberals tell us. This is especially true in a free society with diverse cultures. The sexual practices and music of Samoans are as good as those of DWEMs. The alternative (a correspondence theory of values) produces ethnocentric chauvinism. I mean, if you think values correspond to reality, then it's a small step to supposing that *your* values correspond to reality. To put it differently, it's a small step to supposing that your story is right and everyone else's is wrong and terrible. Which is what produces the racist cultural absolutism that canonizes everything Greek, British and German while demeaning everything Samoan, indigenous and female.

By contrast, moral relativity makes room for the variety and mixture of stories found in our multicultural society. Openness

is the great insight of our times. The true believer is the real danger. The study of history and culture teaches that all the world was mad in the past; men always thought they were right, and that led to wars, persecutions, slavery, xenophobia, racism, chauvinism. The point is not to correct the mistakes and really be right; rather it is not to think you are right at all.[4]

Throughout this book I argue that if truth is relative, then it's no big deal that Hitler killed Jews by the millions and that therefore relativism can't possibly be true. However, these liberals reply that there is a prior step. They claim that if Germans had understood that truth was relative, Hitler would never have been able to whip Germans up to kill Jews in the first place. Racists and chauvinists firmly believe they're right: that's their justification for discrimination and violence. So our task is to understand, not to be right and not to judge, especially not to judge crossculturally. Or so they say.

If Germans hadn't judged Jews, there would have been no Holocaust. What Germans needed to do was read stories and see movies about Jews so that they could feel with them. They needed to learn to empathize and abandon all ideas of one culture corresponding to the good and others to the bad. Their mistake was being closed, where "closed" means thinking that someone somewhere might be right about something.

The alternative to tolerance is terrible, or so they say: it's to be sectarian and tribal (like Hitler and me). Then you have to see to it that all people accept one story (the right story, your story), and you think that those who don't are undermining civilization, causing riots in Los Angeles and committing themselves and their children to shallow, empty lives. They're evil monsters refusing the light.

The Neoconservative Counterattack

"The greatest single threat to America is secular relativism."[5] That's one of the war cries of right-wing intellectuals, who are partial to a correspondence theory of truth. Bashing secular humanism ("Man is the [relative] measure of all things") has long been faddish with them.

Their attack was given a big boost by Allan Bloom in *The Closing of the American Mind.* His most effective critique emotionally is that relativism requires giving the imprimatur to Hindus' burning live widows along with their husbands' bodies.

He also illustrates how relativism adds to the shallowness stressed in this book. When modern people, including educated modern people, "talk about heaven and earth, the relations between men and women, parents and children, the human condition, I hear nothing but cliches, superficialities, the material of satire."[6] And "it was not necessarily the best of times when Catholics and Protestants were suspicious of and hated one another; but at least they were taking their beliefs seriously, and the more or less satisfactory accommodations they worked out were not simply the result of apathy about their souls."[7]

Even more important logically, Bloom points out that if relativists are to be consistent in their tolerance of other cultures, they must be tolerant of ethnocentrism when found in other cultures (which it always is). In other words, if relativists are to be consistent, they have to deny relativism.

Relativism is radically incoherent.

Supplementary Vitamins from the Story of Jah

All of which seems to me to be a decisive case against relativism. Its conclusions are morally outrageous and obviously contradictory. If it's to be at all consistent, it has to accept not only ethnocentrism and widows' being burned alive, but also female circumcision, purdah, women getting all of the work and none of the glory, apartheid and everything else that has ever become standard in any culture. It has to say that the Sisters of Charity are no better than the Gestapo—they just have different customs.

But minority studies departments exist out of a strong moral sense of the terrible injustice and wrongness of teaching DWEM history as history and DWEM literature as literature—and they're right. But it's tragic and ironic that they often wind up combating the injustice by teaching that there's no such thing as justice and injustice, right and wrong. If Martin Luther King Jr. had believed that, he'd still be alive and well, living in a segregated Atlanta.

If truth is relative, why on earth do relativists attack sectarians with such moral fervor?[8] If truth is relative, then truth is relative, and how can relativists go off on moralistic campaigns against ethnocentrism or oppression of minorities?

The reason is that down deep they know that some truth isn't relative; they know they're wrong. They know that racism and wars and chauvinism and persecution of those who think differently are wrong, and they want to fight them. To put it differently, the story of relativism is so unsatisfactory to anyone human that even its advocates naturally fall back on values that correspond to reality.

As Rookmaaker says, in discussing

"one-dimensional man," there is one thing we must never forget. Man will always remain human because he cannot change his own basic created being, whatever he thinks of himself. He can never get away from his place that was assigned to him in the fullness of the created universe. . . . He knows that he is more than an atom—or a rabbit. And so he wants to escape from the box [that the Enlightenment put him in], even if the principles of his own philosophy deny him the possibility of doing so.[9]

That is, secularists and others supplement their story from the story of Jah. The hollow spot within cries out for moral standards, and so minorities (and everyone else) add moral standards to their story even if it contradicts their overall framework.

Racism Justified?

But a natural conclusion from this argument is that minority studies are bad and that the standard study of history and literature is fine. And something like that is what neoconservatives tend to conclude. Their reasons vary, but somehow Jefferson and Homer always turn out to be more important than Malcolm X and Neruda.

One reason given is that the people of a nation have to be able to discourse with each other about questions of importance, and to do that they have to have a reasonably common heritage. So we should all study Jefferson and Homer so that we'll have common points of reference. This is the price of being an American. Any country without a common heritage, a civil religion, is doomed.[10]

If WASP Americans study WASP history, African-Americans study black history, Chinese-Americans study Chinese history and Armenian-Americans study Armenian history, how do we get a common framework in which to make decisions about our common good? Won't we disintegrate into competing self-interest groups like in Lebanon or South Central Los Angeles? There people sometimes literally don't even have a common language. Public education soon becomes impossible—along with all but the most local government. Relativism, designed to combat sectarianism, soon turns into an extreme form of sectarianism.

This is not a silly argument.

Of course, it's kind of hard on African-Americans, Latinos and women.

A Way Out

Once again, we're caught in a false dichotomy. We're caught between relativism and dogmatism, between mush and racism, between two varieties of sectarianism. What'll it be, a mindless, contradictory compassion for others that splinters any country with more than one cultural group, or a heartless, ethnocentric correspondence theory that encourages white males to oppress everyone else? Either choice is fatal.

After high school, I was an exchange student in a British school, and I experienced mild ethnocentrism. Some of my friends clearly thought I didn't speak English well (my accent and idiom weren't just interesting variants on theirs). And they thought that American government was inferior. Which was odd, because I knew that our constitution was the best ever and that Ike was better than Macmillan. Besides, they found it odd how strongly I disliked their class system.

I could have concluded from this that all views and practices are merely customary and that the notion of truth is meaningless. Or I could have concluded that the British are ignorant louts and that everything American was better than anything British. Those are the choices we're offered—relativistic tolerance and ethnocentric dogmatism.

But except in anthropology departments and some departments of minority studies, there's an obvious third possibility: humbly searching for truth. And that doesn't necessitate chauvinism or racism, dogmatism or violence. You acknowledge you don't know everything while continuing to search for better ways of doing things and trying to persuade others of your views.

That may seem impossible to anthropologists, whose story offers limited tools for the job, but most stories give ways of sorting out the good from the bad from the indifferent. Utilitarians do it by sorting out what causes pleasure and what causes pain. Evangelicals do it by sorting out what the Bible itself mandates and what is merely added on by the culture.

Often this process isn't even hard: nobody's accent is better, both forms of government have advantages and disadvantages, and the English class system is even worse than the American. Other times, of course, distinguishing between custom and morality is difficult or impossible. (How, for example, is Western time-orientation to be evaluated compared to Yapese event-orientation?[11]) Custom and morality are extensively intertwined, and sometimes it may take years even to understand the role something has in a culture. And the subtle ways a good story empowers a culture's customs and a bad story twists them can make it hard to evaluate them even when you do understand them.[12]

After all, truth may be absolute, but our human grasp of it isn't. A valid part of the argument of my teacher at UCLA was that we finite human beings never have the whole picture.[13] Without doubt, we see things from our own perspective (which is made worse by our being fallen and twisted), and our knowledge is substantially the imaginative construct of our selves and our culture. So since our grasp of truth isn't absolute, we should tolerate a good deal of ambiguity and uncertainty.

And our human application of absolute truth isn't absolute either. Our grasp of truth has to be applied case by case. During the race riots in the 1960s, I quit graduate school (where I was trying to write a dissertation on moral absolutes) and went to edit *The Other Side*. I needed to quit, but my belief in moral absolutes doesn't mean I think everyone needs to quit academia. The truth has to be applied to different situations and different people in different ways.

I suppose you could say that being in academia is truth for some people, while leaving it was truth for me. I don't like that language because of its meaning in the modern story, but I won't quarrel over words providing we agree that undergirding and joining both those truths is Truth for us all: that racism is always and everywhere evil, that we can't just be concerned for ourselves and our own kind, that we must tear down walls with our own bodies. These truths are absolute truths, truths to which we must all bend our selves, truths which do not depend on my feelings and perceptions. But applying them is a complex and (in a sense) relative matter.

We need to learn about our relative grasp of truth without falling into relativism, without becoming disabled when confronted by crucial moral issues. It's murderous to suppose that customs are moral absolutes, but it's also murderous to suppose that moral absolutes are mere customs. Killing Jews is not just an old German custom; it's murder.

After all, if we say that nothing is good or bad in any culture but only different, then cultures can't learn from each other. And in the mishmash of cultures that is increasingly the United States, that produces paralysis. Calling everything merely different is like trying to patch up a marriage without asking either person to change. We need not only to respect our differences but also to learn from them, to change. Time-oriented folks need to learn from people-oriented folks, and vice versa. And white male culture must learn from other cultures how we oppress them—that's how to bring reconciliation and depth in the collision of cultures that is our time.

So we must sharpen the distinction between custom and morality, not break it down. We must learn the glories of minority cultures and the horrors of DWEM cultures, and that's only meaningful if we distinguish between custom and culture. We must be able to say that racism is taboo no matter how integral to the culture and that love is mana no matter how foreign to the culture. But we must also be able to avoid saying that eating dog meat is evil or that all cultures need a bicameral legislature.

That doesn't mean you coerce those who don't agree. It doesn't justify the Inquisition or witch hunts in Salem, Massachusetts, or Washington, D.C. It doesn't always justify imposing your views through legislation. But it does require you to invite people to accept your story. So those of us committed to the story of Jah need to invite everyone to be committed to it and transformed by it.

Relativists correctly want us to avoid being like the Briton of whom George Bernard Shaw had Caesar say, "He is a barbarian and thinks that the customs of his tribe and island are the laws of nature."[14] But we must also avoid being the sort of person of whom someone might say, "He is a modern person and thinks the laws of Jah are the customs of a tribe and island."

Pie à la Mode
Near the end of the period in that class at UCLA, an African-American woman asked the teacher about Martin Luther King Jr. and the marches he led against segregation. Were the evils of Jim Crow laws relative? He thought they proved his point. Jim Crow laws were now "outmoded," he said, made that way by King's heroic action. Outmoded? *Outmoded!* You mean that at one time they were in mode? That in the 1940s perhaps they were good laws? That whether you have segregationist laws is kind of like whether you put ice cream on your pie? Sort of a question of style?

But the teacher had chosen his word carefully. In a morally relative universe, the strongest possible term of moral disapproval is something like *outmoded.*[15] But then risking your life for someone else is outmoded. If nothing is really right or really wrong, then devote yourself to self-protection.

There are no higher causes to give yourself to; the only thing that matters is what you want. But you can't get very passionate even about that, because nothing is any bigger than you, and you aren't very big. If feelings are all, are anyone's feelings big enough to get excited about? If nothing is really true, can anything be important enough to bother about? So hallucinogens become important, and sex becomes central, because what else is there but feelings? *My* feelings, to be precise. Gradually everything dribbles out, and we have to spend billions of dollars on psychiatrists and massage and tranquilizers because we aren't sure we really exist.

Psychiatrists no longer find many hysterics; the psychiatric ailment of modernity is the identity crisis—because relativity destroys personal identity. The technical term for "identity crisis" is *anomie*, which etymologically means "without law." That is, without moral standards and therefore without purpose.

During the war with Iraq, I heard a woman say on the radio that it wasn't merely that she was unwilling for her son to die for oil; she was unwilling for her son to die for anything.

Now, I wouldn't be real thrilled about my son dying either, no matter what the cause. But in a few cases, it might be better than his living. The mother's response sounds like anomie to me.

Some things are worth dying for. Some things are true. I'm not willing for my son to die for oil, but I hope I'd be willing for him to die so that Iraqi children wouldn't be bombed. You know, during the Roman persecutions some Christians took their children with them into the coliseum because they didn't want them to grow up pagan.

Now that's truth. Otherwise we have nothing worth dying for. And therefore nothing worth living for. Otherwise we have nothing to say to Hitler and Bush and Hussein. I can see Amos after he'd taken a class at UCLA. Arranging a dialogue with the president's chaplain, he'd say: "You tell me how you feel about it, and I'll tell you how I feel about it, and when we're done sharing our insights with each other, each of us must determine truth-for-himself."

Not exactly.

Ol' Amos believed in truth. Otherwise, you can never say anything that needs to be said.

The Wild Truth

I've been fighting both relativism and a DWEM view of reality because I think that accepting either of them is fatal. But at times I've fought them in terms that may have concealed the real nature of truth, in terms that may have sounded like I want a tame view of truth that balances the two views.

And that is not what I mean. It is not what I mean at all.

The truth, you see, is wild. Wild like Amos. Wild like Jesus. For the truth, you see, is Jesus himself. Not just correspondence and not just meaning for me and not just meaning for the oppressed. But Jesus himself.

We imagine truth to be either information or what we feel or custom or what the oppressed need. Whether secularists or romantics, anthropologists or neoconservatives, evangelicals or liberals, we've forgotten about the one who is the way, the truth and the life. We've forgotten our liege lord, the servant king.

Who does wild things to our heads, our hearts, our actions, our imaginations.

When all is said and done the problem with DWEM studies isn't something about correspondence or meaning for me, as crucial as they may be. The problem is our liege lord. And the liege lord of white males is white male. And so we present our side (the DWEM side) of any story and calmly ignore everything else. Our loyalty is to Thomas Jefferson and his kingdom, and so we resist any revisionist history that suggests he was working for his class interests. We resist the idea that "all men are created equal" actually meant all propertied white males. Unless of course we've been radicalized, in which case our loyalty is to *that* kingdom.

And if we're African-American and in the African-American studies department, our loyalty tends to be to Malcolm X and some form of black consciousness. If we're radical white women, our loyalty is in the feminist realm. If we're indigenous, then . . .

The search for truth is shaped substantially by the kingdom we're part of, by whom we accept as liege lord. That's part of what makes truth seem relative. People see truth from the perspective of their liege lord. We bend everything to fit our imagined interests in the kingdom we're committed to. (Truth isn't relative, but our grasp of it certainly is!)

And so making Jesus our liege lord is a large step toward truth. Our loyalty is then to him; so race, gender, nation become finally trivial. That doesn't mean whites who accept Jesus as king are suddenly able to teach black studies. Probably no privileged person, including one who serves Jah, ever fully grasps the situation of the poor and oppressed.

But choosing the Servant King puts everything on a new footing. Our loyalty is now to Jah and his little band of geese, and we have no particular stake in making Thomas Jefferson look good *or* bad, and the same for Malcolm X and Emily Dickinson and every other person and tribe in the world. We know in advance that all cultures have their glories, because all cultures reflect to some degree the glory of Jah, and we'll document that. But we also know in advance that all cultures are utterly depraved and reflect human twistedness, and we'll document that too.

So as slaves of Jah we can know in advance what our natural human biases are and can try to compensate for them. So we're free to pursue truth comparatively "objectively." (Not in Descartes's sense of being free of assumptions, but in the sense of being comparatively free of self-interest.)

We're free to compare Duke Ellington and Wagner on their merits as musicians, not on the basis of their race. (But we won't be free to ignore Wagner's racism, because music reflects the soul: we'll have to ask if his romanticism is connected with his racism.) We'll support studying "minority" cultures, because we have no need to make sure ours is the only one known. (But we may worry about studying too many cultures too briefly, because then people may acquire no real understanding of any culture— no real love for its strengths, no real insight into its evils.[16]) And we won't assume that every drama by everyone who isn't DWEM is as great as *Hamlet*.[17]

Of course, we'll still tend to see things in the distorted perspective we imagine serves our self- and class-interest. Self-deception doesn't end suddenly when we find our rightful king. But letting him loose in our lives opens us to his wild truth. Jesus just doesn't love white men more than indigenous women, and in time that gets hold of us. He adds a wildness that frees, a wildness that draws us toward Truth and therefore toward truth.

Parables and Truth

Did you ever wonder why Jesus told parables rather than give lectures? Well, it was because he wasn't tame. He had a different view of truth. "Truth was a sword in [his] hands and not a yardstick."[18] For him knowledge is personal insight given by the Spirit of God in space/time, in history, and it's transformational. When we encounter truth, we must change, repent and live life formed by that encounter. We live that explosive truth rather than store it away in our heads or turn it into private meaning. Truth is neither a computer nor a heart; it's a sword.

Jesus didn't think truth was facts you memorize from lecture notes. He thought you found truth by entering into stories and grasping their point, their actual point, for yourself. Then the spirit of the stories gets into your spirit and begins to transform you. Unless, of course, you refuse. Parables offer enlightenment to truth-seekers, but they repel those who fear light. And all of life is a parable.

And parables exclude people who aren't truth-seekers. They don't make a point in so many words; so those who aren't prepared to apply them to themselves often have no idea what they're about. To them, parables are just words, a closed book. All of life is like that to those who aren't seekers. Nothing makes sense until we believe.

It's not that we need new information or exciting feelings. What we need is the courage to live out what we already know and insight into why we aren't open to learning more. So Jesus gave us parables. With little new information in them. Their task rather is to expose us to ourselves. To slip through our self-deception.

For example, I start studying the parable of the rich man and Lazarus, interpreting its meaning for others . . . when it reaches out and interprets *me*.[19] Suddenly I realize that *I* am the rich man. It turns the tables on me. The Holy Spirit, the Spirit of truth, moves. And once I allow the Spirit to use a parable to interpret me, I become a different, truer person.

But if you aren't a truth-seeker and hear the parable of the rich man and Lazarus, the best you can do is go write a doctoral dissertation on whether the name Lazarus has any reference to the man Jesus raised from the dead. That has the tremendous advantage of allowing you to avoid the question whether the rich man has any reference to you.

Conclusion

We are in a great war. It's between darkness and light, truth and lies. One web of lies is that truth is merely correspondence to the facts; another is that truth is whatever turns you on. Such lies have squashed us almost flat. But we can regain depth by following the one who said, "I am the way, and the truth, and the life." He is speaking to us from another realm, telling us a true story, the story of Jah, to win back our lives.

14

Mixed Stories: Living off the Capital of Jah or Going Down with the Secular Ship

When I taught at an evangelical college, my theology was evangelical enough, but I had a beard and I opposed the war in Vietnam. And when not actually teaching, I could sometimes be found in blue jeans and sandals.

Then came a faculty meeting where we were discussing why African-American students often didn't feel at home on our campus. I said that the college had difficulty distinguishing between the gospel and middle American culture and that that often made nonwhites uncomfortable.

Within the hour, the president of the college was in my home, trying to persuade me that culture is closely connected to faith. (A point I could hardly disagree with.) Unfortunately, his example was that white shirts and ties are a better reflection of faith in Jesus than are blue jeans and sandals. (A point I could hardly agree with.) He added that even if Nixon and Agnew were not Christians themselves, they represented Christian culture better than hippies did. (This was before either Nixon or Agnew was in danger of indictment.) It's probably fortunate for my self-respect that I don't remember my reply.

Mixed Stories

Why is it that people who say they follow the story of Jah get it mixed up so easily with other stories? I do it too, as do we all. I don't think I ever would have connected hippies with Jesus as closely as the college's president did the Nixon administration, but I certainly connected them more then than I do now. We'd better be careful or we'll go down with somebody else's ship.

The difficulty is that while the college president was right that our stories shape our culture, it's equally true that our culture shapes our stories. So none of us follows a pure form of the story of Jah or of any other story. We live in a diverse culture with multiple, conflicting stories, and we often combine them rather carelessly.

And that's true for all of us: secularists, romantics, evangelical Christians, liberal Christians and everyone else living in modern culture with its smorgasbord of stories. We live odd mixtures of secularism, romanticism and the story of Jah (with a little other stuff thrown in).

So Christians have whole sections in their story that would be repugnant to Jesus or Paul, and something parallel is true for secularists and romantics. Christians are deeply secularized; secularists borrow from Christianity far more than they realize; romantics are half rationalist; and *Kindergarten Cop* has large elements borrowed from the story in back of *Pretty Woman* (and vice versa).

Within reasonable limits this process seems inevitable and even good. Certainly throughout Christian history we've borrowed extensively from other stories. We've borrowed from Plato, Aristotle, rationalism, capitalism, communism, existentialism, Freud, Jung, Gandhi and on and on. And that's what I've done in this book. As an even casual reading reveals, I've borrowed extensively from the stories of people not remotely Christian: Plato, Wordsworth, Sartre, Wittgenstein, Popper, Le Guin, Vonnegut.

As a culture changes, old stories have to adapt to remain intelligible and relevant. For example, as technology develops, you have to apply your story to new situations. What do you do when abortion becomes safe (for the mother)? And between new technology, new ideas and encounters with different cultures, change happens all the time in modern cultures. Just consider the new situations that arise with democracy, birth control, capitalism, mass production, advertising, Dada, bikinis, television, genetic engineering—not to mention cultural encounters with Africa, the Middle East, Asia and native peoples.

Not every new situation was envisioned in the original story, and with some it's hard to see what they even mean in terms of that story. So we have to figure out how to apply the story for ourselves, and sometimes we may even have to sketch a new chapter for ourselves, a new section of story grid for ourselves. And in the process, we're almost certain to borrow from other stories. All truth is God's truth; so let's get it where we can. Right?

The problem is that when we add a part from some other story, we often violate the "inner logic" of the original story. When we import something foreign, even something small, it often has repercussions throughout our story—repercussions never intended. We've been trained to think atomistically, and so we imagine we can pick a piece of rationalism here and a piece of Christianity there and a piece of astrology somewhere else and combine them any way we want. But adding a piece, even a small piece, from another story can have profound consequences.

Stories often have a driving force, an ineluctable inner logic. The logic from a small piece of a foreign story may take over the original story. So if we accept the Schwarzenegger plan of salvation but then notice that that approach was destructive in Vietnam, change tends to ripple through our whole story. Our view of the Vietnam War normally won't be the only thing affected: gradually, we'll apply the same logic to Nicaragua, Iran, blacks, Native Americans, women, government, lectures by teachers . . . till at some point we've accepted the entire Julia Roberts plan of salvation, perhaps without noticing. Or else we'll revert to Schwarzenegger and decide we were wrong about Vietnam. People tend toward a coherent version of a story.

Of course, we can hold on to conflicting parts of stories for a long time. It requires a little fancy footwork, but, for example, we can apply Julia

Roberts to Vietnam and Schwarzenegger to Iraq.[1] Actually it's not hard; after all, the queen in *Alice in Wonderland* "believed as many as six impossible things before breakfast."[2] Kurt Vonnegut's comment applies to us all: "Americans, like human beings everywhere, believe many things that are obviously untrue."[3]

This has the tremendous advantage that we can then use whatever part of whatever story appeals to our self-interest at a given moment. So, for example, governments can use Schwarzenegger's ethics themselves but insist that the enemy use Julia Roberts's ethics.

Of course, this confuses discourse profoundly, especially in a culture with a large selection of stories. People use the logic of one story for a while and then switch over to the logic of another story. Apparently without even noticing. We have so many stories that we can find one to suit our purposes on almost any occasion. This is a central reason for the difficulty of discourse in our culture; people keep switching their stories in midconversation.

But mixed stories are unstable; so for better or for worse, people and cultures tend toward increasingly coherent positions. In time the inner logic works itself out, and while the trappings of the old story may remain, the real fruit of the lived story tends to manifest itself.

Real Fruits of Secularism
This is true for rationalism. Rationalism, like every other new story, borrowed heavily from the previous dominant story of its culture—Christianity. It dumped parts of that century's understanding of Christianity but held on to other parts. From the point of view of the original Christian story, it was right about much of what it dumped and much of what it kept. Christianity, after all, had also borrowed (sometimes badly) from the culture it was part of.

But the question is whether what rationalism kept was compatible with its overall framework. For example, it kept an essentially Judeo-Christian ethic. But rationalism has an ineluctable inner logic: you must be able to test a claim by applying math to the measurable properties of what you can observe. And as I argued in chapter four, that logic destroys any possibility of ethics.

Take progress. The Enlightenment promised wondrous progress: freedom and equality, sexual expression and human rights, medical improvement and intellectual advance. This hope was the driving force of the Enlightenment. And the enormous progress it brought is obvious—from within a moral framework.

But what is progress? What happens to the notion of progress when you apply math to its measurable properties? It goes the way of all other hierarchies, that's what. The idea of progress makes no sense outside some framework in which one direction is mana and the other is taboo. The power of the secular story depends on ideas like progress. Yet those ideas are unintelligible without a directional imperative, without a moral North Pole.

The meaning of *progress* seems so obvious to us that it scarcely seems necessary to explain it, but I suggest that it seems obvious only because we are a people whose culture was cradled in the Judeo-Christian story (and because Jah put a hollow spot with that shape inside us). So as children of Jah (or perhaps great-great-nieces and -nephews of Jah), we naturally sense the moral North Pole. We live in a great cathedral partly built by the Judeo-Christian tradition.

But the Enlightenment rejected the moral North Pole, and its founders did their best to tear down anything pointing to it. Yet even to state their own position, they rely on it. They're dependent on the story of Jah (or on some other spiritual account—like Plato's) in a way that makes no sense in their story.

So without most people noticing (themselves included), secularists borrow the idea of the personal and the moral from older cultures that hadn't yet repressed what it means to be truly human. This makes secularism seem like a compelling, coherent story—as long as no one notices that ideas like progress are firmly anchored in the sort of enchanted framework that secularism scorns.

I suggest that secularists are trying to hold on to the structure of the story of Jah while rejecting the story that the structure depends on. They have a Fall, a plan of salvation and a coming kingdom of righteousness—just like the story of Jah! The Fall is superstition and ignorance; the plan of salvation is rationality and education; and the coming kingdom is the final, assured triumph of science and reason. They hold on to value and moral direction as such while changing many of the particular directions. And they have a passion for their story which looks curiously like religious fervor: they crusade fervently to bring enlightenment and equality through reason.

Our culture emphasized the story of Jah for centuries, and parts of it got so deeply ingrained that people automatically and unconsciously follow them. Parts became habits of the heart, traditions, and they are so natural that they seem to need no explanation, no defense.

In other words, secularists live off the capital of the Judeo-Christian tradition. However, they have no way of replacing that capital. And as happens with all those who spend their capital, in time the money runs out, and they go bankrupt.

That is happening in our culture today.

Perhaps people like Hume and Emerson escaped some of the consequences of their beliefs because they lived in the still grand ruins of a partly Christian world. They threw the accumulated corruption out of the cathedral, not noticing that the way they did it destroyed its foundations. Since they didn't notice, they continued living much as gaitered Christian gentlemen should.

But for the present generation, that grand cathedral is scarcely even a memory. They no longer remember the moral North Pole, and bankruptcy approaches for an entire culture. So whether they are corrupt officers of savings and loans corporations, men who abandon women when they get pregnant, college graduates who refuse to pay off their student loans, candidates for the presidency for whom lying is a habit of the heart (or voters who vote for them), rioters in Los Angeles, voters willing to loot children's school systems to pay for prisons, the 50 percent of our couples who get divorced or teachers who can't be bothered to prepare for their students the next day—all have lost their moral direction.

Not that immoral people haven't always existed, but this time the numbers are huge and more seem not even to sense that they're doing anything wrong. How could they, since they haven't been taught the moral

North Pole? At this moment, the real fruits of secularism are on display on the tree of our culture.

How long can such a culture endure?

Wittgenstein

By some accounts, linguistic philosophy under the leadership of Ludwig Wittgenstein has shown secularists a way out of this predicament, a way to keep ethics without having an enchanted framework. Certainly, Wittgenstein pointed toward an epistemology that frees us from the narrowness of both rationalism and romanticism.

Rationalists taught us to think that the only legitimate use of language is to describe things in a way that reflects the measurable properties of what you observe, but Wittgenstein pointed out that language has many other uses. We also use language to express wishes, make requests, issue commands, tell jokes, curse in frustration, give our word, perform marriages and on and on.[4] These other uses don't have the same logic as descriptive, scientific language, but that doesn't mean they're merely the expression of emotion or that they're gibberish.[5] It means rather that they have their own logic, their own way of being appropriate.

Among these nondescriptive uses of language is moral discourse. Moral discourse has its own procedures, as do the discourses of mathematics and physics, and you can make mistakes in moral discourse just as you can in math or physics.[6] According to Stephen Toulmin, another linguistic philosopher, the function of ethics is to "correlate feelings and behavior in such a way as to make the fulfillment of everyone's aims and desires as far as possible compatible."[7]

So if you say you don't care about the fulfillment of others' desires, you are making a mistake in moral discourse: it's like saying the square of the hypotenuse of a right triangle doesn't equal the square of the other two sides. This time the error isn't an error in the logic of geometry but in the logic of moral discourse. Considerations like whether desires are thwarted by an action are just as binding in moral discourse as are proofs in geometric discourse.

Therefore, nothing more need be said to defend ethics. With Nazis who find concentration camps delightful, you do what geometry teachers do with students having trouble with the Pythagorean theorem. You repeat the logic (the proof) a couple of times, perhaps using different words, but in the end, if they don't get it, there's nothing more you can or need do. Which presents no more problem for ethics than for geometry. So secularists don't need Jah or any other spiritual story to keep ethics. They can add parts of other stories as they please as long as they spell out the logic and limits of each part.

Checkers and Tea

Wittgenstein's power lies in pointing out the silliness of rationalism's imperialistic claim that statements are meaningful only if they apply math to measurable properties. In that way he puts reason on a new footing with a broader application, a broader application of the sort I've been advocating throughout this book. He thereby opens the door from the cell where humanity was squeezed into the one-dimensional confines of rationalism (and then romanticism). New approaches are now possible in ethics, aesthetics, philosophy of religion, law and everywhere else. With a little effort, we can even pry open the doors to story.[8]

Unfortunately, most linguistic philosophers haven't done so. While their arguments suggest that there are more things on heaven and earth than the minds of secular philosophers have dreamed of, they've generally squeezed themselves right back into secularism's one-dimensionality.[9] The logics they've come up with for moral discourse, for example, are almost embarrassingly shallow.

Take Toulmin's description of ethics as "mak[ing] the fulfillment of everyone's aims and desires as far as possible compatible." Not that this is entirely wrong, but I doubt that Buddha, Isaiah, Jesus[10] or Mother Teresa would be impressed (though John Stuart Mill would doubtless have cheered).

While living by Toulmin's formula might be better than most do, and while practicing it might be just barely enough to keep a culture functioning, it is the quintessence of shallowness. The embodiment of one-dimensionality. A prototype for any future soup can.

But it's nice. No need to kill off the false self. No need to take up your cross. No need to sell your possessions. No need to love your enemies. Just work out compromises so that you get a reasonable amount of what you want and everyone else gets a reasonable amount of what they want. No need to repent.

No mention of self-deception or false life projects. No mention of *worthy* aims or *evil* desires, just *aims* and *desires* (nice neutral words). So Hitler's desire to have his mistresses poop in his face was fine as long as his mistresses didn't mind too much. And the aim of most of us not to bother much with other people is fine too, as long as we aren't married to them or something of the sort. Oh, and of course, there's no need to keep marriage vows as long as both parties agree.

Somehow Toulmin sounds like a gaitered English gentleman not quite aware of the real presence of evil. It's as if ethics were a checkers game where you move the pieces around calmly and casually while sipping tea— not a bloody war between good and evil where children are raped and the poor are walked on by those with a fierce commitment to principalities of lying stories.

Somehow one suspects that Toulmin's position would mean little to that near majority who loot S&Ls, Korean grocery stores and our children's schools. He hasn't borrowed enough from the story of Jah to fill the hollowness within or to keep a culture alive. This sort of Wittgensteinian solution is no help in real life.

Why Shouldn't I Be Selfish?

To put it differently, linguistic philosophy has reduced ethics to a procedural matter without any metaphysical or mythic setting.[11] (Which, by the way, is in flat contradiction with the moral discourse of any actual people in history.) As a result, their various ethics have no connection with persons or God or I-thou discourse. They seem to float in midair with no connection to reality.[12] Giving them all the depth and power of a soup can.

To water Jesus down more than a little, morality is caring about others enough that it mitigates our selfishness. Morality isn't keeping rules, though that will happen, and it isn't fulfilling ourselves, though that too will happen. Morality is reaching beyond ourselves to loving and serving others. But if you limit moral discourse to logical procedures, it lacks the vision and the passion that give morality a foothold in the human heart.

Even secular utilitarians say we're to maximize happiness without regard to whose happiness it is. In other words, utilitarians tell us not to be selfish.

But that's costly, and what in the secular story has the power to call us to something so difficult? What in an unenchanted universe will encourage people to sacrifice for the happiness of others? Keeping life genuinely human is like maintaining a garden. Having seeds (moral principles) is essential but not sufficient: you still need the nourishment of water, warmth, sunshine and the means to combat weeds and insects. Can secularism provide such sources of nourishment for selflessness? Can it provide springs of living water to bring the logic of moral discourse to life? Does it offer sufficient moral resources to empower genuinely human life?[13]

The story of Jah has those resources in rich variety. One way to talk about them is to point to the narratives of Scripture, the rituals of the church, the stories in stained-glass windows, the drama of the Eucharist, the beauty of cathedrals, the depth of the *Messiah*. All these were abandoned by the Enlightenment.

What is to replace them? Shopping at the mall. Graduation ceremonies. Rap music. War. Money in the bank. Watching soap operas. Saluting the flag. Massage.

And they don't measure up. They don't fill the hollowness.

Another way to talk about the moral resources of Jah is to talk about the nature of the enchanted universe in the stories and songs of Jah. On the most primitive level, these stories threaten hell and promise heaven. Why shouldn't you be selfish? Because if you are, you'll go to hell, and if you aren't, you'll go to heaven, that's why.[14] The stories also make promises and threats about the approval and disapproval of Jah and about inclusion among his people or else exclusion.[15]

What's more, according to the stories, the universe includes spirit and the personal; therefore selfishness itself takes on horror and taboo. Why not be selfish? Because selfishness is horrible and disgusting, that's why. It violates the spirit and causes I and thou to shrivel and decompose. It is ugliness and emptiness and abomination and boringness. We have a duty to fight this filthiness that turns the human home into Mordor. Selfishness is a beautiful-looking lover who later turns out to have been a decaying corpse.

And for Jah there are resources deeper than that, deeper than duty and the prospect of horrible emptiness. Why be selfless? Because it nurtures the spirit, that's why. Selflessness lets the I-thou flourish and grow strong, in ourselves and in others. It has mana. Which is beauty and reconciliation—and walls broken down. As selflessness becomes a habit of the heart, it has the drawing and sustaining power of love and peace.

But Jah has an even deeper resource—himself. He fills our hollowness not just with the beauty of nature or the contentment of a good family or the attraction of the Platonic ideal, but with himself. Over against selfishness is Jah and love of Jah. We're selfless not just out of an impersonal vision of the good but out of love for Jah, our true master. Our beloved (who saved us from Egypt and promises to keep intervening for us by his Spirit) asks us to be selfless, and we want to please him. And as that primal relationship is fulfilled, selfishness begins to be replaced. It's called grace: we do things not because the law requires them but because love desires them—not out of "labored obedience"[16] but out of free and joyful service. Hollowness filled.

So the story of Jah has a mass of resources to help us grow beyond selfishness: threats and promises, duty for its own sake, the horror of emptiness and defilement, the attraction of the vision of goodness, the hope of fulfillment in selflessness, Jah himself and the love of Jah himself. These aren't mostly rules to intimidate us but visions drawing us on: here is what life can be like if people live out the story of Jah, and here is what it will be like if they don't.

"I have set before you life and death, blessings and curses. Choose life so that you and your descendants may live, loving the LORD your God, obeying him, and holding fast to him, for that means life to you" (Deut 30:19-20).

If thou couldst empty all thyself of self,
    Like to a shell dishabited,

Then might He find thee on the ocean shelf,
   And say, "This is not dead,"
   And fill thee with Himself instead.
But thou art all replete with very thou,
   And hast such shrewd activity
That when He comes He says, "This is enow
   Unto itself—'twere better let it be,
   It is so small and full, there is no room for Me."[17]

The Capital of Jah Again

But modern culture has abandoned those resources, and so we are termi-
nally shallow. The relative deepening of modern epistemology to include
moral discourse is welcome, but until it gets to I-thou discourse and a larger
metaphysical context, until it gets to a larger story—a much, much larger
story, a truly huge story—it hasn't deepened enough to be of use.

As the story of a people changes, traditions and habits of the heart from
the old story don't die overnight—but neither do they live forever uncared
for. To flourish, even to survive, they need sources of loving care.

But the Enlightenment rejected most of those sources. It rejected the old
philosophical framework and the old stories; it rejected the context of
morality. And people like Toulmin haven't replaced them. And without
support, the habits of morality eventually grow weak and collapse on themselves. In time a generation arises that abandons them. Secularism, even
secularism with a Wittgensteinian twist, has nothing to say to a culture
where looting has become almost commonplace.

We're so close to bankrupt that soup cans will soon be about all that's
left.

What Church?

So it's time to turn to the story of Jah and to the churches who live it.
Secularism doesn't have any answers to the ultimate human questions. It
doesn't even ask them. It leaves us so one-dimensionally shallow that it
drives us to the craziness of romanticism.

Which at least asks the questions human beings care about, but it lacks a means of discernment, a crap detector, and so it winds up with all kinds of silliness and destruction.

Which leaves the story of Jah. And by its founder's own statement, that story is to be evaluated by the lives of those who follow him. By the lives of those who have become the church.

Which is a problem—no one seems to have done it. No one much anyway. No large groups, no big denominations. The cost is too high. We've all adapted his story to our culture to the point that the story of Jah has been half replaced by other stories.

This happened most blatantly in our century with the rise of theological liberalism. Theological liberals accepted the secular story that God does not intervene in nature, and so they had to strip their faith of miracles. To all intents and purposes, they became deists. According to them, when Jesus multiplied the loaves and fishes, he was merely sharing what he had, and by doing so he taught us that when we share there is more than enough to go around. And similarly the resurrection was not a physical event but a colorful way of saying that Jesus lives on in the hearts of his disciples (just as Gandhi lives on in the hearts of his disciples). And of course we don't need to take the details of Christian ethics too literally either.

Secularism in drag. A good example of the logic of one story (secularism) taking over another story (Christianity). That people who had been Christians would come to this conclusion is understandable; that they would continue to call themselves Christians is less understandable, an example of Orwellian Newspeak. Especially when they then proceeded to take over most white Protestant denominations and their seminaries.[18]

This was a painful process for those who didn't agree, but it shouldn't have been a surprise. It has happened repeatedly throughout the history of the church: the church is confronted by hostile currents, starts fighting them, but accepts their logic in a little corner (perhaps to fight them better), and that logic soon takes over; so instead of defeating them, it becomes them. Our story gets all mixed up.

The Wilderness

When this form of secularism swallowed most white denominations, fundamentalists and evangelicals were banished to the wilderness. But that's not the worst of it. The worst of it is that those banished to the wilderness also soon swallowed secularism, although in a different way. They too got caught in the secular squeeze. Without so much as noticing. At least liberals knew when they were swallowed, but evangelicals—we never even noticed. We considered ourselves the archenemies of secularism, but on a basic level we were prime allies: we accepted its epistemology and therefore its one-dimensionality. We became as shallow as everyone else.

A worldview has won the day when its opposition accepts its assumptions without noticing. When its assumptions seem so natural they don't seem to need justification. And that happened in the struggle between secularists and evangelicals. Secularism brainwashed us so thoroughly that even our faith became secular. As Roger Lundin has said, secularism "has extended its dominion over so much of modern thought that even when certain groups—like romantic poets and various groups of orthodox Christians—have protested its encroachments, they have largely done so in the language of the . . . [secular] kingdom in which they unwittingly dwell."[19]

Of course, this mixing of stories is an understandable process. Liberals were attacking the Bible for not being good science. And we evangelicals made the natural response: "It is too good science." And then we proceeded to act as if it were *only* good science. Lenses were tightly clamped over our eyes, blinding us to all but the facts.

At which point it was all over. The Bible was reduced to one dimension. Our energy went into showing that evolution was false (not good science) and that the Bible was factually correct (good science). Poetry and parables and beauty got lost. And stories. And everything else right-brained.

Let me put it this way: somewhere there is probably a telephone book with no mistakes in it. But does that make it God's Word? No, because telephone books lack the power and beauty and awefulness of things that come from God.

But in our concern to defend the accuracy of the information in the Bible, we evangelicals lost track of the rest of our story. We reduced the Bible to a set of correct propositions; we began treating it as if it were the sort of book all of whose statements could appear on a true-or-false exam with all of them true. We were limiting our notion of truth to scientific accuracy, to the truth of a telephone book. Somehow, loving your enemies and siding with the oppressed got lost in a flurry of factual arguments.

If liberals accepted the secular dogma against the supernatural, evangelicals accepted the secular dogma that reality is one-dimensional: correct belief systems are what it's about. Formation and transformation are replaced by information.

So the schools we started to protect our kids from secular education are nearly as secular as public schools. They don't emphasize narrative or poetry or letter writing so the kids will be better able to understand the Bible. How could they, when evangelicals never noticed that most of the Bible is narrative and poetry and letters? Nor do they focus on the beauty of the Lord or on anything else of depth; they just ask the kids to memorize different information in biology—different from what they would have in public school. How secular and left-brained can you get? We're going down with the secular ship. The I-thou is as missing in our schools as in public schools.

The same thing is clear in our evangelism, the essence of which is persuading people to accept certain ideas. Few would put it that baldly, but that's our practice. We ask the people next to us on a plane to accept a set of beliefs and to say a prayer, and then we consider them Christian— and abandon them. Or they are evangelized by radio or television—and not introduced to a church that will help them live out their discipleship. Because no life of discipleship is expected. We settle for intellectual acceptance of beliefs, with limited concern for transformation.

Which makes us secular. Secularism has few requirements for how we live, but it does require intellectual acceptance that God doesn't exist: it requires certain beliefs. Just like us. Evangelicals require opposite beliefs, of course, but by reducing faith to beliefs, even opposite beliefs, we unwittingly get flattened in the secular squeeze. So we'll run out of the capital of Jah just a little later than secular society.

And even when our evangelism is connected to a church, notice how much less transformation we ask than Jesus asked. When the rich young ruler asked Jesus for the plan of salvation, Jesus didn't ask him to assent to doctrine plus quit drinking and start coming to church; he asked him to sell his possessions and give to the poor (Mt 19:16-30). He consistently required, even of newcomers, a total commitment of a sort that evangelicals (not to mention liberals and Catholics) have quite forgotten. What Jesus wants is our lives, even to the point of the cross. But secularism has robbed evangelicals of the cross as surely as Constantine robbed the early church.

It's easy to understand how it happened. Secularism was a belief system, a belief system that challenged Christianity at almost every point. Liberals had bought it, but evangelicals were fighting it in order to protect their belief system.

Which was appropriate. After all, belief systems are important: ideas have consequences. So it's essential for evangelism to require intellectual beliefs, but that can't be all it does. It must also introduce people to the beauty of God's creation and to the importance of stopping serving ourselves. It's fine to fight for creationism and the belief that the Bible has no errors. But we can't let those issues squeeze out the other dimensions of the Bible, or before we're done we've accepted a lobotomy that makes us insensitive to the depths of Scripture, to its calls for justice and selflessness. Somewhere in there we're no more Christian than liberals. We too become secularists in drag.

When you're building a house, you need to frame it if you're going to have anything to build on. But you don't stop with the frame, because such a house wouldn't even protect people against cold and rain. A belief system is a frame. If liberalism is an attempt to have a house without a frame, then evangelicalism is a frame with little attempt to build a habitable home around it.

As the inner logic of secularism won out in evangelicals, it made us think of stories as a whimsical waste of time, a sort of entertainment on the level of playing marbles. Because we've been secularized, we don't see the power of story. And that's odd, since so much of the Bible is story.

Odd, too, because the power of story is so obvious. I'll wager that the stories in movies and novels grip and move people more than lectures by academics. I'll wager, for example, that C. S. Lewis's fiction has done more to help people accept the supernatural than his nonfiction books on the topic. (It has helped me more anyway.)

Jesus told stories, and so should we. That will give us more depth and breadth. And it will be a step, a large one, toward not going down with the secular ship.

An odd thing to witness—the flattening of the story of Jah till it's hard to tell from desolation in a soup can. So meager. So thin. So lacking.

Neo-orthodoxy and Pragmatic Evangelicalism

But those battles were fought and lost nearly a century ago. Neither liberals nor evangelicals have remained the same over those years. Liberalism was practically replaced by Karl Barth's neo-orthodoxy, but unfortunately he mixed the story of Jah with existentialism, one of the romantic reactions to secularism. In the process, he did the opposite of what evangelicals do. He emphasized the meaning of the events of Scripture and minimized their factuality, the information in them. Meaning is outside history, independent of facts. For him, the facts are Nothings, the meaning everything. The fruits of this didn't grow fully till the work of Rudolf Bultmann, according to whom even the resurrection wasn't historical. Back to liberal secularism.

Back to half the story again, the half the right brain understands now, but still only half. And we've got that half on blind faith. We're back to *Pretty Woman*. A nice story but no reason to think it can actually happen in my life or anyone else's, because it didn't happen in history.

Meanwhile, evangelicalism has also changed profoundly. My father was a fundamentalist preacher. He believed in truth, which he understood mostly as accuracy. If he discovered that people in his church didn't believe the truth as he understood it (whether that meant they were Masons or that they spoke in tongues), he threw them out, even if it meant splitting the church six ways and losing his financial base. The truth is the truth is the truth.

But not many evangelicals are left like my dad (which isn't altogether bad!). Today's evangelicals are much more likely to be obsessed with pragmatics, with church growth and finances. Consequently, they rarely split churches over truth; they rarely ask for costly discipleship. Making members feel good is more important. If you make people feel good, churches grow (numerically, that is). You may throw in a little guilt to motivate people to give money, but not enough to make them feel bad, because then they give less.

Not that numerical growth is irrelevant. The numbers in the early church were substantial. We must reach as many people as possible. And the great contribution of the church-growth movement is helping us use the culture to attract people. If people are more comfortable culturally with a certain kind of music, use that kind of music instead of traditional church music. If they're more comfortable coming in jeans, that's fine.

But in the story of Jah some things are mandatory because they're biblical. The criteria of what's mandatory because it's biblical and what's optional because it's cultural soon get so flexible that almost anything is optional. If folks are more comfortable with sermons that give them a lift, preach that way, carefully avoiding hellfire. So it's hard to see how Robert Schuller's preaching, for example, is any more Christian than that of old-fashioned liberals.

With the best intentions in the world, the story of Jah gets transmogrified into Americanism. Or blackism, or Chinaism, or the ism of whatever culture we're working in. And Jah gets lost. Church-growth advocates are so committed to reaching people that they sometimes seem to forget who they're reaching them for. For Jah.

And that means calling people to a tough repentance in the context of a straightforward critique of their culture and way of life. At least, that's what Jesus did. And Paul. And John.

Otherwise, we'll go down with the American ship. Which could sink at any moment. Soup cans won't keep us afloat.

Constantine, Nationalism and Shintoism
Throughout history, the favorite story to mix with the story of Jah has been nationalism. Or tribalism or racialism. Not just acculturation, but acculturation that glorifies the local culture and demeans others. Constantine is the classic example. The Roman Empire had struggled with Christians for three centuries. It tried ignoring them, killing them, cajoling them—noth-

ing worked. Till Constantine, a good liberal, joined them. And made Christianity the state religion (thereby making the state a prime object of worship). Which was absurd—an early example of Newspeak. Nationalism dressed up for church.

"Believe or I'll crucify you" is an even worse method of evangelism than asking people to change their belief system. It's not exactly what Jesus had in mind when he said, "Take up your cross and follow me." So naturally the radical content of the gospel evaporated under Constantine. People were following Jesus in order to avoid taking up their cross. Which is to say they weren't following Jesus at all. And Christianity became another painless plan of salvation, a variation on walking barefoot in the grass.

Thus was born upside-down Christianity, where converting emperors and imitating millionaires became more important than helping the oppressed and imitating the suffering servant. The Roman Empire had won, and those who were Christian other than in Newspeak went underground. The church became a branch of the state, legitimizing it, defending it, providing it with a cohesive civil religion.

You see it today in church buildings where a national flag is prominently displayed. Where almost every church endorses almost every war that its country has ever been involved in. Where they sing the local national anthem and songs like "The Battle Hymn of the Republic" in church. Where the church somehow finds a way to explain to the exploited that the interests of Christ coincide with those of the ruling class. This is a false god, whose name is sometimes the state and sometimes Mars, the god of war. (Known locally as Arnold Schwarzenegger.)

Constantinianism of the Left
But the way I'm talking makes it sound as if only those who support the state have mixed their story with Constantine. However, those crusading to reform the state are usually Constantinian too. In that sense Jerry Falwell and the World Council of Churches are as Constantinian as Constantine. By "Constantinian" I mean sacrificing the story of Jah for the sake of success with a political program, even a good political program.

Not necessarily out of bad motives. I know. I spent ten or twenty years doing it. I was really trying to be political in a Christian way, but as I look back on it, I was less than eminently successful. I applied Christian ethics to existing governmental structures, but I didn't finally apply the strategies of Jesus and Paul.

Let me tell you how it's done. You discover some principle that you believe to be biblical, like God is on the side of the poor (in my case) or abortion is evil (in Falwell's case). Then you look around for those with the political program that most nearly reflects that principle, and you join them. You join them whether they're Baptists, secularists, Moonies or witches. You set aside your "denominational" distinctives for the sake of the principle. And in the process you accept the boundaries of standard politics as your working boundaries; you accept its terms.

In trying to promote the principle, you don't get it mixed up with irrelevant issues of faith. You don't get into God and repentance and the church. And you certainly don't get into adultery and resentment and all that. That is, you set aside the overall story of Jah for the sake of one of its substories.

But what do you say at a religious demonstration in favor of your principle: "Support this principle and join the church or coven of your choice"? I can see it now. "Elijah and High Priest of Baal Call for Hunger Education Week: Ahab Agrees."

We just sank with the secular ship. Religion is optional compared to politics.

We don't call everyone to repent and serve their rightful king. We settle for asking them to accept one of that king's principles. For the first time in history, we imagine it's possible for people to behave Christianly without being Christian. We imagine it's possible to have a Christian nation without a Christian people. Our task is to make Christian social ethics palatable to sensitive people everywhere, no matter what their religious beliefs or lack thereof. Our task is not to call them out of their unbelief.

Well, what Jesus and Paul and Isaiah had to say was *not* palatable.

If Jesus taught anything, it was that the only question of importance is who you serve, how you try to fill the hollow spot within. And that means that the most important thing for Jesus' followers to do is to call everyone to accept Jesus as their liege lord.

Now that doesn't mean that Christians shouldn't join non-Christians as cobelligerents in political causes. But when we're among them, let's call them to leave their covens and join the church of Jesus Christ. And anytime we get a microphone in our hands, let's call people to repent and fill themselves with Jah. Nor does it mean we should stop demonstrating. Let's by all means demonstrate against injustice. It's a method of street-corner evangelism that gets beyond fundamentalist clichés and shows by its very form part of what salvation is.

And let's lobby senators. But let's not just tell them to vote our way or they'll lose our vote. Let's ask them to vote our way because we think that's the way of Jah, their rightful king. Whom we beg them to serve. And let's have soup kitchens for the poor, but let's not just give them bread and run. Let's also offer them the bread of life. Like Jesus, let's talk to them about their Father. Which is far more important.

Anything less is Constantinian.

Of course, those of us who are evangelical Constantinians may still "evangelize" to save souls from hell, but we see political salvation as lying in electoral politics. We have limited the story of Jah to a little spiritual compartment.

Pastoral Counseling Centers

Evangelicals also do that in all kinds of ways that aren't political. Take pastoral counseling centers, which generally assume that salvation lies in psychology. Not eternal salvation, of course. That comes by grace through faith. But here and now we're saved by getting over our maladjustments. Not by repenting of our sins, but by having repressed memories healed. Or our self-esteem increased. Or our family system improved.

Funny. I just don't remember Jesus advising Nicodemus to work on his self-esteem. Nor did he ask the Sadducees how their fathers treated them. He told them all to repent.[20]

And that is the problem. The church, whether evangelical, liberal or neo-orthodox, doesn't often ask people to repent anymore. So when church members have terrible, self-inflicted problems in their lives (which we all do), their pastors don't know what to tell them. They can't tell them to repent; so they start pastoral counseling centers. There folks at least have someone to talk to about their pain.

The story of Jah keeps getting squeezed down to something smaller and smaller and flatter and flatter and thinner and thinner. It's so mixed with logic from other stories that the other stories often seem to have taken over, to be where we really look for salvation.

50-Percent Churches and Anomie

But that's not to say that the story is completely lost. Most churches are probably still 50-percent churches. They still believe in a moral North Pole, albeit one seriously transposed by other interests. They still generally believe in the family, in sexual fidelity and in minimizing violence, which helps keep the pain in our world from being a whole lot worse than it is.

Besides, almost any moral North Pole is better than none. Which is to say, even a civil religion is usually better than anarchy. (In the United States, we may soon find out what it's like to have no civil religion.)

Let me illustrate the point with art. Official churches (50-percent churches?) long retained enough of the story of Jah to allow art to flourish. Giotto and Michelangelo, Handel and Bach, Dante and Chaucer—all had access to the capital from the story of Jah. And so their art gave us icons reasonably worthy of worship, or at least respect.

For that is the function of art. At its core, art is the depiction of icons, of the story a culture lives, or even of epiphanies.[21] This is clear in depictions of Jesus and Mary and Venus and even in the idealized landscapes of the romantics, but it's equally true of soup cans and centerfolds. Those are all that's left for us to serve. When a culture has no icons of anything worthy, soon the art isn't worthy either.

Not too long ago the art of our culture was about the stories of Jah or of classical civilization, or else it was romantic icons of nature. But in the middle of the nineteenth century we got realism. Some clever souls began to wonder why you couldn't just paint or write what you saw. Who needs the old stories to write poetry or to paint or to compose? Just write what you experience, paint the ordinary things, the things people actually see.

So we got Dickens, Zola, Courbet, Manet. It seemed reasonable, especially to those of Enlightenment bent. We don't need any icons to focus what we see,[22] no stories anchored in the unobservable to tell us what things mean. And so we got depictions of the real world, some of them excellent.

And then seventy years later we started getting nonsense. Dada. Broken glass from Duchamp, entitled "To be looked at (from the other side of the glass) with one eye, close to, for almost an hour." Nonsense. Nothing. Nothing.

Within seventy years. From Courbet to Duchamp, from realism to Dada, from painting ordinary things the artist could see to not being able to see anything to paint. In one single lifetime. It took just a few years once we had no icons beyond what we could see, once we had Nothing to focus our seeing.

I think it's called anomie. Or soup cans.

Oh, for a 50-percent church!

Conclusion

But it isn't enough. Fifty percent is a lot better than Nothing, but we need a church with more of the story than that. We'll never get the whole story, of course, but half . . . it doesn't fill enough hollowness. It never reaches critical mass. If our broken world is to have any peace, if people are to have any chance of finding Jah, we need at least a 75-percent church. Or a remnant of such a church. Perhaps enough of it would rub off on the surrounding culture to keep the culture from destroying its people in an orgy of anarchy.[23]

But for that we need at least the remnant of a 75-percent church.

Which is the topic of the final chapter.

15

On Becoming
Part of the
Warm Spot

I f we took God out of the picture, what kind of change would it make? Most of us imagine that God is an item in the upper right-hand corner who can be removed without fundamentally changing anything. Kind of like taking one of the jagged hills out of the background of a painting like Mona Lisa. The balance in the painting would be altered, no doubt, but if done carefully it would be no big deal.

But in this book, I've argued that removing God is more like replacing the painting of the woman with an anatomical drawing from a medical textbook. The painting won't fall off the wall, at least not right away, and each part is still there, but all the mystery, all the depth, all the beauty, all the life is gone.

We are left with a one-dimensional corpse.

Which I suggest is exactly what secularism has left us with. We have been squeezed flat. Through a process of reverse sublimation, we have repressed the great questions and squeezed our lives down to trivia. We settle for self-esteem workshops in place of confessionals, *Playboy* in place of *The Imitation of Christ*.

Not that any other time or place was a whole lot better. The average medieval male would probably have preferred *Playboy* to *The Imitation of Christ* any day, and I don't suppose confession has ever been popular. Still, a fundamental shift has occurred. Modern people are haunted by the notion that the only proper way to answer questions is by "applying math to the measurable properties of what we observe." And since none of the great questions can be answered that way, we're left without answers.

In particular, we're left without God. And without Plato's Forms. And without a story of much more depth than "L.A. Law." Without grace or any of the resources for a life of love and depth. All we have left is feelings. But the lives of romantics from Rousseau to Hitler suggest that feelings are a little thin.

We took God out of the picture, and before long the picture fell off the wall.

Perhaps the difference between us and people of other times and places is that they at least *had* a picture. In the Middle Ages, people would have been as tempted to commit adultery as we, but they had a picture to judge themselves by. If they committed adultery, they knew they had sinned and needed to confess it. But in our age we have no picture, at least no coherent picture with substantial life direction (unless you want to count "L.A. Law"). As a result, confession is getting as hard to imagine today as self-esteem workshops would have been in the Middle Ages.

Success of Science, Failure of the Church

So we have a problem. Our whole culture has a problem. We're geniuses at science and technology but failures at pretty well everything else. Science has cracked secret after secret of the physical world: the laws of motion, the nature of matter, germs, genetic structure, mesons and galaxies, relativity. And it has made awesome advances in technology: flush toilets, electric light, penicillin, television, jet planes, hydrogen bombs, heart transplants, computers.

But we have no larger picture: everything else has failed. Or at least nothing else has succeeded. Government, the arts, church, voodoo, the family and relationships, astrology. None of them has delivered. The church talked love but gave us televangelism. The family advertised beatitude but produced as much misery and abuse as happiness. Modern government looked promising at first, but it has given us as much war as peace. Astrology promised everything but delivered nothing. And the arts . . . well, the arts reflected the lostness of the culture before the culture knew it was lost.

And that is why our age is essentially secular. The paradigms of science worked while all other paradigms failed. Often spectacularly. So naturally we applied the paradigms of science to all of life. And became secular.

But the paradigms of science didn't do so well in life. They left silence. A reverberating silence.

And human beings won't put up with silence. We're all questers. In quest of the Holy Grail. In quest of the warm spot at the center of the universe. If science doesn't lead us to it, then we try something else. Romanticism. Sex. Voodoo. Anything is better than Nothing.

Which is about what romanticism proved to be.

The solution seems obvious. We need a church. A real church. One where a people together live out the story of Jah. The whole story. Or at least 75 percent of it.

Unmixing Our Story

And there's the problem. How do you get a people to live out more of the story? The main problem is undoubtedly sin and selfishness: the cost of Christianity is so high that many reject it outright. Even most of those claiming to be Christians seem not to make a good-faith effort to live out things like the Sermon on the Mount. When you put a crucified God in the picture, most people don't really want to hang it in their living room: it's not pretty.

But that's not the whole problem. Part of the problem is that it's not easy to sort out what the whole picture is. Let me explain. If people in a pagan culture become Christians, the next day they don't just start living the story of Jah. Their lifestyles and thought processes are still essentially determined by the story of their culture. The best they can do is adapt their lives a little at a time to their newly adopted story.

That's obvious with a tribal culture, but it's no different if the tribe is Western. If people live in a secular culture and become Christians, their lifestyles and thought processes are at first essentially determined by secularism, not by their newly adopted story. The best they can do is slowly work their way out of secularism—or out of romanticism or whatever story they happen to have accepted before.

And that's us.

Of course, we immediately adapt in some major ways. We accept intellectually that God exists, and we deal with some easily observed behaviors like adultery and alcoholism. But it may take a long time to get to the less easily defined parts of the story of Jah, the less rule-based parts. It may take decades to get to the real genius of the story, like loving God and our neighbors, like stopping living for ourselves, like extending grace to other people. In fact, even when we start reaching for things like that, they're always beyond any final grasp.

And that's OK; in fact, it's good. Any worthwhile story, any story approaching the depth of Jah, can never be fully understood, let alone fully lived, by human beings. Growth consists in discovering increasing levels of depth. Growth consists in letting the logic of our story take over more and more of our lives. Growth consists in our taproot reaching deeper and deeper into Jah and the story of Jah. That way our lives will be determined less and less by the competing stories of the culture.

What's not OK is leaving our taproot in some other story. Which is what's happening with Christians today. And it leaves us functioning at about the 50-percent level. So we rarely live lives of truth and grace and love. And few walls are broken down. We remain half empty, and others remain without clear witness to the warm spot at the center of the universe.

Soup cans reign.

Checking Our Stories

We're always going to carry around baggage from our culture's stories; so the question is, How do we minimize that baggage so we get most of our nourishment from Jah? How do we get at least our taproot solidly in the story of Jah?

If Descartes were right, we could just set aside all stories, all presuppositions, and build the right story from the foundations up. But for better or for worse, that doesn't seem possible. All we can do is work with the stories we have, the presuppositional constructs we start with. Which we acquired mostly from our tribe.

Not that we're trapped on the merry-go-round of whatever version of whatever story we already have. We start with it, but then we can check it out; if we're Christians, we can check our version of the story of Jah. We have three ways to do it. We can check our story and our lives for coherence (left-brained logic); we can check them for empirical adequacy (right-brained theory formation plus left-brained observation); we can check them for depth (observation and right-brained imagination).[1]

Furthermore, within limits, we can step into other stories and versions of stories and check them out too. We can ask of each: Does it meet its own criteria?[2] Does it deliver what it promises? Does it fit the universe it claims to explain, including me? Does it have the depth and grandeur to account for the wonder and horror of our universe and our selves? Does it produce a life of grace and truth?

That makes it sound complicated, and I suppose it is in a sense. But in another sense it isn't, at least for Christians. All Christians have to do is read the Bible and see if what we do fits its story (coherence). All we have to do is ask if our practice fits the story told and lived by Jesus and Paul. And usually the answer is pretty straightforward.

You don't have to be a genius to see that standard evangelical evangelism has little to do with the way Jesus talked to the rich young ruler. You don't have to be a genius to see that Jesus is hard to confuse with Arnold Schwarzenegger or Julia Roberts. You don't have to be a genius to see that Jesus never dealt with people's problems by healing their childhood memories. You don't have to be a genius to see that Jesus never spent five minutes trying to change political structures the way Christian political activists do.

It's usually pretty obvious . . . if you ask the question. All you have to do is soak yourself in the Word of God while questioning yourself about your work, your habits, your beliefs, your church—and the Spirit of God will make clear what you need to know. If you seek, Jah promises that you will find what you're in quest of: the story of Jah will get clearer and clearer. It's pretty easy really—if you give your heart, your mind, your life, for as long as you live.

Of course, I'm begging all kinds of questions. On the one hand, what I'm saying is almost simple-minded. I'm assuming that the Bible doesn't need to be demythologized. I'm assuming that Paul is authoritative for our lives. I'm assuming that we can generally tell the difference between what's normative in the Bible and what's cultural. (I'm assuming, for example, that since Paul had Jews and Gentiles in the same church, we should have African- and European-Americans in the same church, but at the same time I'm assuming that Jesus' wearing sandals doesn't mean Eskimos should.)

But on the other hand, what I'm saying is also extremely complex. I'm assuming that our understanding of the story of Jah isn't just read off the Bible in some inductive/deductive process the way evangelicals tend to think it is. Our understanding of it is an intellectual construct profoundly shaped by our culture, our church, our class, our upbringing, our commitment to self-deception. But I'm also assuming that our stories aren't completely independent of reality. So if we struggle with our whole lives against self-deception while being open to the Spirit, then the text and experience and the Spirit will eventually reshape our intellectual constructs and our lives (though it will take decades).

Life and Love

And then there's testing versions of the story by their fruit (the right-brained process). The key test of the story of Jah or any version of it is the people it produces. Jesus says: "Beware of false prophets. . . . You will know them by their fruits" (Mt 7:15-16). And since he says this near the end of the Sermon on the Mount, we should be looking especially for the fruit he asked for there. Like poverty of spirit, peacemaking, loving enemies, not being concerned about money and not being judgmental, treating others the way we want to be treated. If a story produces people like that, then they've got the story of Jah right. Otherwise, they don't.

It's simple really. If someone is telling a version of the story of Jah, you ask whether it produces love and depth or whether it produces meanness and a spirit of judgment.[3] You can usually tell right away. If they're short on love and long on pettiness, then you know that somewhere they've got the story wrong. But if you find a people in touch with the horrors and wonders of the universe, if you find a people of compassion who therefore speak truth plainly, if you find a people who give grace to each other and who like each other as well as love each other, then you're on the way home.

The Church

But Christians aren't left to sort out truth all alone. We're part of a people, part of Jah's little band of geese. And it's a good thing, too, because by ourselves we could never uncover our self-deception. We could never see what parts of our story are from Jah, what parts from our culture, and what parts from our selves. We need each other if we're to find truth, and we need each other even more if we're to live it.

But unfortunately this notion is almost unintelligible to modern people. From the Renaissance on, the Western world has been profoundly individualistic. And the Reformation didn't help anything. Luther's stand for truth was of necessity lonely. It was too easily understood as each individual interpreting the Word individualistically, with little role for sisters and brothers in the process.

Calvin and Luther understood the church to be where the Word was properly preached and the sacraments properly administered. They gave little emphasis to koinonia, to the tribal aspect of Christianity. They emphasized the individual and neglected the peoplehood of the people of God.

But after all, the most important New Testament metaphor for the church is the family, and the next most important metaphor is the body. That doesn't sound like a building. That doesn't sound like a place where you go to sit in rows to listen to sermons. It sounds instead like a people, a people together taking care of each other, helping each other, and growing each other up. We're not meant to be independent individualists with an essentially private relationship to God, but a family, a body that experiences its parts depending on each other.

Those of us who follow Jah are part of his body. So we discern *together* what parts of our story come from Jah and what parts are merely cultural. We don't need to sort it out all by ourselves. We have the discernment of our brothers and sisters throughout the ages, the discernment of our brothers and sisters throughout the world, and, most important, we have the discernment of our brothers and sisters who are part of our local tribe, of the local family of God.

The Holy Grail

In the New Testament the task of Christians is clear and simple. It's to become disciples in a local church that has other disciples and to call everyone else to do the same. It's to become part of a local body of Christ and thereby to grow bodily together into the "measure of the stature of the fullness of Christ" (Eph 4:13 RSV).

And that's about all we have to do. Which is one of the best-kept secrets in the history of the world. The Holy Grail, the secret of life, the warm spot at the center of the universe, fullness and depth, riches beyond counting— they're readily available to anyone willing to become a disciple in a local church that has other disciples. That's it. That's all. Then we're on the way home.

But to do that, all other priorities have to go. The focus we put on our jobs has to go (they're of no importance, because our only vocation is to become the church). Any commitment to where we live has to go (we might have to move in order to find a church with a reasonable number of other disciples). The centrality we give to our families has to go (they will only flourish when they've found their proper place as second to the Servant King). Any priority we give to intellectual interests has to go (they're of no importance except as they serve local churches). Our love of comfort, security and entertainment has to go.

Because becoming the church of Jesus Christ is all.

And that isn't usually exciting like resisting apartheid or hiding Jews from the Nazis, though those things happen in a faithful church. Mostly it's living as a repenting sinner among repenting sinners, many of whom you wouldn't be caught dead with if you weren't part of their little band of geese. But as you open your life to them and the Holy Spirit and as they open themselves to you and the Holy Spirit, you together grow up into the fullness of Christ—more depth than you ever imagined. The people in the church will be irritating, troubled, sinful, maddening. And the secret to life is laying down your life for them as Christ did for you. To help them (and you) get through the trouble and the sin into lives of depth.

That's the Holy Grail. Nothing romantic. Nothing thrilling. Mostly just hard work. The hard work of breaking down with our own bodies the jagged walls that divide us. Daily. Then comes the joy.

And when we start doing it, something funny happens. Those of us questioning the story of Jah get questioned ourselves. The judge becomes the judged. "Is there a warm spot at the center of the universe?" is no longer an academic question about something else. It's a question of me. Am I a warm spot? Am I part of a church that provides the warmth and the challenge and the comfort that human beings need so badly in our horrible, wonderful world?

If I am, then the story of a warm spot is true and our deepest desires are well founded.

Soup cans no longer reign. The crucified God does—the Servant King.

Notes

Chapter 1: Hollowness Within and Hollowness Without

[1]However, the late Greek and Roman empires came close, and Restoration England must have looked that way to the Puritans. Perhaps that's the fate of any civilization in decline.

[2]My Anglo-Catholic college (Keble) and therefore my philosophy tutor (Basil Mitchell) were important exceptions, but they didn't control the university syllabus.

[3]See, for example, "A Free Man's Worship," in *Mysticism and Logic* (London: George Allen and Unwin, 1917), especially pp. 55-57.

Chapter 2: The Dimensions of Our Emptiness

[1]Some other things can fill it to some degree—a family that looks beyond itself, the struggle for justice for others, some varieties of mysticism—but modern people rarely follow them. In any case, they don't really fill the void, but only make it more bearable in the proportion that they share aspects of the story of Jah.

[2]American manufacturers shipped $15.7 billion (wholesale?) in sugar and confectionery in 1983, not including baked goods (U.S. Bureau of the Census, *Statistical Abstract of the United States, 1985* [Washington, D.C.: Government Printing Office, 1984], p. 751). That year American consumers spent $28.3 billion on tobacco and $51.4 billion on alcohol (p. 435). U.S. foreign aid was $8.7 billion, one third of which was merely loaned. That same year Americans claimed $31 billion in tax deductions for giving to religion (p. 385), 5 percent of which (or $1.55 billion) went overseas (David B. Barrett, "Silver and Gold Have I None: Church of the Poor or Church of the Rich?" *International Bulletin of Missionary Research* 34 [October 1983]: 149). Meanwhile, worldwide arms manufacturing for that year is estimated at $771.1 billion.

[3]In 1990 there were 2,248,000 marriages and 1,175,000 divorces (National Center for Health Statistics, U.S. Department of Health and Human Services, quoted in

The World Almanac and Book of Facts 1992 [New York: Pharos Books, 1991], p. 942).

[4]"Kurt Vonnegut: The Faith of a Skeptic," *National Catholic Reporter,* May 16, 1986, p. 10.

[5]Each age also has characteristic ways of expressing its illumination. If the Middle Ages had the Franciscans, we have Greenpeace (thinner though it may be).

[6]I don't mean that school is always that bad, but school does tend toward maximizing information and minimizing meaning because that's the orientation of the culture. Some teachers break out of the cultural mold, of course, but unfortunately they're usually romantics like Robin Williams's character in *Dead Poets Society.*

I'm not saying that rhyme and rhythm have no aesthetic value but that they're rarely the place to start, especially since their measurability is what's usually being taught rather than their beauty.

[7]I don't mean to suggest that things like Greek and New Testament introduction are irrelevant. They're vital, but they're no substitute for the idea of the holy. We need both, and the dichotomy is one of the worst parts of the legacy of secularism.

[8]Thomas à Kempis *Of the Imitation of Christ* 1. 1. 3. Of course, Thomas wrote this in the fifteenth century, before secularism. Perhaps under Greek influence, Western thought has always had a tendency to focus on the merely rational. This may also be a tendency of males, like in seminaries (till recently) and monasteries.

[9]How trivia relate to the great questions is itself one of the great questions, and the romantic answer reflected in my game is as disastrous as it is common. See chapters five and six.

[10]Donald Nicholl, *Holiness* (New York: Seabury, 1981), p. 4.

[11]See chapter fourteen.

[12]Martin Buber, *I and Thou,* trans. Walter Kaufmann (New York: Scribner, 1970).

Chapter 3: The Implacable Tide

[1]Plato *Apology* 26.

[2]Or at least it thought it did.

[3]This wasn't true for the Hebrews, for whom God was transcendent. However, from their point of view, God was responsible for everything; God's hand was behind everything.

And it's an oversimplification for Greek philosopher-scientists like Aristotle. Though they rejected Anaxagoras's views, they nonetheless didn't give mythological, personal explanations of events. They explained things in terms like "purpose" and "essence" and "unmoved mover," which though far from the approach of modern science are even farther from mythic explanations. (For a discussion of this point, see A. C. Crombie, *Medieval and Early Modern Science,* 2 vols., 2nd rev. ed. [Garden City, N.Y.: Doubleday/Anchor Books, 1959], 2:4-5.)

[4]My Nothings are related to Plato's opinions.

[5]See, for example, Arvin Vos, *Aquinas, Calvin and Contemporary Protestant Thought: A Critique of Protestant Views on the Thought of Thomas Aquinas* (Grand Rapids,

Mich.: Eerdmans/Christian University Press, 1985).

[6]Galileo, Kepler, Descartes and Locke articulated this theory at most length. (It's what Locke meant by primary and secondary qualities.)

[7]I am omitting one aspect of the change: the uniformity of the universe. It's crucial in the growth of science but not crucial in understanding the rise of secularism. For a wonderful explanation, see Alfred North Whitehead, "The First Physical Synthesis," in *Science and Civilization*, ed. F. S. Martin (New York: Oxford University Press, 1923), pp. 161-79.

[8]"voices to voices, lip to lip," in *Complete Poems, 1913-1962* (New York: Harcourt Brace Jovanovich, 1972), p. 264. I have omitted an opening parenthesis at the beginning of the first quoted line.

[9]For a discussion of this idea, see *Alphaville*, a 1965 film written and directed by Jean-Luc Godard; the filmscript is published as *Alphaville, a Film by Jean-Luc Godard*, trans. Peter Whitehead (New York: Simon and Schuster, 1966), especially p. 49.

[10]The French *philosophe* Julien La Mettrie proposed it in his book *Man the Machine*, published in 1747, but his position seemed indefensible to most people till Darwin's work more than a century later.

[11]In fact, I don't find it convincing myself, but fighting that battle isn't the point here. The point is rather the historical and logical one that evolution was crucial in the rise of secularism. Before Darwin, most people thought it irrational not to believe in a creator, but after Darwin, deism practically died out and thorough secularism became common. (Increasing awareness that things were not as orderly as had been thought also played a role; stars, for example, can collide.)

[12]Stephen Crane, "A Man Said to the Universe," in *War Is Kind*, reprinted in *Poems and Literary Reviews*, ed. Fredson Bowers, University of Virginia Edition of the Works of Stephen Crane 10 (Charlottesville: University Press of Virginia, 1975), p. 57.

[13]J. A. C. Brown, *Freud and the Post-Freudians* (Harmondsworth, Middlesex, U.K.: Penguin Books, 1961), pp. 13-14.

[14]Carl G. Jung and depth psychology are examples of psychology reaching for something else. I consider them a variety of romanticism, which I discuss in chapters five and six.

Chapter 4: Secularism Triumphant

[1]*Webster's New Collegiate Dictionary* (Springfield, Mass.: G. and C. Merriam, 1980), q.v., defines the Enlightenment as "a philosophic movement of the eighteenth century marked by questioning of traditional doctrines and values, a tendency toward individualism, an emphasis on the idea of universal human progress, the empirical method in science, and the free use of reason." In England its proponents were people like Locke and Hume, in France Voltaire and Diderot, in the United States Jefferson and Franklin.

[2]Epitaph intended for Sir Isaac Newton. Pope vigorously opposed the Enlighten-

ment, but this quotation shows how deeply the thought of an age invades the thinking even of its opponents. Notice how, in contrast to the early Middle Ages, light is now understood as science and scientists.

[3]Another factor was the Reformation insistence on the goodness of all creation and on jobs being vocations whether secular or churchly. Other factors, not entirely intellectual, were things like the rise of capitalism and the discovery of lands where crowded Europeans could settle.

[4]*Meno* 82-86.

[5]Plato *Republic* 7. 514-18.

[6]By this I mean to include both the Platonism mediated by Plotinus and Augustine and the Aristotelianism mediated by Thomas Aquinas. For the present purposes they are alike in giving metaphysical standing to forms that can be known.

[7]The Platonist metaphysic saw physical reality as suspect, and this led to a negative evaluation of the physical, mentioned above. Perhaps even worse, the metaphysic lent itself to hierarchy since something that is purer Form (a rational man) is going to be better than something that is less pure Form (dirt—or an emotional woman!). And the epistemology put an emphasis on reason that impoverished both observation and emotion, which in turn impoverished both science and personal relationships. It also saw changeableness as bad, thus giving us the odd and unbiblical idea that God doesn't feel, move or change in any way.

[8]I owe much of this to Charles Taylor, *Sources of the Self: The Making of the Modern Identity* (Cambridge, Mass.: Harvard University Press, 1989).

[9]Rembrandt's painting himself crucifying Jesus wouldn't have been possible because that requires a view of evil and forgiveness foreign to Plato (and to everything outside the Judeo-Christian-Islamic tradition).

[10]The relationship between pleasure and happiness, between pain and unhappiness is much debated. I'm going to ignore the issue and treat them as comparable. Though that's not correct, it shouldn't affect this argument.

[11]They have also replaced God's law, but that is not the topic of this chapter.

[12]However, utilitarianism is only a part of the difference between supporters and critics of abortion. Utilitarianism doesn't explain why the pain of the fetus is not taken into account by supporters of abortion. The disagreement is also a metaphysical one over whether what is aborted is a person, over whether its pain counts.

[13]Especially Anglo-Saxons. That is why at Oxford so much energy is invested in the meaning of the word *good*. So my studies there turned out to be far more important than I said in chapter one.

[14]The classic statement of the issue is in G. E. Moore, *Principia Ethica* (Cambridge, U.K.: Cambridge University Press, 1903). Logically, the point is clearer in the negative. "It's not good to maximize happiness" seems to make sense, but it turns out to be self-contradictory. If *good* means *maximizing happiness*, the sentence then means, "It's not maximizing happiness to maximize happiness," and that clearly isn't what it means since the first form isn't self-contradictory.

[15]William Wordsworth, "Ode: Intimations of Immortality from Recollections of Early Childhood," in *The Oxford Book of English Verse 1250-1918,* ed. Arthur Quiller-Couch (Oxford, U.K.: Clarendon, 1957), p. 628.

[16]I am trying to avoid metaphysical dualism by seeing spirit as one aspect of reality and matter as another aspect of that same reality. I suspect that that is the account of both the Old Testament and the New Testament.

[17]For a discussion of how recent late philosophers resolve this problem, see chapter fourteen, starting with the section on Wittgenstein.

[18]A standard reply is that values are a "social contract." Apart from the fact that no such contract has ever been made, the argument is circular. The notion of a moral obligation to keep contracts must come before the contract and so can't be based on it.

[19]*Alphaville*, a 1965 film written and directed by Jean-Luc Godard; filmscript published as *Alphaville, a Film by Jean-Luc Godard,* trans. Peter Whitehead (New York: Simon and Schuster, 1966), p. 69, adapted. The film is a parable about a technologically powerful culture without values. That's also the theme of *That Hideous Strength* by C. S. Lewis and in a sense *1984* by George Orwell.

[20]H. R. Rookmaaker, *Modern Art and the Death of a Culture* (Downers Grove, Ill.: InterVarsity Press, 1970), p. 173.

[21]John Russell, *Francis Bacon* (London: Methuen, 1965), p. 1, quoted in Rookmaaker, *Modern Art,* p. 174.

[22]A good example is Bertrand Russell, "A Free Man's Worship," in *Mysticism and Logic* (London: George Allen and Unwin, 1917), especially pp. 56-57.

[23]I've always attributed this to a sonnet by John Masefield, but I can't find it among his sonnets.

Chapter 5: A Feeling of Passionate Mercy

[1]The revolt started just sixteen years after the publication of Descartes's first major work: he published *The Discourse on Method* in 1637, and the ideas for Pascal's *Pensées* probably crystallized in 1653. At that time Galileo had just died, Newton was thirteen, Locke was twenty-three, and the Enlightenment and the birth of Voltaire were half a century off. (However, the *Pensées* weren't actually published till 1670, eight years after Pascal's death.)

[2]Blaise Pascal *Pensées* 277.

[3]Ibid. 152.

[4]*L'esprit de géometrie* and *l'esprit de finesse.*

[5]That is, of course, a terribly broad use for both of these words. (I'm including empiricism in rationalism, and existentialism in romanticism, for instance.) I'm aware that this usage goes well beyond the academic definitions of the terms, but it's a common use of the words and is in any case a clear way of marking off two distinct streams of thought for which we have no other standard terminology.

Clearly that is to paint the intellectual landscape in strokes so broad that it involves some oversimplifying, but I hope it clarifies the structure of our intellectual mountains and valleys in a way that gets lost when each tree and leaf is painted in detail.

[6]The great work in pure physical science is creative theory formation. So pure science has more in common with creative art than with sequential calculation based on collecting data from observation. Perhaps that's why the greatest of physical scientists often have not embraced the rationalistic vision of science. Perhaps that was left to minor scientists like Francis Bacon.

[7]If you're right-handed, that's how it works; it's reversed if you're left-handed.

[8]So if right-handed people with the connections severed between the two hemispheres see something with the right eye, they can name it and draw the parts accurately. However, the parts won't be joined together well. If they see the same thing with the left eye, they won't be able to name it but they'll be able to draw it well. For a popular discussion of this topic, see Betty Edwards, *Drawing on the Right Side of the Brain: A Course in Enhancing Creativity and Artistic Confidence* (Los Angeles: J. P. Tarcher, 1979), especially pp. 25-43; Erica Eerdman and David Stover, *Beyond a World Divided: Human Values in the Brain-Mind Science of Roger Sperry* (Boston: Shambhala, 1991); Roger W. Sperry, *Science and Moral Priority: Merging Mind, Brain and Human Values* (New York: Columbia University Press, 1983). Jung made a similar distinction between those oriented to truth and the sensate compared to those oriented to feeling and intuition.

For a more technical discussion with evaluation of the physiological evidence see: D. Frank Benson and Eran Zaidel, eds., *The Dual Brain: Hemispheric Specialization in Humans* (New York: Guilford, 1985); *Proceedings of the Sixth International Symposium of the Centre de Recherche en Sciences Neurologique of the Université de Montreal: Neurology and Neurobiology*, vol. 17: *Two Hemispheres, One Brain: Functions of the Corpus Callosum* (New York: Liss, 1986); Colwyn Trevarthan, ed., *Brain Circuits and Functions of the Mind: Essays in Honor of Roger W. Sperry* (Cambridge, U.K.: Cambridge University Press, 1990).

[9]I'm not making a serious claim that people fit neatly into one of these types or the other. I suspect that these lists include a number of independent factors, that it's not just one continuum.

[10]e. e. cummings, *Complete Poems: 1913-1962* (New York: Harcourt Brace Jovanovich, 1972), p. 290.

[11]Pascal *Pensées* 265.

[12]Ibid. 489.

[13]It's only accurate to say that near the end of his life, Rousseau seems to have approached clinical paranoia; so some of his penetrating analysis is actually nastiness.

[14]Jean-Jacques Rousseau, "Discourse on Inequality," in *The Social Contract and Discourses*, trans. G. D. H. Cole (London: Everyman Library, 1938), p. 207.

[15]William Blake, "Great Things Are Done," in *The Complete Poems*, ed. Alicia Ostriker (Harmondsworth, Middlesex, U.K.: Penguin Books, 1977), p. 624.

[16]Jean-Jacques Rousseau, *Emile, or Education*, trans. B. Foxley (London: Everyman

Library, 1938), p. 253.

[17]Ibid., p. 249.

[18]Ibid., p. 239.

[19]William Wordsworth, "The World," reprinted in *The Oxford Book of English Verse 1250-1918*, ed. Arthur Quiller-Couch (Oxford, U.K.: Clarendon, 1957), p. 626.

[20]At this point, the chapter becomes more obviously autobiographical. My story isn't especially important, but I hope its concreteness will make it easier for people to understand the power of romanticism.

[21]Kierkegaard's comment about someone else (*The Journals of Kierkegaard 1834-1854*, ed. and trans. Alexander Dru [London: Fontana Books, 1958], p. 57).

[22]Ibid., pp. 56-57.

[23]Ibid., p. 48.

[24]I'm not attempting to explain here the more technical parts of Kierkegaard's thought. He's much more than a romantic.

[25]Kierkegaard, *Journals*, pp. 252-53.

[26]Ibid., p. 44, emphases Kierkegaard's.

[27]I found it in *Existentialism from Dostoevsky to Sartre*, ed. Walter Kaufmann (New York: Meridian Books, 1956), pp. 255ff., reprinted from *Being and Nothingness*, trans. Hazel E. Barnes (New York: Washington Square, 1966), pp. 71ff.

[28]I'm not referring here to Nothing as used by Sartre and many other existentialists.

[29]Barth didn't say that the resurrection was irrelevant, but that's the logic of his position as worked out in Bultmann.

[30]I owed the line to Francis Schaeffer.

[31]e. e. cummings, *Complete Poems.*

Chapter 6: The Romantic Dead End

[1]My title was *Taking Jesus Seriously*, but Harper & Row renamed it *Your Money or Your Life*.

[2]Mt 12:7 RSV, quoting Hos 6:6.

[3]Mt 9:13; 1 Sam 15:22; Ps 40:6; Is 1:11-13; 40:16; 66:1-4; Jer 7:21-24; Hos 6:6; 8:11-14; Amos 5:21-24; Mic 6:6-8.

[4]Kenneth Patchen, *Hallelujah Anyway* (New York: New Directions, 1967), last page (page numbers not given).

[5]The arguments that follow aren't in the chronological order in which I became convinced of them. Rather, they're the arguments that seem decisive to me now. Some of them I knew all along (I was never a full-blown romantic), and others I arrived at later, but the writing got too cumbersome when I gave the arguments chronologically.

I fear it took me some time to sort out that Jesus never offered a general justification of acting on feelings; he merely told us to feel *with* others. I need to feel with the mother *and* the baby and also with an unmarried couple wanting to have sex, but that doesn't mean their feelings are all that matters. They're part of the data in making ethical decisions but not all of it.

[6]Quoted in H. R. Rookmaaker, *Modern Art and the Death of a Culture* (Downers Grove, Ill.: InterVarsity Press, 1970), p. 90.

[7]Ibid., p. 92. Gauguin lived it out in an extreme form, but Ralph Waldo Emerson said the same thing: "I shun father and mother and wife and brother when my genius calls me. . . . I must be myself" ("Self-Reliance," in *Essays: First Series,* 1841). Jesus agrees that father and mother and wife and brother sometimes have to be abandoned, but for the sake of *my genius,* for the sake of *being myself?* Hardly. Kids probably no longer read this essay in high school the way we did when I was young, but no wonder my generation is given to self-indulgence masquerading as art.

[8]We don't know whether his children died, because he sent them away without any identification; so no one knew which ones they were, Rousseau included.

[9]Caryn James, "How Woody Let Us Down," *San Francisco Chronicle,* September 13, 1992, Datebook p. 21.

[10]José Arguelles, *The Mayan Factor: The Path Beyond Technology* (Santa Fe, N.M.: Bear and Co., 1987). This is the publisher Matthew Fox backs.

[11]See, for example, *The New York Times,* August 11, 1987, Science Times p. 1, and *The New York Times,* August 17, 1987, main section p. 1.

[12]e. e. cummings, *Complete Poems: 1913-1962* (New York: Harcourt Brace Jovanovich, 1972), p. 736.

[13]Ibid., p. 769.

[14]Romanticism couldn't fully arise until secular rationalism began sweeping all before it—for romanticism is primarily a reaction against rationalism. So romanticism defines itself substantially as the negation of rationalism (though keeping its individualism and optimism), attacking reason in a way no one would have done if rationalism hadn't gone so badly wrong.

[15]Jacques Louis David designed the costumes for the ceremony at Notre Dame where reason was crowned.

[16]I recognize the extremely subjective nature of these sweeping generalizations. It would be better to spell them out in detail, but that would take a whole book, and besides I'm not sure I know enough to do it.

They are at best hints. At worst, they may be nonsense. In the first place, I don't know the work of some of the people well enough to speak with authority. In the second place, that Shakespeare and Goethe and Michelangelo are better than the romantics doesn't prove a lot: they're better than anyone. The question is whether that has any connection with their being neither romantics nor rationalists, or is it just their greatness as artists? If they had fallen into the abyss on one side or the other, would they have been less great?

Yet I'm struck by the fact that when you consider the great artists and writers, few of them have been romantics. (Perhaps only Dostoyevsky and Van Gogh, at least on my list, though perhaps I should include Wordsworth and Stendahl.) Can that be an accident?

[17]cummings, *Complete Poems,* p. 377.

Chapter 7: Authenticating Story by the Lives of Storytellers

[1]It's no accident that the first classic statement of the modern position (published in 1637) was entitled *Discourse on the Method of Rightly Directing One's Reason and of Seeking Truth in the Sciences*, by René Descartes.

[2]Descartes, *Discourse*, pt. 2, in *Descartes: Philosophical Writings*, ed. and trans. Elizabeth Anscombe and Peter Geach (London: Thomas Nelson and Sons, 1954), pp. 15-16.

[3]In order to make this book more intelligible to modern people, I spent one of the most frustrating summers of my life trying to write first about methods. I couldn't do it. My fundamental commitments were to content, or perhaps to a whole picture; so it was hard to get a foothold starting with methods.

In fact, the hardest part of writing this book was that with a commitment to a whole picture, it was hard for me to get a toehold *anywhere*. When every piece depends on every other piece, which piece do you start with? This is especially tricky when many readers are liable to be committed to dispassionate, atomistic foundationalism and are therefore opposed to the sort of presuppositions I think you need at the start.

[4]Immanuel Kant, *Critique of Pure Reason;* Hermann Dooyeweerd (see, for example, *In the Twilight of Western Thought* [Nutley, N.J.: Craig Press, 1965]); Nicholas Wolterstorff, *Reason Within the Bounds of Religion*, 2nd ed. (Grand Rapids, Mich.: Eerdmans, 1984); Karl R. Popper, *Conjectures and Refutations: The Growth of Scientific Knowledge* (New York: Harper & Row, 1963); Alasdair MacIntyre, *Whose Justice? Which Rationality?* (Notre Dame, Ind.: University of Notre Dame Press, 1988); Thomas S. Kuhn, *The Structure of Scientific Revolutions* (Chicago: University of Chicago Press, 1962); Jacques Derrida, *Of Grammatology*, trans. Gayatri Chakravorty Spivak (Baltimore: Johns Hopkins University Press, 1974). I, of course, don't mean to imply that all these people would be comfortable being called presuppositionalists, but each of them realizes that we add a great deal to our perceptions and worldviews; we don't just read them off the world.

[5]In *The Story of Philosophy*, Will Durant devotes a whole chapter to Bacon while hardly mentioning Locke or Hume ([New York: Simon and Schuster, 1926], pp. 75-112). In fact, Durant seems to say (p. 107) that Bacon understood scientific method better than Galileo did!

[6]This discussion is based on Popper, *Conjectures and Refutations*, especially pp. 33-65; see also his *The Logic of Scientific Discovery* (New York: Harper & Row, 1959).

[7]Popper himself was reasonably aware of this.

[8]I'm aware of the effort of post-Wittgensteinian analytic philosophers to show this particular fly the way out of the fly-bottle. (See, for example, O. K. Bouwsma, "Descartes' Skepticism of the Senses," *Mind*, n.s. 54 (October 1945): 313-22. However, for reasons too complex to explain here, I find this specific application of Wittgensteinian method utterly unconvincing.

[9]The Wittgensteinian method is a little more convincing here. See, for example, Paul Edwards, "Bertrand Russell's Doubts About Induction," in *Logic and Language:*

First Series, ed. A. G. N. Flew (Oxford, U.K.: Basil Blackwell, 1960), pp. 55-79.

[10]*Intellego ut credam* (I understand in order that I may believe).

[11]*Credo ut intellegam* (I believe in order that I may understand), to use Augustine's classic phrase. The tapestry I'm weaving is substantially Augustinian, but I'm even more indebted to those mentioned in note 4 above. I should also mention H. R. Rookmaaker, *Modern Art and the Death of a Culture* (Downers Grove, Ill.: InterVarsity Press, 1970), and Francis Schaeffer (see, for example, *Escape from Reason* [Downers Grove, Ill.: InterVarsity Press, 1968]); Alvin Plantinga and Nicholas Wolterstorff, eds., *Faith and Rationality: Reason and Belief in God* (Notre Dame, Ind.: University of Notre Dame Press, 1983); all the work of Stanley Hauerwas, perhaps especially *A Community of Character: Toward a Constructive Christian Social Ethic* (Notre Dame, Ind.: University of Notre Dame Press, 1981).

[12]I don't mean to say that our observations are irrelevant to our imaginative constructs, but only that since we have to fit our observations into our existing constructs, our observations are partly shaped by those constructs. As a result, the line between where one begins and the other ends is not precise. However, the time comes when certain observations are so intrusive that we have to alter our constructs or admit confusion. "Observation and experience can and must restrict the range of admissible scientific belief. . . . But they cannot alone determine a particular body of belief" (Kuhn, *Structure of Scientific Revolutions,* p. 4).

[13]J. S. Brunner and Leo Postman, "On the Perception of Incongruity: A Paradigm," *Journal of Personality* 18 (1949): 206-23, referred to in Kuhn, *Structure of Scientific Revolutions,* pp. 63-64.

[14]Kuhn, *Structure of Scientific Revolutions,* pp. 53-58.

[15]*Credo quia impossibile,* to paraphrase Tertullian. He was saying something closer to Augustine when he said, "Truth persuades by teaching but does not teach by persuading" (*Adversus Valentinanos* 1).

[16]As we will see in the next chapter, it has enough precision to falsify most forms of Christianity. For the classic discussion of Popper and the falsifiability of Christianity, see Anthony Flew, R. M. Hare and Basil Mitchell, "Theology and Falsification," in *New Essays in Philosophical Theology,* ed. Anthony Flew and Alasdair MacIntyre (London: SCM, 1955), pp. 96-108.

[17]For more on factual evidence, see also Mt 11:22-24; 15:30-31; Lk 1:1-4; 5:4-11; 9:41-43; Jn 1:50-51; 2:18-19, 23; 3:2; 4:29, 39; 7:31; 9:28-34; 10:21, 24-25, 38; 11:14, 45-48; 12:9-11, 18, 37; 15:22-25; Acts 2:22; 1 Cor 15:1-34. John emphasizes evidence especially. The quantity and clarity of texts on factual evidence should overwhelm those Christians inclined to dismiss the importance of factuality.

[18]See, for example, John Warwick Montgomery, *The Shape of the Past: An Introduction to Philosophical Historiography,* vol. 1 of *History in Christian Perspective* (Ann Arbor, Mich.: Edwards Brothers, 1962), pp. 138-41. Actually, even in this form the argument is closer to Popper than to Bacon.

[19]*The Jefferson Bible: With the Annotated Commentaries on Religion of Thomas Jefferson,* ed. O. I. A. Roche (New York: Clarkson N. Potter, 1964).

[20]Basil Mitchell suggested a scenario something like this to me in a tutorial in 1962.

[21]I regularly hear this attributed to Ralph Waldo Emerson, but he actually said, "A *foolish* consistency [emphasis mine] is the hobgoblin of little minds ("Self-Reliance," in *Essays: First Series*, 1841). I suspect he was saying that only little people avoid contradicting themselves to avoid admitting error. That would be refusal to grow—and the sign of a very little mind indeed.

[22]Ironically, rationalistic secularism seems to be an exception. With its rejection of assumptions, its denial that it has a metaphysic behind its science, with its affirmation of value, it involves itself in endlessly silly self-contradictions. This is clearest with logical positivism, according to which everything that can't be confirmed by the verification principle is meaningless—and then the verification principle turned out to be unverifiable.

[23]As Descartes said, "Fables make one imagine various events as possible when they are not; and the most faithful historians, even if they do not alter or exaggerate the importance of matters to make them more readable, almost always leave out the meaner and less striking circumstances of the events; consequently the remainder has a false appearance, and those who govern their conduct by examples drawn from history are liable to fall into the extravagances of the paladins of romance and conceive designs beyond their powers" (*Discourse*, p. 11).

[24]Plato suggests that the soul is like a chariot with the emotions as the horses and reason as the charioteer trying to control them (*Phaedrus* 246. a. 6ff.). The force of his metaphor is that certain emotions, like rage and resentment, presumably do need to be held in check; most of us are suspicious of them, and rightly so. But what about pity and awe? Should they also be held in check? The poverty of the West is revealed in treating all emotions as if they were alike. We have an incredibly impoverished anatomy of passion. Plato's metaphor had at least two horses, one good and one bad, but dispassionate foundationalism is not so profligate in its taxonomy and neither is romanticism.

[25]See Mt 9:36; 14:14; 15:32; 20:34; Mk 1:41; 6:34; 8:2; Lk 7:13. See also Mt 18:27; Mk 9:22; Lk 15:20; 2 Cor 6:12; 7:15; Phil 1:8; Philem 7, 12, 20.

[26]See, for example, Rom 6:6; Rom 7—9; Gal 4—5; Eph 4:22-24; Col 3:9; see also Jn 6:63. Of course, none of these passages separate feelings from actions any more than Jesus did.

[27]You shouldn't even try to do this by yourself. In Catholic spirituality, you do it with the help of a spiritual director. In Anabaptist spirituality, you do it with the help of a discerning community.

[28]This is derived from Augustine, but in different language the idea is in Jesus. He speaks of what fulfills us as life, as springs of living water, eternal life, the pearl of great price, true bread. And Augustine's hollowness is equivalent to Jesus' death, selling your soul, bread that perishes.

[29]Augustine *Confessions* 1. 1.

[30]However, this can be tricky. At first, true life may feel like it is empty because the old self doesn't want to die.

Chapter 8: A Cross with Nails

[1]Notice that I'm suggesting that the lives of individual Christians by themselves can't quite authenticate the story; Jesus' criterion requires a loving people, not a series of loving individuals ("love one another"). Christianity at its very heart is corporate and has no truck with Western individualism.

Remember too that by "authenticate" I don't mean some sort of geometric proof of the sort Descartes wanted. That seems to me to be both impossible and irrelevant.

[2]I owe this and much of the rest of this book to Francis Schaeffer. For this chapter, see *The Church at the End of the Twentieth Century* (Downers Grove, Ill.: InterVarsity Press, 1970), pp. 133-53. That section of the book also appears separately as *The Mark of the Christian* (Downers Grove, Ill.: InterVarsity Press, 1970). I don't mean to imply, however, that my use of the phrase is exactly the same as his.

[3]This isn't meant as a criticism of the Odd Fellows. I choose them because what little I know of them is quite positive; they're a reasonable standard to measure a church against.

[4]Francis Schaeffer says, "Jesus is not here saying that our failure to love all Christians proves that we are not Christians. . . . What Jesus is saying, however, is that, if I do not have the love I should have toward all other Christians, the world has the right to make the judgment that I am not a Christian. This distinction is imperative" (*The Church at the End of the Twentieth Century*, p. 137).

I hope this is correct, but I'm not sure it takes into account 1 John, especially 2:1-11 and 3:14.

[5]See also Jn 15:12-13; 1 Jn 2:9-11; 3:11-15, 23; 4:7-8, 11-12, 19-21.

[6]See also Jn 17:11; 14:31.

[7]To anyone familiar with the work of Stanley Hauerwas, it will be obvious that he influences me profoundly—not, however, at this point. In my critique of organized religion, I accept what Troeltsch calls "sectarianism" (*The Social Teachings of the Christian Churches* [New York: Macmillan, 1931], 2:993). That is a choice Hauerwas is accused of but which he steadfastly refuses to make. If I could agree with him, it would solve much of the problem in this chapter.

[8]Antoine de Saint Exupéry, *The Little Prince* (New York: Harcourt Brace and World, 1943), pp. 41-47.

[9]*In hoc signo vinces.*

[10]Even fundamentalists who believe that the Sermon on the Mount is for a later age still have to deal with parallel teachings in the Epistles.

[11]Mt 5:39-42.

[12]"Servants, be submissive to your masters with all respect, not only to the kind and gentle but also to the overbearing. . . . If when you do right and suffer for it you take it patiently, you have God's approval. For to this you have been called, because Christ also suffered for you, leaving you an example, that you should follow in his steps. . . . When he was reviled, he did not revile in return; when he suffered, he did not threaten; but he trusted to him who judges justly. He

himself bore our sins in his body on the tree, that we might die to sin and live to righteousness. By his wounds you have been healed" (1 Pet 2:18, 20-21, 23-24 RSV).

For more on rights, see chapter eleven.

[13]Romans 12 starts with an appeal to "present your bodies as a living sacrifice." Then Paul says, don't "think of yourselves more highly than you ought to think," for the church is a body, and the parts of the body have different roles. We should fill the role God has given us. Then, "Bless those who persecute you; bless and do not curse them" alongside of "Live in harmony with one another; do not be haughty, but associate with the lowly; do not claim to be wiser than you are. Do not repay anyone evil for evil." And that's alongside of "If it is possible, so far as it depends on you, live peaceably with all." Which is right beside "Beloved, never avenge yourselves, but leave room for the wrath of God; for it is written, 'Vengeance is mine, I will repay, says the Lord.' No, 'if your enemies are hungry, feed them; if they are thirsty, give them something to drink; for by doing this you will heap coals of fire on their heads.' Do not be overcome by evil, but overcome evil with good" (vv. 19-21).

[14]By and large, Christians have weakened the stringency of Jesus' teaching beyond recognition. That argument deserves more space than I give it here, but I have made the point in detail in *Your Money or Your Life* (San Francisco: Harper & Row, 1986).

[15]Some claim that he became Christian cynically, because in a divided empire he needed the support of this growing group. However, Christians weren't powerful enough in the empire for that to seem likely. See A. H. M. Jones, *Constantine and the Conversion of Europe*, 2nd ed., rev. (New York: Collier Books, 1962), pp. 73-74.

[16]Susan Howatch, *Glamorous Powers* (New York: Fawcett Crest, 1988), p. 127.

[17]Ibid., p. 130.

[18]Ibid., p. 132.

[19]Tertullian *Apology* 39. 8.

[20]Gerhard Lohfink, *Jesus and Community: The Social Dimensions of Christian Faith*, trans. John P. Galvin (Philadelphia: Fortress/New York: Paulist, 1984), p. 175. I am heavily indebted to Lohfink throughout this chapter.

[21]Origen *Contra Celsum* 3. 33, trans. and ed. Henry Chadwick (Cambridge, U.K.: Cambridge University Press, 1953), p. 150, quoted in Lohfink, *Jesus and Community*, p. 179.

[22]Athenagoras *Plea for the Christians* 11, in Alexander Roberts and James Donaldson, eds., *Justin Martyr and Athenagoras*, vol. 2 of *The Ante-Nicene Christian Library*, trans. Marcus Dod, George Reith and B. P. Pratten (Edinburgh: T. and T. Clark, 1867), p. 387, quoted in Lohfink, *Jesus and Community*, p. 177.

[23]Rolf Hochhuth, *The Deputy*, trans. Richard and Clara Winston (New York: Grove, 1964), p. 14.

[24]Ibid., p. 289.

[25]Nechama Tec, *Where Light Pierced the Darkness: Christian Rescue of Jews in Nazi-Occupied Poland* (Oxford, U.K.: Oxford University Press, 1986), p. 84, especially note 15. Israel officially recognizes 1,505 Righteous Christians (people who risked their lives for Jews) in Poland, and they estimate that at least ten times that number would be if they were known and nominated. According to some, the number might be as high as 100,000. At least 343 Poles are known to have died defending Jews.

[26]"Confrontation: Adolf Hitler/Bruderhof 1933," *The Plough: Publication of the Bruderhof Communities* 21 (March-April 1989): 7-17.

[27]Popper and Flew wouldn't be impressed. (See chapter seven.)

[28]George Bernard Shaw, preface to *Androcles and the Lion* (New York: Brentano's, 1922), p. xiii.

Chapter 9: Two Plans of Salvation

[1]How many stories you think deal with salvation depends on how explicit it has to be to count. I'm inclined to say that a story deals with salvation any time, for example, a person is portrayed as succeeding or when that theme is parodied. I'm also inclined to count any story that implies moral advice, like marry the person you love, and any story that assumes that a particular way of life is ideal, like being white and upper-middle-class. I also count stories that end in despair—that say there is no plan of salvation.

[2]This is, of course, simplistic. To give it a semblance of truth, you have to treat stories like "The Three Little Pigs" (whose plan of salvation is industriousness) as part of the Schwarzenegger plan, and you have to treat stories like *Mississippi Masala* (whose plan of salvation is to forget status and marry the person you love that week) as part of the Julia Roberts plan.

[3]Why are stepmothers so seldom good and witches so seldom male?

[4]Most fairy tales fit here. If they don't have wicked women as the problem, they still usually have strong men as the savior.

[5]Contemporary versions of the story often change some of the symbolism under pressure from the civil rights movement, feminism and the like; so powerful women and blacks are now relatively common. Schwarzenegger's *Terminator 2*, for example, portrays a good, muscular woman and a good, black man. And when someone as politically correct as Kevin Costner makes an evil woman central in *Robin Hood*, he balances her by adding a black man as underhero.

This seems to me to be changing for the better how evil is perceived, but the central message of salvation by power remains unchanged. Crucial as racial, gender and handicap are, that symbolism is culturally conditioned, and symbols can be revised or even reversed while leaving the plan of salvation otherwise intact. That seems to me to be much of what's happening in *Thelma and Louise* and *Malcolm X*. There are two sorts of change: one changes the plan of salvation (as in *Pretty Woman*), the other keeps the story but changes the symbols. Black power and feminist power keep the story but allow blacks and women in on the same footing as white males, though both *Thelma and Louise* and *Malcolm X* have more to be said for them than that.

[6]Especially her recent books: *Always Coming Home* (New York: Harper & Row, 1985) and *Tehanu: The Last Book of Earthsea* (New York: Atheneum, 1990).

[7]Rockford is admittedly a very male version of the story, but his incompetence and failure ever to get paid moves him from Schwarzenegger's camp to Julia Roberts's. In "All in the Family," Archie (a white male) is anything but a savior, and Edith (an ineffectual woman) is a source of goodness. Similar arguments could be made for "Scarecrow and Mrs. King," and in "M*A*S*H" the white male heroes are heroic precisely in being Schwarzenegger reversed.

[8]These were all major films in 1991. Major ones from previous years are *Dances with Wolves, Emerald Forest, King of Hearts* and *Barefoot in the Park*.

Schwarzenegger's *Kindergarten Cop* is an interesting combination of the two plans: he saves a helpless (and beautiful) woman and child by power but is saved himself by becoming a sensitive kindergarten teacher. This combination of the two plans may be our culture's first choice for a plan of salvation, at least for the moment.

[9]To be fair, this story isn't all bad. (An archetype as popular as this one must have something to it, or I doubt that it would be so central in our culture's unconscious.) At least, it sees the struggle between good and evil as primal, and it offers the hope of salvation. And often the hero is kind and gentle except possibly when facing evil.

On some level, we all love this story. "Gunsmoke" and "Star Trek" are among my favorite television programs (though that's partly because television has a dearth of programs with Julia Roberts's plan of salvation). And Robin Hood—well, he's the hero after whom all white male social activists model their lives.

Or take Matt Dillon of "Gunsmoke." He's a kindly man who treats women and lame people well. And he never uses violence except as the last resort. He's the father we've always wanted. In fact, along with Walter Cronkite, I suspect he's my generation's image of God. Strong, tough, compassionate and fair. (If only he'd run for president!) But by the end of almost every program, he reached the last resort—and shot someone. Power is the final key.

Power which belongs only to God.

[10]The culture is pretty close to that of certain California Indians. The K in Ursula K. Le Guin stands for Kroeber. Her father was the great anthropologist Alfred L. Kroeber, who cared for Ishi, the last wild Indian in the United States. Le Guin's mother, Theodora Kroeber, wrote *Ishi in Two Worlds: A Biography of the Last Wild Indian in North America* (Berkeley: University of California Press, 1961). Le Guin's work tends to follow her parents' ideals, with her latest books giving those ideals a feminist twist.

[11]See, for example, Suzanne Gordon, *Prisoners of Men's Dreams: Striking Out for a New Feminine Future* (Boston: Little, Brown, 1991), though the ideas are much older than that book.

[12]*Pretty Woman*'s plan of salvation is rarely used by hard-core secularists, because for it to be at all plausible requires some sort of spiritual underpinning. But that doesn't mean romantics always use *Pretty Woman*. Hitler preferred Schwarzenegger for his version of romanticism, as do romantic skinheads and many in hard rock.

And Schwarzenegger's story is older and more appealing than secularism and rationalism. It was the standard story of Greece and Rome (the favorite of Homer and Virgil with a little cultural adaptation), though Socrates and Plato opposed it; Constantine made it the standard story for standard Christianity; and idealized medieval knights devoted themselves to it. It is, however, an uneasy fit for any Christian who takes Jesus seriously, whereas it's the only positive story available for secularists. (Secularism does have a story that fits it better: the story with no plan of salvation by Sartre, Beckett and company.)

[13]It was Richard McSorley, S.J., who suggested to me that this might be what I was doing. Though to be accurate, I sometimes had severe doubts about evangelical theology, and in the early eighties I briefly rejected it consciously.

[14]The engine for almost everyone's life is job or family or comfortable security.

[15]I assume that's an illustration of how we don't notice facts unless they fit our imaginative construct.

[16]Part of the power of the symbol of walking in the grass is that it's a great symbol for life in the eschaton. However, it's a terrible symbol for the journey to the eschaton.

[17]He said something like this on "A Prairie Home Companion" in the early 1980s, but I don't have the exact wording.

[18]I don't mean to imply that most stories in which the women are better than the men mean to say that women are in principle better than men. A few do, but most of them are just portraying the world accurately: men are in power and therefore do more harm. Furthermore, since the main story in our culture is about strong white men saving the world, critics of that story will inevitably make part of their point by reversing its symbolism and portraying women as good and men as bad.

[19]This in fact was the next film she made, only it was called *Sleeping with the Enemy* and didn't costar Richard Gere. This at least portrays fighting evil as more costly, but the evil is still exclusively in someone else.

[20]The movie explicitly recognizes that. Julia Roberts asks her hooker roommate, "Who does [this life] really work for? . . . You give me one example of someone that we know," and the roommate answers, "Cindef------rella." For a popular movie, *Pretty Woman* is unusually open about being a myth. Right near the start a blind man goes by singing, "Everyone who comes to Hollywood has a dream. What's your dream? What's your dream?" and he reappears with his song at the end. Furthermore, one of its central metaphors is a "knight on a white horse, " "colors flying," rescuing a maiden from a tower.

[21]J. R. R. Tolkien, "On Fairy-Stories," in *The Tolkien Reader* (New York: Ballantine

Books, 1966), p. 68.

[22]The Schwarzenegger plan often does better than *Pretty Woman* here. The Schwarzenegger heroes sometimes suffer a great deal. In *Terminator 2*, for example, Schwarzenegger actually gives his life. The ease with which Perry Mason saves the innocent is more common, however.

Chapter 10: On Being Woody Allen

[1]This isn't entirely fair. The male "hero" has lost his power and is made to look a little silly because he minds. I suspect that Le Guin intends to say that salvation is rooted in more womanly virtues like love and constancy and tenderness and that power should rarely be used, but having Tehanu summon power for the eucatastrophe weakens the point, to say the least.

[2]I'm assuming that the "heroes" in Woody Allen movies are portrayed as klutzes, incompetents and neurotics rather than as sinners. That doesn't mean that some of their neuroses wouldn't be better understood as sin from within my presuppositional framework; for example, they're often promiscuous and keep being nasty to their girlfriends.

[3]I owe this way of putting it to Stanley Hauerwas, who uses it as a joke on modern Methodists.

[4]The primary cost is in broken spirits, but that cost is reflected in a secondary way in the national budget. Think of the economic cost of AIDS, divorce and abandoned mothers.

[5]I don't mean to suggest that the idea of an earth-mother goddess produces the same idea of sin as Judeo-Christians have or that it connects to the personal as I have tried to do in this book. But the earth-mother idea of taboo and the Judeo-Christian idea of sin are closer to each other than either is to our culture's reduction of sin to sickness.

[6]The baker is in Tolkien's *Smith of Wooton Major*. The issue here is partly the classic theological problem of the incarnation. Naturally, not many stories try to tackle that topic. But Aslan isn't God incarnate; he's God using a lion's body. Which is very different. It means Aslan, unlike Jesus, doesn't experience the limitations of having a body. He's fully God, but only partly lion. *Smith* is a better account of the incarnation, but it omits God's dying for his people.

[7]Which, however, lacks an account of God's dying for his people (unless you count Gandalf's death and resurrection). That's part of why I say the story of Jah is too large for human stories. Lewis tells parts, Tolkien tells parts, Richard Adams tells parts, Madeleine L'Engle tells parts, but no one tells the story as a whole or even most of the basics.

[8]In Richard Adams's *Watership Down*, evil is also defeated by assuming the Schwarzenegger story. A group of militaristic rabbits attacks a warren of good rabbits, and the militaristic chief is about to defeat the largest rabbit the good guys have. The good rabbit mentions his chief, which makes the attack collapse because the militaristic rabbits assume that the chief would be even bigger than the one they're

fighting. How else could he have gotten to be chief?

Madeleine L'Engle also tells another piece of the story of Jah in *A Wrinkle in Time*. In it, Charles Wallace (a child) brings salvation in weakness, and the essence of that weakness is that he begins to love his enemy. Combined, all these stories come close to the story of Jah.

[9]For that matter, power isn't even much use in dealing with other people's evil. Oh, Matt Dillon can stop bad guys from hurting others (power has a role in policing), and it can have a limited role in teaching good habits (power when combined with love has a role in parenting and education), but it doesn't win people over. That's done only by love and goodness.

[10]Tolkien, "On Fairy-Stories," p. 68.

Chapter 11: Playing with FIRE

[1]We live in a large house with nine other committed Christian adults. (It's our church.) Combined, they do as much with Vicki as we do.

[2]Seven thousand dollars annually in direct payments; probably twice that on educational expenses (a staff person for every child in her present school); free hospitalization and therapy if you fight for it; extensive physical and psychological exams; the time of a courtroom and court investigators; interviews with social workers (over and over and over again); staff meetings with half a dozen expensive professionals. In the first twelve months we knew Vicki, her hospital bills alone were over twenty thousand dollars.

[3]One of the basic ideas of liberal democracy is to limit oppression by a tiny minority by appealing to the selfishness of the many. So if you're a woman, it's clearly in your self-interest to believe you're equal to men, and since there are at least as many women as men, in time women will make major strides toward equality. And it's in the interest of people of color to believe in equality, and since there are many more people of color than whites, given time they'll progress. At least a little.

It's rather sordid, but it's better than a tiny majority of selfish rich white males oppressing everyone else. Much better. That's the genius of modern liberal democracy. It doesn't depend on people being good but on people being actively selfish—which is something you can count on. So when the ruling class oppresses the majority too much, you can count on the majority eventually getting fed up and trying to throw them out.

In life in general and in liberal democracy in particular, each person's selfishness is an automatic mechanism tending to limit the selfishness of others. So you produce change not by preaching goodness but by organizing various (self) interest groups into a rainbow coalition to resist the ruling (self) interest groups.

It's not pretty. Selfishness struggling with selfishness. But it works better than the alternatives. However, it has nothing to do with the kingdom of God.

[4]For a scholarly statement of this point, see Isaiah Berlin, *Four Essays on Liberty* (London: Oxford University Press, 1969), pp. 121-33.

[5]First raised by John Paul Jones on December 3, 1775.

[6]Understanding this is especially important for people in helping roles.

[7]Equal opportunity, the right of each person to discover where he or she excels, is different from the sentimental egalitarianism that assumes that each person excels in everything. But here I'm not concerned with equality of opportunity but with moral equality, by which I mean that even beside the worst person, "there but for the grace of God go I."

[8]Plato comments on what happens when people become "devotees of equality" and "liberty":

> The father habitually tries to resemble the child and is afraid of his sons, and the son likens himself to the father and feels no awe or fear of his parents so that he may be forsooth a free man. . . .
>
> The teacher in such a case fears and fawns upon the pupils, and the pupils pay no heed to the teacher and to their overseers either. Young and old are alike, and the young are on a level with the old and are ready to compete with them in word and deed. The old condescend to the young and are full of pleasantry and gaiety, imitating the young, for fear they may be thought disagreeable and authoritative. (*Republic* 8. 562-63, my translation)

Part of this is quoted in Robert Brustein, "The Case for Professionalism," *The New Republic* 160, no. 17 (1969): 16-18. I owe several of my ideas and illustrations in this section to Brustein's important article.

However, Plato (if not Brustein) uses these illustrations to defend oligarchy. He is attacking the idea that women, resident aliens and slaves are equal to free Athenian males. That is not my point. Surely we have more choices than conservatism and liberalism.

[9]And it became even harder after we saw what happened when people bent the knee to Hitler, but the fact that authority can be misused doesn't mean it always is.

[10]Josh 5:14; see also Ex 3:6; Judg 6:22; Is 6:5; Ezek 1:28; Lk 1:12; Rev 1:17.

[11]This is of course a complex linguistic claim. Some modern translations assume that Hebrew and Greek had the dynamic equivalent of *rights*. That's not unreasonable, but it's a serious mistake. So, for example, one word translated "right" in some modern translations of the Old Testament would be more precisely translated "power." See, for example, Ex 21:8 in the New Revised Standard Version, the Revised Standard Version, the New International Version and the Jerusalem Bible. (The NIV uses *right* or *rights* this way eighteen times.) Interestingly, the terms appear only six times in that sense in the more literal translation of the New American Standard Version. Nor do they appear in the King James Version (except in "birthright"); after all, that was forty years before Hobbes made them current and seventy years before Locke made them standard. They seem to appear in the King James in 2 Sam 19:28 and in Neh 2:20, but the translators of 1611 would have understood *right* to mean *rightness*.

[12]For a more detailed discussion of the origin of rights, see Alasdair MacIntyre, *A

Short History of Ethics (New York: Macmillan, 1966), pp. 120-77.

[13]In fact, judging from how free God was in taking their lives, they didn't have an inalienable right to life either.

[14]Is it significant that English has only negative antonyms for individualism? We have collectivism and communism, but neither has even a neutral connotation. Language reflects the biases of the culture it grows out of.

[15]It's no accident that Hobbes was the one to give prominence both to rights and to the theory of social contract. If individuals are primary he has to devise an explanation for why individuals would give some of their power and rights to the state. (See his *Leviathan, or the Matter, Form and Power of a Commonwealth, Ecclesiastical and Civil* 2. 17.) However, if you take the group as primary, the situation is reversed: no theory of social contract is needed and the problem is why groups have such a hard time functioning together.

For similar reasons, as society's common moral basis erodes, marriage counselors, schools and therapists rely more and more on individual contracts to produce a semblance of cooperation. They have nothing else to appeal to; they certainly can't appeal to covenants of the sort found in the Judeo-Christian tradition.

[16]Especially when the rights story is combined with the determinism of the physical and social sciences.

[17]The sabbatical year reflects the same idea of freedom. Every seventh year, the children of Israel were to release any Hebrew slaves they had, but they weren't to send them out with nothing the way white Americans did to blacks. God told Israel to "provide [for your slave] liberally out of your flock, your threshing floor, and your wine press" (Deut 15:14). And the reason for this was not some abstract, intrinsic good; it was bound up with their history. The passage continues with the rationale: "thus giving to him some of the bounty with which the LORD your God has blessed you. Remember that you were a slave in the land of Egypt, and the LORD your God redeemed you; for this reason I lay this command upon you today" (v. 15).

And then there's the year of Jubilee. The Liberty Bell is inscribed "Proclaim liberty throughout the land to all the inhabitants thereof." That's a quotation from the Jubilee legislation (Lev 25:10 KJV). Naturally, in the 1700s Americans understood that as freedom from a king, as negative liberty. But that's not what Jubilee was.

Political liberty wasn't being talked about at all. Jubilee was for the poor. When Israelite families became poor, they sometimes had to sell their land to pay their debts. But such sales were not permanent; every fiftieth year, on the year of Jubilee, all land was to be returned to the family God had given it to. So everyone got their land back. That was what liberty meant.

But that was not all it meant. The year of Jubilee started on the Day of Atonement, when sins were forgiven. So on this day all Israel started over, liberated from their sins as well as from their debts. Furthermore, all were to take the year off, allowing them *and* the land to rest. And since the whole family was returning to the land, they had a yearlong family reunion to reestablish their closeness and unity. It also allowed them time to revere God.

[18]The word isn't used until the legislation for the sabbatical year (Ex 21). From then on it's used extensively in relation to sabbatical and Jubilee years (Deut 15 and Lev 25) and rarely elsewhere, though a Greek equivalent appears in other senses in the New Testament.

[19]Ex 4:23; 7:16; 8:1, 20; 9:1, 13; 10:3.

[20]This interpretation is supported by the form of the first request: "Let my people go, so that they may celebrate a festival to me in the wilderness" (Ex 5:1). In the standard interpretations of the text, Moses never asks Pharaoh for more than time to go out into the wilderness for a religious festival. In the negotiations that follow, a feast seems to be what Pharaoh is refusing to allow (8:8, 25-28; 10:7-11, 24-26; 12:30-32; 14:5). However, Pharaoh clearly fears that if he grants this relatively minor request, they'll never come back. Is this because he thinks Moses is trying to trick him, or does he understand the request to serve God as a request to stop serving Pharaoh?

[21]At the very least, the text is making an elaborate wordplay on two meanings of *serve*.

[22]This is usually translated "the servant of God," but that's a euphemism growing out of our embarrassment at the thought of anyone being a slave. For Moses as the slave of God, see Ex 4:10; 14:31; Num 11:11; 12:7-8; Deut 3:24; 34:5; Josh 1:1-2, 7, 13, 15; 8:31, 33; 11:12, 15; 12:6; 13:8; 14:7; 18:7; 22:2, 4-5; 2 Kings 18:12; 21:8; 1 Chron 6:49; 2 Chron 1:3; 24:6, 9; Neh 1:7-8; 9:14; 10:29; Ps 105:26; Dan 9:11; Mal 4:4.

[23]Rom 1:1; Gal 1:10; Phil 1:1; Tit 1:1; Jas 1:1; 2 Pet 1:1; Jude 1.

[24]*The Living Bible*, Williams and Jordan are the only ones I've found that use "slave."

[25]It continues, "and early American times" (*A Greek English Lexicon of the New Testament and Other Early Christian Literature*, trans. and adapted from Walter Bauer's 4th ed. by William F. Arndt and F. Wilbur Gingrich; rev. and augmented from Walter Bauer's 5th ed. by F. Wilbur Gingrich and Frederick W. Danker [Chicago: University of Chicago Press, 1979], s.v. δοῦλος). Abbott-Smith doesn't even mention *servant* as a possible translation for the word (G. Abbott-Smith, *A Manual Greek Lexicon of the New Testament* [New York: Charles Scribner's Sons, 1956]). Neither does *Liddell and Scott's Greek-English Lexicon*, 7th ed. (Oxford, U.K.: Oxford University Press, 1988).

[26]J. Blunck, "Freedom," and R. Tuente, "Slave, doulos," in *New International Dictionary of New Testament Theology*, trans., with additions and rev., Colin Brown (Grand Rapids, Mich.: Zondervan, 1986), s.v.

[27]The point is repeated in 1 Cor 7:22; 10:29—11:1; 1 Pet 2:16.

[28]Even if we have excellent insurance, modern hospitals and insurance regulations usually become faceless mazes.

[29]William Ernest Henley, "Invictus" ["In Memoriam R. T. Hamilton Bruce"], in *The

Oxford Book of English Verse, 1250-1918, ed. Arthur Quiller-Couch (Oxford, U.K.: Clarendon, 1957), p. 1027.

Chapter 12: Castles of Darkness, Castles of Wonder

[1]Berke Breathed, "Bloom County," *San Francisco Examiner and Chronicle*, July 23, 1989, comics section.

[2]Graham Greene, *The Lawless Roads* (Harmondsworth, Middlesex, U.K.: Penguin Books, 1947), p. 200; originally published in 1939.

[3]I am indebted in this section and throughout the book to Ernest Becker, *The Denial of Death* (New York: Free Press, 1973).

[4]The comments of William and Mary Morris on Watergate are typical: "Virtually everyone involved in the whole messy affair was at least a college graduate, with most of them holding graduate degrees in law. What this says about the level of literacy in our institutions of higher learning must give anyone who cares about language a bad case of the wimwams" (*Harper Dictionary of Contemporary Usage* [New York: Harper & Row, 1985], pp. 615-16).

[5]C. S. Lewis, *The Last Battle* (New York: Macmillan, 1956), chap. 13.

[6]C. S. Lewis, *Perelandra*, 2nd ed. (London: Pan Books, 1960), p. 112, called *Voyage to Venus* in this edition.

[7]Its only variation from the Schwarzenegger story is that in it it's good to die fighting with honor. You don't need to win in Schwarzenegger's sense.

[8]Graham Greene, *The Confidential Agent: An Entertainment* (London: William Heinemann, 1939), chap. 2.

[9]I don't mean to say that the traditional problems of epistemology are irrelevant. They still need to be dealt with, as I tried to do earlier in the book, and as I will try to do again in a moment. But solving the theoretical issues does little without repentance from sin; we just misuse the solutions.

And it's also only fair to say that both rationalism and romanticism had some sense of the problems caused by sin (usually using different language, of course). The rationalist objection to feeling was based in part on the correct observation that (sinful) emotion often causes people to calculate badly, and the romantic emphasis on the falseness caused by repressing feelings was in part based on the correct observation that repression is a denial of reality, of truth.

To put it differently, Jesus and Descartes agreed that self-interested feelings block us from truth, but they had radically different ways of dealing with the problem. Descartes, I suggest, proposed repressing feelings—a long Greek tradition. But Jesus proposed getting them into the open so you can repent of the bad ones and use the good ones—also a long tradition, this time a Jewish one. (Jesus was not big on repression. Remember, he was the guy whose first miracle was turning water into wine, and he was called the son of David—the king who got so excited dancing before God that he exposed himself.)

Jesus and romantics agree that you ought not to lie to yourself about how you feel, but they have radically different ways of dealing with the problem. While romantics tend to think you should follow your feelings, Jesus thought that some feelings (like hatred) are bad and will deceive you.

The problem isn't too little feeling or too little reason: a self-deceived person who follows his feelings isn't going to accept the truth, and neither is one who tries to follow his reason. It's simple to deceive ourselves with either emotion or reason. The problem of knowledge is that truth requires us to change our lives (repent), and that's so costly it makes self-deception compellingly attractive.

[10]See Jn 1:4-9; 3:16-21; 8:12-20; Rom 1:18-23; 2 Cor 4:1-6; Eph 5:5-18.

[11]For more passages on the New Testament idea of accepting or rejecting truth, see Mt 24:4-5, 24; Mk 3:1-6; 6:52; 8:17-18; 13:5-6; 16:14; Lk 12:54-56; 21:8-9; Jn 1:4-9; 3:16-21; 8:12-47; 9:24-34; Rom 1:18—2:16; 2 Cor 4:1-6; Eph 4:17-25; 5:5-21; 2 Thess 2:9-15; 2 Tim 3:7-9; 4:3-4; Heb 3:7-19; 1 Jn 1:5—2:11; 5:10.

Etymologically, the Greek word for *truth* means unveiledness, unhiddenness; it's the negative of escaping notice, causing to forget. It is often used to mean "not a lie." Some Greek philosophers use it to mean truth vs. appearances, though it's doubtful it could mean that in the trade Greek in which the New Testament was written.

The main Hebrew word for truth means fidelity, stability, covenant keeping, what you can rely on. A secondary meaning of *truth* in Hebrew is not a lie, not deceit, not taking a bribe.

I trust that careful exegetes will forgive the way I may appear to be prooftexting here, but this is not the place for a lexicographical and cultural study of Greek and Hebrew. Those who want to see it done properly should read A. C. Thiselton, "Truth," in *New International Dictionary of New Testament Theology,* ed. Lothar Coenen, Erich Beyreuther and Hans Bretenhard; trans., with additions and rev., Colin Brown (Grand Rapids, Mich.: Zondervan, 1978), 3:874-902. For a rather romantic attack on the scientific view of truth, see Rudolf Bultmann, "ἀλήθεια κτλ," in *Theological Dictionary of the New Testament,* ed. Gerhard Kittel and Gerhard Friedrich, trans. Geoffrey W. Bromiley, 10 vols. (Grand Rapids, Mich.: Eerdmans, 1964-76), 1:232-51.

[12]Of course, it was presumably offensive to the Pharisees as well.

[13]See, for example, Jean-Paul Sartre, *Being and Nothingness,* trans. Hazel E. Barnes (New York: Washington Square, 1966), pp. 56-86.

[14]See, for example, Karl Mannheim, *Ideology and Utopia: An Introduction to the Sociology of Knowledge,* trans. Louis Wirth and Edward Shills (New York: Harcourt Brace and World, 1936).

[15]See, for example, Jn 7:17; 8:12, 31-32.

Chapter 13: The Wild Truth

[1]*American Heritage Dictionary,* 2nd college ed. (Boston: Houghton Mifflin, 1985), s.v. "truth."

[2]This is of course my old problem in the Nothing game.

[3]When I talk about a correspondence theory of moral and aesthetic truth, I don't

mean to say that some property, independent of all physical characteristics, corresponds to the value. G. E. Moore seems to have thought this, but I don't. I mean that moral laws are like physical laws in that both are functions of reality independent of the observer (though how observers understand them will be influenced by their story).

⁴Allan Bloom, *The Closing of the American Mind* (New York: Simon and Schuster, 1987), p. 26. Bloom is of course criticizing the position he's describing. I owe much of this discussion of relativism to his book, especially pp. 25-29. However, he's a neoconservative who opposes minority studies, and I suspect he's living off moral capital borrowed from his Jewish grandmother, capital that no longer fits his story.

⁵Dennis Prager, "The *Door* Interview: A Civilization That Believes in Nothing," *The Door*, November-December 1990, p. 11.

⁶Bloom, *Closing of the American Mind*, p. 60.

⁷Ibid., p. 35.

⁸And why do they, the "open-minded," have such fundamental contempt for fundamentalists?

⁹H. R. Rookmaaker, *Modern Art and the Death of a Culture* (Downers Grove, Ill.: InterVarsity Press, 1970), p. 48.

¹⁰To be fair, Robert N. Bellah coined the term "civil religion," and he is hardly a neoconservative. (See *The Broken Covenant* [New York: Seabury, 1975].) Furthermore, neoconservatives aren't just saying we have to have some story in common and this one is America's; they're also often saying that this one is true, or at least the best one going.

¹¹Sherwood G. Lingenfelter and Marvin K. Mayers, *Ministering Cross-Culturally: An Incarnational Model for Personal Relationships* (Grand Rapids, Mich.: Baker Book House, 1986), especially pp. 36-51. We have to ask ourselves to what degree the Western orientation is the source of stress and of ignoring people, and to what degree the Yapese orientation contributes to failure to complete vital tasks.

¹²Unlike anthropologists, I suspect that few customs are completely neutral morally; all cultures have fundamentally rebelled against God, and that rebellion is reflected in all sorts of aspects of every culture. Take language, for example. Few would want to say that any language is morally bad, but can a language that uses the male gender disproportionately be morally neutral?

¹³He was also right that teachers are often so arrogant that they crush the spirits of their students, especially students on welfare. And he was right that we should often be more respectful of those we disagree with, especially those who do not respect themselves. It's especially important for white men to learn this.

¹⁴George Bernard Shaw, *Caesar and Cleopatra*, act 2.

¹⁵Even if you think I'm overstating the case, it seems significant how often modern intellectuals slip back and forth between absolutist moral language and language reflecting extreme moral relativism. We're not clear on our story, on the logic of our moral discourse; so we switch back and forth. See, for example, Matthew Fox,

"The Door Interview," *The Door*, May-June, 1992, p. 8. There a morally, spiritually passionate man like Fox calls the system confronted by Rosa Parks "outdated," though for him that is a little more reasonable than for my teacher, because in his story the Spirit is bringing progress.

[16]This is especially important for oppressed groups so that they overcome the sense of worthlessness that for some reason comes with being sinned against.

[17]I have to wonder whether a limited percentage of the drive for minority studies isn't the fear and rejection of being evaluated. In our egalitarian culture no one can evaluate others without violating their narcissism. Besides, a classic speaks to the whole of humanity and isn't narrowly limited to being appreciated by one subculture.

[18]Walter Rauschenbusch, *The Righteousness of the Kingdom*, rpt. ed. (Nashville: Abingdon, 1968), p. 92, quoted in Hauerwas, *A Community of Character*, p. 46.

[19]William H. Willimon, *The Bible: A Sustaining Presence in Worship* (Valley Forge, Pa.: Judson, 1981), pp. 35-38.

Chapter 14: Mixed Stories

[1]This could of course be valid—providing you saw a morally relevant difference between Vietnam and Iraq. However, it's hard to see what that would be. Iraq's lack of jungle for guerrillas to hide in is relevant within the Schwarzenegger story but not within the Roberts story. That's a question of pragmatics, not of principle.

[2]Lewis Carroll (Charles L. Dodgson), *Through the Looking Glass*, chap. 5.

[3]Kurt Vonnegut, *Slaughterhouse-Five: or, The Children's Crusade* (New York: Dell, 1969), p. 112.

[4]Not all the credit for this should be given to Wittgenstein. It is in fact the direction of the whole linguistic philosophy movement of which he was the most influential, but not the only, practitioner. At the least, G. E. Moore and J. L. Austen should be given some credit.

[5]He argued, however, that private language is impossible, which raises questions about some varieties of romanticism, including private messages from God that some Christians think they get.

[6]Just what these procedures are varies from philosopher to philosopher. For R. M. Hare, the logic of moral discourse involves choosing a moral principle you are willing to universalize. He thereby gets quite close to Kant and the existentialists. I find Stephen Toulmin's version, which I explain next, more reflective of the objective nature of actual moral judgments; it's therefore harder to deal with from my perspective, and so I try to show the weakness even of a position like his.

[7]Stephen Toulmin, *An Examination of the Place of Reason in Ethics* (Cambridge, U.K.: Cambridge University Press, 1950), p. 137.

[8]Although my concept of story was greatly deepened by Stanley Hauerwas, it was studying Wittgenstein while reading *Lord of the Rings* that first led me to a story-based epistemology. Though Wittgenstein never suggested such a thing himself, R. W. Hepburn and Iris Murdoch come fairly close in "Vision and Choice in

Morality," in *Proceedings of the Aristotelian Society,* supp. vol. 30 (1956), reprinted in *Christian Ethics and Contemporary Philosophy,* ed. Ian T. Ramsey (New York: Macmillan, 1966), pp. 181-218.

⁹This is less true than it was twenty years ago. Iris Murdoch, Alasdair MacIntyre, Charles Taylor and Stanley Hauerwas are all exceptions to the rule, but as a result they probably aren't linguistic philosophers anymore.

¹⁰Actually, I suspect that Jesus would have laughed himself silly just before asking Toulmin to go stand with the Pharisees.

¹¹This is clear in a book like John Rawls's *A Theory of Justice* (Cambridge, Mass.: Harvard University Press, 1971).

¹²The point is too technical to pursue here, but the standard interpretation of the is/ought problem by analytic philosophers makes this almost necessary. They believe that since ethics is its own sort of thing, ethics doesn't and can't grow out of human nature or God's nature; their epistemology cuts the connection between ethics and metaphysics, leaving all three impoverished. This puts them in the position, almost unintelligible to everyone else, that ethics is disconnected from all other reality.

¹³I learned to ask these questions from reading Charles Taylor, *Sources of the Self: The Making of the Modern Identity* (Cambridge, Mass.: Harvard University Press, 1989), especially pp. 91-107. He gives a more balanced, less polemical answer than I do.

¹⁴Obviously, threats and promises are rather primitive and not presently in style in morality. The problem with them is that they are finally selfish: sacrifice now so that after you die you'll be happy. You do things not because they're good but because they pay. This extrinsic motivation isn't ultimately moral; in fact, it seems to reduce morality to selfish calculation. (See, for example, Walter Kaufmann, *The Faith of a Heretic* [Garden City, N.Y.: Doubleday, 1961], pp. 223-26.)

However, we all use external motivation with children and the morally immature (which is all of us at times). Sometimes, threatening and cajoling are the only ways to get decent behavior out of people, and they at least teach postponement of gratification and some decent habits. The story of Jah meets people where they are, providing motivation for those who won't respond on better grounds, and in time they may develop habits of the heart lifting them to another moral level.

¹⁵We moderns may no longer sense the importance of being part of a people, but I suggest that it's a basic human desire reflected well in a desire for companionship and badly in our desire to be part of an "in" group. But this would require a chapter in itself, if not a book.

¹⁶George Eliot, quoted in Hepburn and Murdoch, "Vision and Choice," p. 192.

¹⁷Thomas Browne, quoted in Madeleine L'Engle, *A Ring of Endless Light* (New York: Farrar Straus Giroux, 1980), p. 20.

¹⁸It seems obvious that J. Gresham Machen was right that "modernism" is not Christian at all but an alternative story. See *Christianity and Liberalism* (Grand Rapids, Mich.: Eerdmans, 1923).

[19]Roger Lundin, "Our Hermeneutical Inheritance," in Roger Lundin, Anthony C. Thiselton and Clarence Walhout, *The Responsibility of Hermeneutics* (Grand Rapids, Mich.: Eerdmans, 1985), p. 6.

[20]This section essentially reflects the views of Jay E. Adams and nouthetic counseling. (See, for example, *Competent to Counsel* [Nutley, N.J.: Presbyterian and Reformed, 1970].)

[21]See Taylor, *Sources of the Self,* pp. 419-93.

[22]Of course, in another sense their icon was the ordinary person, the working man.

[23]That doesn't mean that keeping our culture from collapse is an important role for the church; if the culture is bad enough, perhaps it should collapse. Our task is to be the people of God and let that affect the state and the culture as they choose to let it affect them.

Chapter 15: On Becoming Part of the Warm Spot

[1]As I understand it, the last two ways of checking are actually functions of checking coherence. We can't check the stories we've constructed against reality in some objective manner. We can only check them against our perception of reality, which is also a construct determined in part by our story. So in a sense what we do is compare the stories we've constructed with perceptions we've constructed. This is therefore ultimately a coherence theory of truth. But if reality is too different from our story, we'll eventually be unable to fit parts of it into our constructs—at which point our stories will be seen to be incoherent, depending, of course, on our gifts at self-deception.

What tests you use depend in part on your story, but almost all Western stories, even those that claim otherwise, in fact require coherence and empirical adequacy.

[2]This is a trickier process than we sometimes realize. When you step into another story or version of a story, you inevitably understand it in terms of your own story. Your perceptions of reality are substantially influenced by the story you live day to day. But that doesn't mean that stepping into another story is meaningless: as you try a story and live in it and interact with people whose story it is, you can begin to approximate understanding it on its own terms. What you can't do is understand it in no terms at all, in terms independent of any story.

[3]Of course, you have to distinguish an appropriate and accurate evaluation of something bad (like Jesus' condemnations of the Pharisees) from a general spirit of meanness and negativity. Because of our cultural story of liberal tolerance, we have difficulty making this distinction.